BEAUTY
AND THE
DARK

A Cancer Memoir of Traveling, Grieving,
Loving, and Living

ANGELA AMOROSO AND CAROL HORDIS

ISBN Paperback: 979-8-218-74974-3

ISBN E Book: 979-8-218-81661-2

Library of Congress Control Number: 2025921271

Book Design: Sarah Lahay www.cestbeaudesigns.com

Editorial Services: Renee Nicholls www.mywritingcoach.net

Cover Photography: Liesl Clark www.lieslclarkphotography.com

Author Photography: Liesl Clark www.lieslclarkphotography.com

Web Design: Kimberly Watters www.kwgraphicsandweb.com

Printed in the United States of America

Published by Carol Hordis

www.beautyandthedark.com

Testimonials about Angela's blog, Beauty and The Dark

"[These] words are so majestically written [they] captivate me from the first sentence."
—Nicole Brock

"Thank you, Angela, for such a beautiful piece of writing and for making those of us without cancer think about our own quality of life."
—Karen Chase

"I have never known anyone as Fierce, Uplifting, Persevering, and BadAss."
—Linamaria Gallego-Valencia

"A purposeful, healing call for all of us to live more deeply, to love more generously and to believe that evolution wants us to fulfill the uniqueness that is our birthright."
—Jan Brown

"The embodiment of a spirit, an energy, a force that is here as a message to all of us."
—Terri Wlaschin

For Angela

"What greater grief can there be for mortals
than to see their children dead."
—EURIPIDES

Contents

Preface

February 2021: My daughter, Angela, and I have driven to our cottage in Maine. Ange, as she is often called, is recovering from another two weeks of brain radiation, the last treatment that is available for her. She has metastatic breast cancer, which went directly to her brain, bypassing all the usual areas first. We are standing outside talking. It is a beautiful sunny day, but it is still February in Maine, so we are bundled against the cold. Angela is having a good day—more energy, thoughts clear—and her speech is good, with few word-finding problems. I am enjoying this time and holding a thread of hope that the treatment will give her a few good months. Everything about the day feels blessed.

Angela looks at me and tells me she thinks I should write a book—that I should tell my story. I remind her that she is the writer, not me. Still holding my gaze, she says that she knows I can and that I should. After thinking about it for a few minutes, I say that maybe I could use her blog and include my experiences and perspective. She gives me one of her big smiles: she approves.

. . .

I now wonder if, when Angela told me she wanted me to write this book, she thought that it would help me process the seven years she lived with cancer. I also believe that she may have felt that it would help me process my grief when she passed away. This would make sense, because writing helped her to process living with metastatic cancer and her own grief. In our talks, she was worried about me. This suggestion was her way of helping me once she passed away.

When Angela developed cancer, she journaled regularly, until the effects of cancer prevented that. In fact, Angela had been an inter-mittent journal writer since she was in elementary school. Angela started a blog in September 2015, about a year and a half after her initial diagnosis and prior to knowing she had metastasis. She was taking a cross-country trip with her dog, Oskar, and she decided to blog about her trip. She felt it was a way to share her experiences and photos with family and friends. Her original title for the blog was *Cancercation*, which she changed to *Beauty and The Dark* after she developed metastasis.

On her return home from the initial trip, Angela decided to continue with her blog. I believe that it gave her purpose. It was about travel, living with cancer, traveling with cancer, and—most importantly—liv-ing life.

This book is both Angela's story, in her words, and my story as a mother of an adult child with cancer who became her advocate and caregiver and who continues to journey with grief. Foremost, during those seven years and now, I am her mother.

I kept journals when Angela was receiving treatment, recording test results, medication changes, recommendations, and our questions for her oncologists. Only rarely did I record my own thoughts and feelings during that period. Then I started journaling regularly after

Angela's death in 2021. Journaling became a way for me to live with grief. Initially it started as my Happy Journal, a space for me to record stories about Angela that people wanted to share with me and stories I remembered. Rereading them on my darkest days helped with the grief. Eventually, the journal included everything I was experiencing, much of which became the basis for this book.

This book is organized into five parts.

Part I: Beauty and The Dark. This is Angela's blog. The chapters I've taken directly from her blog appear here with only a few changes. In some instances, I have corrected spelling and punctuation to avoid distraction to the reader. Spellings of names and places have been corrected when needed, and sources of quotes have been identified when possible.

When Angela started writing her blog, she was not using capital letters. You will see that she explained this in one of her posts. I recognize that this style makes it a bit more challenging to read, but I felt that it was important to allow her words to stand as she wrote them. I also have not corrected any of the medical information that Angela included. What she shared represents her understanding at the time.

Some of her blog posts are quite long, and eventually she did start to include an "Intermission" in her writing. This was often due to the time between posts, the amount of information she wanted to share, and, I believe, the effects of brain cancer treatments. If, at times, you find that she jumps around in her posts, please note that I have chosen not to make changes. That was the effect of brain cancer.

In some passages, I have included links instead of the full song lyrics and poems that she originally included in her blog; this has been done because of copyright restrictions. I have also included only a few of her photos in this book, but in passages where she indicated that photos would follow, I have included footnotes with a link to her collection of photos, which can be viewed at www.beautyandthedark.com.

When appropriate, I have added my voice and experience to hers. I have also provided an update on the two years when Angela stopped writing, prior to her death. As noted in the book, I am the author of the last two blogs included in Part I. Angela had talked about the importance of having a blog for her followers posted after she passed away. Her friends also completed the final part of her photo essay on cancer, which we added to her blog after she passed away.

Part II: Further Reflections on Angela's Blog. This part further expands on issues Angela frequently discussed in her blogs—breast cancer culture, finances, and insurance—including my thoughts.

Part III: Living with Dying. Included in this section is my response to her comments on deciding when she wanted to stop treatment. This discussion focuses on the importance of keeping open communication, the burden of living with cancer, and my thoughts on cancer being a blessing or a curse.

Part IV: Living with Grief. My experience of being a bereaved mother.

Part V: Life Celebration. The steps I have taken in rebuilding my life.

As I believe Angela intended, writing this book has helped me to process her life, illness, and death. It has allowed me to focus my pain with the hope that it would lead me on a path to finding a way to live with grief and still build and live a fulfilling life. If you or your loved ones are going through a similar experience, please know that you are not alone. I hope that as you read our story, our words will offer you validation, comfort, hope, and peace.

Acknowledgments

To Angela's health care team: Thank you to her primary care providers, oncology team, surgeons, nurse practitioners, physician assistants, nurses, medical assistants, phlebotomists, receptionists, radiology technicians, and all whom I have missed who were a part of her team. All of you took the time to get to know Angela and listened to her when she talked about how she wanted to live her life. You supported and respected her decisions, although I am certain you did not always agree with them.

In this current health care system, time is important to patient and provider, although it is difficult to fit into crowded schedules. Angela and I both recognize and cherish that valuable commodity—time—which allowed you to see her and know her. It is my belief that knowing and respecting her values and how she wanted to live her life, along with your expertise, contributed to giving her many good years and to giving me more time to spend with her. Medications and treatments are only a small portion of what she needed, and you provided those. Most importantly, you gave of your time, to know Angela and respect her choices and the life she chose to live. I am grateful. We were blessed to have such a wonderful team caring for her. You are all forever held close in my heart.

To Angela's counselor and my own counselors: Your kindness, support, and presence in our lives was invaluable during Angela's years with cancer and since she passed away. You provided us with a safe place to talk about everything, including current concerns and remote issues. I believe that your guidance also helped us to improve our relationship.

Thank you to Liesl Clark, Ben Proulx, and Charlie Chronopoulos for completing Part III of Angela's photo essay. It was beautifully done and a perfect ending to her project.

I would like to acknowledge the courage of those who have written their memoirs about cancer, living with cancer, having a child pass away, and grief. Angela and I learned from your stories, and your stories are helping me find a path in my life now. For those who study grief and bereavement, your work has been a source of comfort and hope that I will build a future without Angela's physical presence.

To the staff and animals at Selah Carefarm, you provided me with a safe place to grieve and learn, and a support system that keeps me upright most days. You will find much of what I learned in these pages.

Thank you to my coworkers and everyone who worked in the office. You were a constant source of support. You were all available to help, support my patients, and cover calls without question when I needed to be out of the office with minimal notice for Angela. You relieved me of the office stress and worry, which allowed me to focus on Angela.

Thank you to Renee Nicholls, editor, who agreed to work with me on this project. Her input and guidance were invaluable to me as a non-writer.

Acknowledgments

Acknowledgments would not be complete without thanking both Angela's pillars and my pillars, family, friends, coworkers, acquaintances, and everyone who has touched our lives. You have all made our lives fuller and richer.

Introduction

My daughter Angela passed away from metastatic breast cancer at the age of forty-one. She lived with cancer for just over seven years. Angela always said she didn't want to just survive: she wanted to LIVE! Angela accomplished that.

As a child, Angela was always fiercely independent with a stubborn streak. When she was three, upset that I told her we needed to clean up after an afternoon baking cookies, she packed her suitcase, put on her raincoat, picked up her umbrella, and headed for the neighbors, returning only when she found they weren't home. At four or five, frustrated that she had not been able to master riding a two-wheeled bike, she brought the pliers outside, took the training wheels off, tossed them across the yard, and taught herself to ride. My assistance was clearly not needed. After she eventually came in, we went back outside so she could show me, both very proud. Little did I know how much Angela's strength and determination would benefit her thirty years later.

A few years after that triumph, when Angela was old enough to fly on airlines as an unaccompanied minor, she started traveling alone to visit her grandparents or her father. I always stayed with her until she boarded, although she quickly became very comfortable with airports.

During one delay in Boston, we overheard two airline employees arguing over which one of them should use the single first-class ticket that was available on Angela's flight. Angela immediately decided the ticket should be given to a paying customer, such as herself. While I sat and watched, she walked over to the counter and spoke with the attendant, stating her case. As the attendant looked around, clearly hoping a parent would appear to rescue her, I simply continued to watch. Angela liked to fight her own battles, and I felt that the attendant should be able to explain the policy to Angela in a way she would understand. I was also hopeful that these two employees would recognize how ridiculous they looked to a child as they fought over a first-class ticket for a one-hour flight. In the end, Angela still flew coach, but I was proud of the way she felt comfortable fighting her own battles and expressing her beliefs.

In the years that followed, Angela and I enjoyed traveling together, also. Our joy was in immersing ourselves in the culture of the area, meeting people, and roaming a grocery store to pick up food for a meal. We would share a studio apartment, use public transportation, eat at local cafes, and skip museums for outdoor sculpture gardens. Even as an adult, Angela would come home from every trip with new friends, whom she stayed in touch with. One person said, "You come home from every adventure with new friends because people are drawn to you. They know you are a force, and they want to be close to you, to experience you, even if just for a few moments or days." After Angela passed away, I realized how many lives she had touched because messages flooded in from around the world.

When Ange was thirty, we spent two weeks volunteering at a remote medical clinic in Africa. I got to know my daughter differently during those weeks in Africa. Although I was working as a nurse practitioner,

Angela had always been averse to medical issues. However, in Africa, she not only held babies while their mothers were being seen but also helped with procedures and triaged patients. One day, as she helped a gentleman with a severe foot wound, she reassured me that it did not contain any maggots—all without her usual grimace.

During our stay in Africa, Angela was also comfortable living without running water and electricity, washing with wet wipes, and wearing semi-clean clothes. I believe we both developed a greater appreciation for our lives and the comforts we had at home. At the time, I also developed a deep sense of compassion for all of the mothers who had lost children. Many presented as fragile, hollow shells, and I worried about their well-being in light of their heartbreaking loss. After Angela's death, I sometimes looked back to those days in Africa and reminded myself I must not become a shell but, rather, whole again—to live.

. . .

As you will see, Angela's blog does not include her first year of treatment: surgeries, chemotherapy, and radiation. During that period, she continued to work full-time. She needed her health insurance, and she had a house with mortgage payments, car payments, and medical co-pays. During that year, she simply existed, life on hold. There were many times I was concerned that she would not survive. Twice, chemotherapy was put on hold to allow her to regain some strength and hope that her weight loss would stabilize. We were cautioned that she was at risk of burning out if she did not take time off. At that time, Angela would not accept help from me to allow her to reduce her work hours.

Once she completed treatment, the burnout we'd been warned about happened to us both. I realized I had been mistaken to think that the door to our pre-cancer lives was simply sitting ajar and that we could both reenter once treatment was completed. Neither of us was the same person after treatment as we were before diagnosis. Angela was living with the lifelong side effects of surgery and treatments. She was dealing with an altered body image. She was grieving a life she had dreamed of pre-cancer and now knew she would never have. I was still holding my breath as I became hypervigilant for any changes and grieved Angela's experience and loss. Neither of us was prepared for these monumental changes despite all we had learned about cancer.

After that first year of treatment, Angela was not cured, even though she was no longer in active treatment. She was considered NED: no evidence of disease. At the end of that year, she was not certain she wanted to return to her pre-cancer life. Consequently, she decided to sell her house, move home with me, take time off, and use the equity from her house not only to pay off her car and medical expenses, but also to travel for a year while she figured out her next step. Cancer had changed her perspective and outlook on the life she wanted to live. She spent a week in Ooray, Colorado, ice climbing with First Descents, a group of twenty- to forty-year-olds with cancer. We spent a week together in Turks and Caicos on her chemo graduation trip. Angela spent a week in Costa Rica at a yoga retreat.

Then Angela started planning a two-month-long cross-country trip with her dog, Oskar. Initially, I was concerned. I had confidence in her ability to travel alone and manage unforeseen events, but I was worried about her health, particularly whether or not she would recognize she needed medical care and seek it out. Despite my concerns, Angela had something she needed to accomplish or find, and she

4

could only do that on her own through this trip. As I reflect now on her need to be alone, I recognize that she was struggling with grief from losses over the first year of treatment. Being alone with grief is something we have both needed. She started her blog, originally titled *Cancercation,* about eighteen months after her initial diagnosis, during that cross-country trip.

On her return home, about two years after her initial diagnosis, we found out she had brain metastasis. She decided to continue her blog with a new title, *Beauty and The Dark.* Her blog continued to chronicle her travels, while also including her medical status and the many issues she encountered living with cancer.

. . .

Angela became disabled and went through the first of four craniotomies. Over the next five years, she had radiation treatments, multiple chemotherapies, and two clinical trials. Each time there was a change, we would gradually adjust to her new normal. Eventually, disease progressed so quickly we were no longer able to adjust. We rapidly learned that "cancer was the real boss" (Hallenga, 2021).

It would have been easy to allow our relationship to fracture when Angela was living with a terminal illness, and we were both grieving. I believe that we kept our relationship intact by talking openly about the medical needs, recommendations, and emotions. We were both realists and left the push from others to only be optimistic out of our relationship. Angela and I also had our own support systems we could lean on and talk with if we did not want to share with each other. We learned to embrace the blending of beauty and darkness in our lives and to recognize that they coexist. Life is/was not either/or.

I have reread Angela's blog multiple times since she passed away. This has allowed me to feel closer to her and gain a better understanding of her feelings and what she was living with. Each time I read it, I learn something new. I find peace in the joy she found in traveling, living, and capturing and sharing life's beauty in her photos. Through her blog, I seek a path to help me navigate through my own days. As Angela found a way to live her life with the grief and the losses she experienced as a person with a terminal illness, she has also provided me with tools that help me with my own grief.

Neither of us stayed the same people we were before Angela got cancer, and I am not the same person I was before she died. I now understand that trauma changes us. I believe that there will always be sadness in me; grief will continue. Yet I am also able to experience happiness and joy. They coexist. Writing this book has helped me begin to heal, to start to feel whole again, to accept that my life is forever altered, and to recognize that I am forever changed.

I hope that our story will offer comfort, support and validation through your own challenges, joys, and journey— and that alongside the darkness, you will gain as much wisdom, light, and peace from Angela's words as I have.

BEAUTY AND THE DARK

I Have Arrived!

September 11, 2015

i woke up this morning in Abiquiu, New Mexico, where I will stay in an authentic village casita for 15 days.

so, my very good friends and family keep requesting that i do a blog while traveling. despite all the anxiety of actually doing this and feeling not funny enough or even good enough at using a computer, i will give it a go. please be gentle 😊 i love you all.

today i drink a bottle of merlot from a new mexico winery. it's excellent. i color, in my modern mandala coloring book, a gift from mom. there's something about this that makes me feel light and far away and inspired. i write in my journal. i take oskar for a walk through the pueblo down the hill, past the churches, and i try to take in everything that's happening and everything i see and hear and smell and I'm overwhelmed. i'm moved by the architecture and rustic reality that still remain in this country. i'm so grateful to be lucky enough to see this. it also reminds me of how very different our lives are.

i walk back to the casita slowly and i see people working in their yards, that are made of sand and rock and cactus and random yellow daises. i hear a lot of dogs barking. i feel the heat of the desert and the welcoming breeze. i feel the pull of oskar in his harness, pushing on for more and more adventure. i try to take it in and start thinking about everything i want to do here, should do. i'm overwhelmed. so i color and drink wine and do a little yoga in the courtyard. i will enjoy a quiet night, under the desert stars and a beautiful bedroom looking out over the canyon. i will do no more than this, because look at how much experience and cancercationing i did in just this one day. today i was cured. i have more days and more time ahead.

Cliff Notes

September 14, 2015

i awake feeling heavy this morning here in New Mexico. i didn't sleep well, but i never sleep well. i feel this overwhelming need to write today, to fill in the gaps a bit for my family and friends, so you understand what this journey is about for me. there's something very uncomfortable about putting all this out there for you to see and read and judge but that's part of nature, really, however sad and unfair it is at times. i went back through my journal i have kept since 'it' happened, the cancer, and pulled some of the most significant entries out. i don't want to frighten everyone away with my cancer craziness but screw it, i want you to know. Please be advised that profanity is used widely throughout this post.

when asking someone whose opinion i respect about my blog and the direction i should take, they said i should focus on the 'ange-ness'. this makes total sense. i don't want to be anyone but myself and everyone that knows and loves me understands that underneath my surface there is darkness and there is light in my soul. I was told to focus on "what perspectives you have that make you uniquely you. Your thought process. This is a huge, horrible, defining event in your life, but it doesn't define you as a whole. There's, much, much, more. You on the other hand are in some genuine shit and are part of something. The epidemic among women with breast cancer is staggering. You're

11

part of something, a greater good and I think you have a strong voice and unique perspective and it deserves to be heard regardless of the audience size." I appreciate this feedback, and it provides the needed encouragement for this post.

an excerpt from journal day 1, the lump. happy new year.

angela marie amoroso

life changes. 2014. age 34. amherst, nh

1/2/14 – i found a lump. no, it found me. it stabbed me in the arm, it was screaming at me. "i am here, I am hurting you". I already knew. I started sweating. i felt it more closely. It was hard. It wasn't round. It had an edge like a triangular, jagged rock. it didn't hurt. I called my mom, took a shower and decided to call the doctor the next day which of course I didn't do because I was too busy or just too lazy.

1/17/14 – it was friday, around noon, and the phone call started with, "Angela, unfortunately, it's not good news…" said dr. a, the sweetest, meanest woman id ever met. I knew this was coming. I never even began to imagine what it would feel like to hear it. But I already knew it. I laughed and cried and hyperventilated in my office at work, for what seemed like an eternity, called my mother and left work in a fog because I wasn't surprised but yet i never expected it. my mother and i go meet with the surgeon. she believes that it's a 'well behaved' cancer based on the findings thus far. oh you mean the findings of the biopsy that i had on tuesday, when the radiologist thought it was ok to say, "you're totally fine, I've done a thousand of these, it's 100% benign." dr.

a's recommendation is a bilateral mastectomy. i have an mri and gene testing that day. chemo and radiation are questionable at this time, as is most everything.

the mri was about as unpleasant as the mammogram. how surreal it was laying there, to have to lay there, listening to the instructions on the intercom, staring at a fake underwater fish scene, that's supposed to help relax patients. they give me headphones to listen to music and i choose channel 69- ESCAPE. this is all to try and hide the noise of the machine, well that is fucking impossible. dr. a calls me at 9 pm that evening with the results. Another "unfortunately" the MRI showed several areas of enhancement in both breasts and lymph node area. more tests need to be scheduled. I will soon learn to loathe the word unfortunately. Anyone that listens to pandora and has the version that comes with commercials is familiar with this phrase…unfortunately. thanks to the american cancer society for making me re live that moment after every 5 fucking songs.

my well-behaved cancer has not been so fucking well behaved after all. as we all know, time is a thief. Jump forward to my surgery and the findings. as it turns out, my cancer is not well behaved and neither are my genes. the cancer has spread into my lymph nodes and i have 3 tumors all aggressively graded and my right breast is almost entirely cancerous. it is shocking to me that after all the tests they make you go through even prior to the surgery, they couldn't see this?! what the fuck kind of bullshit is this?! this is modern medicine?! after 2 ultrasounds, 2 mammograms, an mri, a ct and a bone scan and you couldn't see this? stop calling me a 'conundrum'. so now, not only am i more cancerous than they thought but i also incidentally have a large mass on my liver, which i have been told 'not to worry about' and a genetic 'variance' as they call it due to the lack of data that exists about my particular messed up gene. As you can tell by now, I'm slightly jaded and bitter about 'medicine'.

Just to give you a little info about my stupid gene as i like to call it, there are genes called the msh2 and msh3 gene. these genes combine to form a protein that fixes mistakes in your dna sequence. when someone's msh2 gene doesn't function correctly it results in excessive tumor growth with links to very specific cancers, at an early age. now, my msh2 gene as it stands is classified as a 'variance', due to the lack of data. this could change at any point. with every new genetic test that is performed all this info goes into a data pool where it sits until things can be re classified after more data is obtained. the unfortunate thing about this process is that a lot of people choose not to undergo more extensive genetic testing because it's information that we can't necessarily do anything with, just yet. they can't go into my genes, into my dna and make my stupid gene say c instead of a, which is an easier way to understand it. most people have c's in this gene and i have an a, or vice versa. so i just sit here and wait for my stupid gene to be re classified as a benign variance or wait for it to become a true mutation.

as my mom said recently and i say this with so much love and affection, because she is now learning to make cancer jokes too and swear, which makes me happy... "either way, you're screwed." i love you mom. she struggles with the unfairness of it all. i understand. i spent a year having surgeries, 20 weeks of chemotherapy, 6 weeks of radiation, and all i get is this? these odds, which i don't particularly want to talk about or even try to explain. i have spent the last year being cut up, slashed, stuffed, poisoned, burned from the inside out. i realize how horrible this sounds but i feel as though the treatment for many cancers, especially breast is barbaric, it's violent and there has to be a better way. i truly believe that it's out there, but I'm just gonna say it… "CANCER IS A BIG MONEY MAKER, A BIG BUSINESS, MAKING A LOT PEOPLE A LOT OF MONEY." except the people that actually have it.

just a little about the financial impact cancer has had on my life. cancer made me broke, even more broke than i was before. in the last year, cancer has cost me over $12,000 out of my own pocket. i worked through my treatment because i had to, more than one job. the bills don't stop just because you have cancer. not only has cancer turned my world upside down and inside out, now I'm broke?!

i apologize for the length of this entry but i can't exactly leave any of this out, it's all part of my story, my reality.

I think I'll write a bit about the breast cancer culture and how disgusted I am with a lot of it. I apologize if this upsets people that have a different opinion. This is just mine. I hate pink. I can't stand all the fundraisers to find a cure. we need to find the cause for god's sakes. i resent being called a fighter, the pressure it puts on me is too much. i didn't fight, "i showed up, i did what i was told." society makes us feel that if you just try hard enough you can beat it, that's the message, just try harder. i reject the word survivor. it's a put down of those women who don't survive. i might go through all of this and it might not work anyways? we can't prevent it if we don't know what causes it. how can you cure what you don't know? it's my own terrorist that grew within me, attacking me. every 69 seconds someone dies from breast cancer.[1]

---

1. CAROL'S NOTE: My reflection about breast cancer culture, with updated statistics, appears on page 252.

I felt alienated because i wasn't wearing pink, i wasn't attending fundraisers, i wasn't using my voice. i locked myself in my room for a year and did nothing except watch netflix, cry and wish for it to be over. i know there are women that feel alienated by the overly optimistic approach. I'm one of them. "in order to be a survivor you must maintain this optimistic outlook and articulate in the tyranny of cheerfulness." then there's tamoxifen and the relation to pesticide manufacturing by the same company. The women with estrogen-fed breast cancers have to/should continue treatment for 10 years to stop the body from producing something that it does naturally, that normal women need to continue life. i am turning into a scarecrow, they replace my damaged parts with unnatural forms, they use other drugs to suppress what my body does naturally. am i even still a woman?

sometimes when i have to tell someone what kind of cancer i have i whisper, like i am ashamed, embarrassed that i have a super lame, overdone, popular breast cancer. we are all sick and yes some more so than others and yes breast cancer is overdone, and we should be grateful and feel lucky that we have one of the most studied and researched diseases, but it doesn't make it any less significant or any less hard. and then there's the guilt. for the moment i am here in this life and don't ever for a second not have that in the back of my mind. the knowledge and proof, that comes from my bitter/sweet existence on this earth. there are others who are not here but i am.

please don't look at my photos or read this and feel sorry, don't feel sad. i am more happy in this moment than any before. feel happy for me because of this, regardless of the origin or the cause. i feel free now. i feel love. i have grown. i have let go. cancer is my blessing and my curse. i have been cured in so many moments just with a smile by someone i love or a random message of hope from someone i barely know. i have been touched by so much unexpected kindness. i cant finish writing this without acknowledging the connection i had with my oncology team. the nurses have become my family and when i was so suddenly forced to live without them, i struggled. i love them all so very much.

i feel I've made peace with the idea of death. i understand the consequences of not following medical advice at the moment and to be completely honest I'm ok with it. it's my life not theirs. i just don't want to leave this earth feeling like there was a little piece of me still missing. i feel like i am filling up; somedays faster than others. most days now i am happy but I'm traveling around the world for the next year. i still feel like i have something to do down here. I have decided to put certain treatments on hold. i feel more healthy and more happy without them right now. My body is begging for a break, my soul is begging and i will now give it what it is asking for. it's a hard fact to process, knowing that your own body is harming itself and there's nothing i can do about it except keep taking pills, injections, removing organs to help prevent a recurrence. maybe if i just focus on being happy and being out living it (THANK YOU FIRST DESCENTS!), maybe that is a better treatment for me, not for everyone but for me.

So, jump forward to where the worst part is supposed to be over. However, sometimes the worst part begins after treatment, and I know a lot of people will understand this. I'm left with the effects of treatment. these things don't go away. they are here to stay. so i had a year of treatment to help kill the cancer in my body but the potential effects of the actual treatment itself could be more detrimental.

backing up to the beginning of this year, i struggled to find my place within the cancer community. i was too young for some groups, too old for others, too single, too childless, too advanced in disease. Many of these groups or programs were not beneficial for me at all and to be completely honest, made me even more angry. I finally participated in a program through an amazing organization called First Descents. i spent a week with other 'cancerful' people my age and it changed my life immediately. i finally felt like i belonged, i fit and it was ok to make bad jokes, it was ok to be quiet, it was all ok no matter what. I came home from that and left my job, sold my home and decided the one thing i want to do with the next year of my life is travel so that's what I'm doing. I have already been to Colorado ice climbing, a beach vacation with Mom to Turks and Caicos, a yoga retreat in Costa Rica. Next March I'm heading to South America, to travel through Patagonia by horseback. I recently left NH to take 2 months to travel through the Southwest United States. My horoscope that weekend said this: "envisioning the future is a creative act that comes naturally to you. because of this vision, you are the perfect person to lead a group of people with similar goals and interests. you're willing to travel across the country if need be, but are you willing to travel to the most complicated parts of yourself? should you decide to take the risk, extraordinary things will happen." holy shit right?!

to end this post, i want to re-iterate that i have found something better in this life, something worth exploring and that's myself. i am finding my new self and i like what I'm finding. it's ok if i don't go back to what was. i will move forward with hope for happiness and nothing more because after all, "the only side effect of fighting for recovery, is finding happiness". (Author unknown)

**"The truth is, life is full of joy and full of great sorrow,
but you can't have one without the other."**
—ANDRE DUBUS III

Now that i got that out, I'm off to climb a mountain in the desert!
That is my medicine today and for many days to come.

Stones & Imagination...

September 25, 2015

"Claim your experience, don't let it claim you."
—AUTHOR UNKNOWN

I have one more night, here at Casa de Artista, in Abiquiu, New Mexico. I leave tomorrow for Taos, NM where I will stay in The Stargazer Earthship for 10 days. This off grid, solar powered home was the first Global Model Earthship constructed in 2008. It was built within a 650 acre community, the world's largest sustainable subdivision. I can't wait because I have a huge interest and passion for alternative living.

It is with mixed feelings that I leave this pueblo, however. I have been amazed every day by the places I have seen. Even with 15 days here, i feel as though i have barely scratched the surface. But I have done and seen almost everything I originally wanted to or that was on my 'list'. If I was to properly write about my experience here, this blog would be longer than one of my favorite books, *East of Eden*. So, in 15 days, these are the places I visited:

- Georgia O'Keeffe's home and studio
- Ghost Ranch; Chimney Rock; Museum of Paleontology/ Anthropology

- Plaza Blanca
- Dar al Islam Mosque
- Christ in the Desert Monastery
- Abiquiu Lake
- Poshuouinge Ruins
- Santa Rosa de Lima Ruins
- Penitente Morada
- Ten Thousand Waves Japanese Bath House
- Tesuque Pueblo Flea Market
- Traveler's Market in Santa Fe
- Purple Adobe Lavender Farm
- Echo Amphitheater

I have done a lot of living in 15 days, without cancer in my face. This is an incredible gift the earth is giving me. My favorite area was Plaza Blanca, the 'White Place'. The following is what I wrote in my notebook about Plaza Blanca that day.

> *plaza blanca. the white place. Georgia O'Keeffe painted here. the colors of the white canyons remind me of her home and the color palette she uses. it's like someone poured left over watercolors over the top of this canyon, a watercolor sundae, chocolate, vanilla, strawberry. the vastness of this place is truly deceiving, a hidden gem. the crazy blue sky and the white canyons remind me of the colors of Greece, that I've seen in magazines anyways. the colors of coffee and grapefruit, this place is unlike anything I've ever seen and i think I've had the good fortune and blessing to be able to say that a lot in my life. i say it out loud to myself. why are there not more people here? this confuses me. why people pay a fortune to go to amusement parks and other places that cost money, I'm here, for free, and it's all mine, for the afternoon*

anyway it just makes it a more special day. not that i dislike people, or amusement park rides for that matter.

i hike in an old dried up river bed. i try to envision what this place would have looked like in the past. the rocks under my feet glow and sparkle, like crystals. i pick one up, carefully choosing the right one, and hold it in my hand while i walk. it's so warm and pretty. it's the color of a pearl with peppermint stripes, like Steels salt water taffy on the ocean city boardwalk and the tops of these canyons are covered in what reminds me of sand castle drippings and childhood memories. the wind through the canyons, the sounds of the crows and vultures makes it feel more isolated. i can't write fast enough. as my very good friend said the other day in response to my last entry "i love that you hardly use punctuation because it needs to come out of you so fast."

we are not supposed to take things from these lands but georgia o'keeffe did it all the time! she collected rocks! my secret inner sheller freak is surfacing and i can't help it. if i find a heart shaped stone it's mine. here's something you guys may not know, except my mom of course, i collect heart shape stones and shells and rocks in the figure of animals. i know, super weird, but i have some impressive pieces! whatever, some people collect spoons, i collect rocks and stuff.

i hear water. in the middle of the day in this crumbly canyon there is a tiny little trickling waterfall. i will still refer to it as a waterfall, even though it is tiny. i can't see it but i can hear it. so, like a 10 year old i scale the canyon wall, almost fall a bunch of times but i can finally see it. i see the darkness of the pale colored rock, stained from flowing water and i look even further and i see bright green algae. it occurs to me as i try precariously to take a selfie, which i really dislike, but who else is gonna do it, that i am very much alone, should anything happen. like me falling off this canyon. my heart beats a little faster as i climb down, back to the riverbed.

an hour after i start the hike i finally get out my 'real' camera and i am suddenly stumped. i love to take photos. whether or not I'm any good at it, well that's another issue. how the hell am i going to photograph any of this? i put the strap around my neck, because knowing me ill drop it and my hands feel clumsy as i just blindly start shooting left and right, up and down. it's as though i have never held a camera before. i don't know how to even begin capturing this place in a photo. so i think of it like slices on an mri scan or a 3d mammogram. weird analogy i know, but look at the writer.

i think i am smiling the whole time. i feel so free and alone, but not lonely. it makes me sad to leave this place. i will come back here with oskar. the road out of the canyon is unpaved and it follows what i think is the chama river. it is beautiful and as i drive i imagine having a tiny casita along this river, with vegetable gardens and flowers and maybe a couple horses. that is my childhood dream, so i guess not much has changed.

"It was just my imagination, running away with me." While I am making dinner tonight this song by the Temptations comes on and it is the perfect way to end this day. Today, I am thankful. Today, I didn't have cancer. Today, I didn't think about 'odds' and if it entered my mind even for a moment, i didn't care. I realize that I have been given a gift, many in fact. There are people in my life that show me there is a different way to live, to be grateful, to be happy. People that have shown me that it is ok to love my cancer, to make peace with it, to embrace it and use it as motivation to receive everything i want in this life. So as much as I am doing this trip for me, I do it for them and for those who cannot.

Signing off for the night...I'm going to rent the movie city slickers and drink some local wine. Apparently, Ghost Ranch, where I hiked today, is a hot spot for movie making. Denzel is filming here! Pretty cool...

Sweet dreams, my friends and family.

Signs, Spiders and Sinus Infections

October 4, 2015

"choice is a very powerful gift."
—AUTHOR UNKNOWN

it is my last day in taos, nm. i will be driving to payson, az tomorrow to stay at a cabin in the tonto national forest. this past week has had some real ups and some real downs. i haven't written much the last few days and I'm actually struggling a bit right now trying to get the words to come out. they're stubborn things, those words.

the rain is starting and i am sitting in the living area of this earth ship and i can hear the drops so closely above me. i turn my music off so i can listen to it. this reminds me of the double rainbow i saw yesterday while i was walking oskar. there have been a lot of weird coincidences this week, signs. I'm not sure what they mean but i do believe they exist.

my mind feels a bit heavy. it is breast cancer awareness month. i had a tough time with it last year, still being in treatment. i am having a tough time with it this year as well. i guess the only good thing is that I'm traveling and most of the time far from anywhere where i would be reminded. i was reading some things online the other day that i found through a fellow 'cancerful' friends' fb page. it was a link to an organization called Metavivor. Their sole purpose is raising awareness and funding research for stage iv metastatic breast cancer. i read that 30% of breast cancer patients will have a metastasis. 13% of the money raised goes towards stage iv research.[2] this is horrifying. all the numbers hit me. i think of 'cancerful' friends and family and i remember them. these numbers need to change, now. the rain has stopped. as quickly as it came, it disappeared.

i came to taos with expectations. this is the place i was most excited for but i was never really sure why. it makes me think about this trip in general and why traveling has been so important to me. i know the obvious reasons are to experience beauty and other cultures. but i think there is another side to my traveling. am i running away? this is the biggest escape of my life. I've run across this country and others several times for several different reasons and here i am running away again, but from cancer. or is it more a matter of having an adventurous spirit? at least that's what the fb quiz told me. I'm going to think it's a little of both for right now.

this week i got to see the rio grande gorge bridge and hike along the rim of it. i locked my phone and my keys in my car in the desert and then it rained. i have contracted a wretched virus. i spent a day at Ojo Caliente Hot Springs and had a tub in the canyon all to myself. I did a

---

2. CAROL'S NOTE: As Angela points out, only 13 percent of money raised by traditional breast cancer organizations goes toward Stage 4 (metastatic) research. 100 percent of donations to Metavivor fund research into metastatic breast cancer. For more information, please visit https://metavivor.org.

short hike there to see the P'osi Pueblo ruins. I saw the eclipse. I spent the day at the Taos Pueblo for the San Geronimo Feast Day. I walked around the Taos Plaza and Farmer's Market. I have seen adorable bunnies, creepy spiders and heard coyotes calling in the night. I saw one of the oldest churches in America.

And for those of you who can read between my lines…i took a road trip to colorado one afternoon, only an hour by the way. i went to a place where i purchased something legally, something controversial. the one thing that gave me any amount of relief during treatment last year. who knew? instead of 16 medications a day i only actually need-ed that stuff. it was surreal. it was fun. and i felt like at any minute i was gonna get in big trouble. it was a good afternoon, in colorado.

so, it has been a good and not so good week. i have learned a lot. I've struggled a lot, physically and emotionally. It didn't occur to me that climbing a small hill to see some beauty in the desert would take my breath away literally. i have been reminded of the effects of treatment. i don't want to feel bad and i know i shouldn't but i do that I'm not where i want to be physically after treatment. i will try harder to give myself a break. even if i have to stop every 5 minutes on the way up, at least I'm still moving forward. for me, it's not about making it to the top anyways. it never was. it's about seeing and recognizing the beauty along the way. the beauty in simple things, as my great-grandfather said. that's the best part, the simple things. so, if i do make it the top, well. that's just an extra bonus. Sending love and light to you all.

Caves, Contusions and Cows

October 10, 2015

**"we travel, some of us forever, to seek other places,
other lives, other souls."**
—ANAIS MIN

so, i did it. 3 days after staring at it every day i got on the tire swing in payson, arizona. and it didn't break. and, while for a moment i know i had a mischievous smirking grin on my face, it occurred to me very quickly that a tire swing does not feel good. also, drinking a margarita while on a tire swing that doesn't swing back and forth it just twirls around in circles isn't much fun either. I'm still smiling, because on my cancercation this week, i played on a tire swing in arizona, while a cow stood next to me, while drinking a margarita, and i didn't fall down.

the whole week wasn't full of blue skies. in the first 24 hours of arriving here I experienced hail, torrential downpours, flash flooding, mud ankle deep and wind gusts like a hurricane. the town I'm staying in next is actually called hurricane, utah. is this because i spilled the salt last week?

the last few days have been beautiful though and i have seen some unexpected magnificence out here in Rim Country. i spent half a day at the tonto natural bridge, believed to be the largest natural travertine bridge in the world. this park is like a secret garden in a secret garden cave. also, for those of you thrill seekers…who needs amusement parks when you have free roads like this to drive on. i felt sick and part of me thinks there should have been a big black trash can at the end so i could barf into it. where's the dramamine when i need it?

i hiked down to the eden and was so impressed by what was all around me. as if i wasn't overstimulated already by the bridge itself, there were small pools of water, ferns everywhere. i go off the trail a few feet and find a spot on a fallen log hovering over the water. i see dragonflies, butterflies, birds. everything seems larger than it should be down here. the prickly pears are the size of large lemons and bright purple like young grapes. there is life growing out of everything everywhere i look. could i live here? i think i could be very happy down there. prickly pear margarita?

the sound of the flowing water is awesome. it eases my anxious heart and i try to take a couple photos but the secret garden feeling i have is not coming through. i take out my notebook and write. i look and listen instead. i can feel the warmth of the sun on my face, poking through the tree canopy. it is reflecting off a small pool of water nearby. i spot a couple dragonflies chasing each other across the stream. one is blue. one is red. i smile. everyday i am amazed by how beautiful our country is. how lucky and blessed we are to have this and to have the freedom to be here. on the way out of eden i got backhanded by an alligator juniper. nasty trees, but beautiful. at least i have a nice souvenir. i am officially hard core. gash across my cheek…

yesterday i hiked around woods canyon lake on the mogollon rim. it was there, pretty early on, that i was given the gift of walking beside an elk, a cow? she kept sneezing and i actually said to myself or i may have even said it out loud, because traveling on your own will do that to you.. "got a cold huh? me too". we walked together for what seemed like 5 minutes but it was probably more like 2. she was so beautiful and close to me. her wildness made my heart race when i saw her instantly. her size, intimidating. despite my excitement and a bit of fear, we shared a couple moments in this place together.

it was a perfect sunny day on the lake. i needed to be around water. the sunlight glimmered across the top all day. i stopped halfway to write and enjoy some ice cold grape juice. i was alone there and i could have stayed all day. i thought about the future a bit. what is the best way to live this life I've been given? i am not sure yet but what i am doing in this moment feels right. i know it is somewhat wasteful to ponder the what if's of the future. for now i will do my best to think about this lake, this trail, those birds, and the ripple in the water that the wind is pushing my way.

when i arrived home there was a cow in my yard. later on, sitting on the front porch, after the tire swing, there were 5 cows. it is becoming very city slickers here. should i like call someone? oskar is very angry ☺ clearly, they are trespassers and clearly, he needs to take care of the problem. i think they are black angus. I'm remembering this from an animal science course i took at a college in oregon. i switched majors after i saw the dead horse and wrecked my car right after. anyways, i think their udders are black. one of them is so close i can hear his horns rubbing against the wood of the porch.

it's hard to believe i will be home in one month, back in new hampshire. doctors appointments, surgery, recovering blah blah. which reminds me of the daily small dose of chemo i am supposed to be taking but not and the wrath and disappointment of dr. f when i return and the look in her eyes. i have made my decision for now and there hasn't been a day in the last month that I've questioned it. i don't want to disappoint her or anyone but i know my closest loved ones understand and that's all i need for now.[3]

tomorrow, i head to hurricane, utah & zion national park! for 4 days i will explore this wondrous area and I'm sure be taking lots of photos. Until next week.

All my love xo

A

---

3. CAROL'S NOTE: My reflection on making a choice to pause or discontinue treatment is included on page 289.

Alis Volat Propriis

October 17, 2015

**"I am homesick for a place that I am not sure even exists.
A place where my heart is full, my body loved,
and my soul understood."**
—MELISSA COX

it is breast cancer awareness month. you know what that means…
this is gonna be a long one! breast cancer is why i am taking this trip.
i must acknowledge that and talk about what having breast cancer
means to me, hence the title of this blog entry…she flies by her own
wings. i don't want to talk about the culture, the cure, the pink, the
blessings etc. i just want to write about what it means to me today,
good and not so good.

my mind feels tired. my body too. I think knowing this trip is coming to a ridiculously fast end and knowing why i am going home, is
weighing heavy. today, because of cancer, breast cancer, these are all
the things that i thought about, on this cloudy, windy, rainy day in
colorado, on my cancercation. i think about my family history and
my lack of genetic link and the disbelief. but how can we truly know?
i have a lot of cancer in my family. Brain, breast, prostate, colon, skin.

i think about my own genes and what they're doing in there and the ironic link to those types of cancers with this particular genetic mutation, which they're not sure i have but maybe but probably not. i think about the decisions and choices i have to make, had to make and the consequences. i am not invincible and everyday i am readjusting to a new life after treatment, emotionally and physically.

i look back at journal entries from this month last year, the last month of my treatment. i was half way through 5x a week radiation treatments. i was exhausted. i was struggling emotionally and physically. my journal entries were short and sad. On this day last year I said, *"I feel bad all the time now."* last year on this day i had more genetic testing. last year on this day it rained. i am emotional looking back at these entries.

i can see it now, the gradual decline. everything dr. f warned me about in terms of working, not resting enough blah blah, happened. she warned me about the effect and toll treatment would take at the end. in the moment i always thought it can't get any worse than this, but it always did. it was the emotional effect from treatment that came out of nowhere. within 2 weeks of finishing almost an entire year of treatment, i was diagnosed with ptsd. i did not see that coming. i laughed at it but it is a very real thing that happens. like tig notaro makes jokes about in her documentary, "God can't give you more than you can handle..." as a side note, 3 weeks before my diagnosis, right around christmas, the pipes in my home burst and destroyed a lot.

so, for ending treatment as a gift to myself last november i rented a cabin in the catskills. the day after i arrived there, i fell apart and i had absolutely no idea why and i couldn't make it stop. everyone kept saying "aren't you so excited to get back to normal?" i wanted to cry every time someone asked me this. i think there are some that assume that after treatment is over "normal" comes back immediately and I'm sure it does for a lot of people. but it didn't for me and i didn't want it to. i wasn't happy in that normal and i felt more alone than i ever had in my whole life.

dr. f was right. my world came crashing down. I had hit bottom. i accepted it, eventually, and worked hard to recognize it, acknowledge it, work through it and move forward, some days. to understand where the emotions were coming from, my therapist, my amazingly wonderful therapist, reminds me that i have been through a 'trauma, an assault', on my body, my mind. i am grieving loss and i feel guilt. and i now know that i am not alone which is an incredible relief.

i had people in my life that i didn't even know sending me gifts and notes of support and baking me blondies every week. there were so many of you that helped me in hard moments with just a smile. just to see the care in your eyes was enough to brighten my dark days. even for a quick moment. people who cared for me instantly, like my oncology team, other doctors, family and old friends. i have a few tremendously important people in my life. each one of you giving me a different kind of support and i love you all so much. as much as this month is about breast cancer awareness for me, it's about recognizing you. i would not be here, this happy again, without any of you.

there's another side of what becomes of personal relationships, while having cancer. some people start to fade away, some people come back and forth. it wasn't until after treatment was over that i recognized that this was happening. at first i felt hurt and angry and disappointed and confused. but i have to remember that i truly believe that everyone comes into your life for a reason, no matter how long or short the duration of their stay.

i realized that people, even me, have voids that they need to fill. a cancerous friend fills a lot of voids. but then when you're not so cancerous, those voids aren't for you anymore. if this makes any sense at all. i really hope it does. i can't remember where i read this recently but i wrote it down, "be willing to go alone sometimes. not everyone who started with you will finish with you. and that's ok." this is very true of having cancer and the change that occurred in my life with personal relationships, friends, family.

no wonder i feel so fatigued, body and soul, still. maybe it will be like this for awhile. I'm going to assume that my therapist will tell me this is all very normal. she told me there are people that experience physical illness, just driving by the cancer center. i believe it, even though i love everyone in there.

so anyways, a few days ago when i went to zion national park, i thought, screw it, I'm gonna see if this works. I've heard it does sometimes. i drive up to the gate and the park ranger says that'll be $30.00. And i say, it is breast cancer awareness month and i have breast cancer. can i have a discount? he didn't even chuckle, despite my big smile! maybe i am not funny. he said do you have a fourth grader with you? i laughed and said no because i knew where this was headed and i knew i was gonna want to punch the guy so hurry up and take my $30 and fuck off. apparently i could have gotten a discount if i had a 4th grader in the car. i think of tig notaro in this moment. her comedy brings me relief, a lot. her ability to make humor from our disease, i am so grateful for her. watch her documentary on netflix, please.[4]

---

4. CAROL'S NOTE: More information appears at https://www.netflix.com/title/80151384.

hurricane utah and i got off to a rough start. i say that being presently in colorado, having cut my trip to utah a few days short. the owner of the zion rental is a bit off and has changed her pet policies recently. let me mention she did not communicate those changes with me, so long story short, i decided to leave hurricane, utah early and just get to colorado. it was bound to happen sooner or later, a bit of drama. again, is this because of the salt or the black cat? so on the way out, i let oskar eat a bunch of her pretty green grass and barf on the rug. oops..

with my all too short 2 days in utah i went for a drive up to the kolob reservoir and spent a day at zion national park. i love the landscape of southern utah. at the top of the reservoir, it feels and looks like new england, like home. the leaves are changing. at the bottom, it is red canyons and open green land. it is so incredibly beautiful that i actually looked online at land for sale when i got back to the crazy lady's house. the land up there is everything i always wanted. but i have to mention, as i think i have in every post, these roads are fucking terrifying.

zion was impressive. zion was crowded. zion was $30.

on my drive to colorado i listen to stevie nicks and i hear her sing "sometimes it's a bitch, sometimes it's a breeze…" this makes me laugh and i say "amen". i drive the scenic road outside bryce canyon and i wish i could have figured out more time there. bryce has a special feeling to me.

i think about this trip and its purpose and the pressure i was putting on myself, almost unknowingly, to "figure things out". have i figured out the rest of my life or unlock all of my life's mysteries? nope. but i have seen incredible beauty every day, something i didn't see a year ago. i have a better idea of things that i value in this life, things that are important to me and the way i want to live. i always wanted these things but now i know i want them even more.

there is a lingering decision and issue resulting from having breast cancer that i am presently struggling with immensely. i guess to some it would be a private issue, but when you have cancer it's hard for things to remain private. and i totally welcome feedback. during my bilateral mastectomy last year i received immediate reconstruction. meaning i went to sleep and they slashed off my old parts and implanted new parts, all in one go! at the time i was grateful that this was an option, as many others do not have the same. there was no time then to think, to consider how i would really feel about 'them'. at the time, i thought or didn't think that i had an emotional connection to my breasts. i was always one of the ones who would say, "someday i'll get a lift!" now i was getting that, sort of.

i had problems with 'them' from day one. i have not grown to love them. in fact, my body even kicked one out for a while. 6 weeks of antibiotics later and my implant won the battle. but a year later the damage of that fight is clear and i need one new implant. i am conscious of 'them' all the time. i never feel comfortable and i am literally numb from my chest to the middle of my back. i am contemplating and have been contemplating removing them all together. i would have no breasts. there is a huge part of me that wants this relief. but my surgeons feel as though i should give it a shot with a new one and then see how i feel. i have decided to do this but believe with every bit of me that i won't feel 100% secure with this choice. so i continue to think, continue to read, continue to make decisions that are best for me.

the other issue that weighs heavily is removing my ovaries and the treatment related to that for 7-10 years still. After my mastectomy but before chemo started i met with another oncologist who asked me questions i was not prepared to answer. the issue of motherhood hadn't really come up yet and it should have before that moment. if i desired to ever have a child of my own i had to make the decision to harvest eggs before chemo. there were so many factors i had to think about in a 30 minute consultation. if i harvest eggs, realistically the chances they will ever take, are slim. if i harvest eggs i have to take hormones. hormones feed my cancer. if i want to harvest eggs the chemo has to wait. if i want to harvest eggs i need another surgery. I'm sorry, i just found out i have aggressive breast cancer and it spread into my lymph nodes and now i have to decide if i want to be a mother?

no. the answer is no. why, for me, would i ever produce a child of my own? so no, i didn't harvest eggs, i will never have a child of my own. i could always adopt but feel like that would be a pretty stupid move too. so i'll probably just have dogs. i really hope someday to have 2 horses. this would be a dream. i have made peace with not being a mother to a child.

In my new 'normal', some days i am fantastic and some days I am a hot mess. some days i am so overwhelmed with the blessing of this trip and some days I am overwhelmed over why this trip is even happening. some days i stay in that place and struggle to get out. some days i hike up a mountain or large hill. some days i stay in my pajamas and read all day in a rocking chair. i have been letting my soul feel what it needs to and to experience what i need to. some days are just easier to place one foot in front of the other.

the other night when i arrived in colorado, i saw Robert Frost's *Anthology of Poems* on the coffee table. i was curious what poem i would open up to and this was it:

The Road Not Taken

"Two roads diverged in a yellow wood,
And sorry I could not travel both
And be one traveler, long I stood
And looked down one as far as I could
To where it bent in the undergrowth;

Then took the other, as just as fair,
And having perhaps the better claim,
Because it was grassy and wanted wear;
Though as for that the passing there
Had worn them really about the same,

And both that morning equally lay
In leaves no step had trodden black.
Oh, I kept the first for another day!
Yet knowing how way leads on to way,
I doubted if I should ever come back.

I shall be telling this with a sigh
Somewhere ages and ages hence:
Two roads diverged in a wood, and I—
I took the one less traveled by,
And that has made all the difference."

Goodnight sweet world and to my cancerful family...

A

Wasps, Weather and Weed

October 23, 2015

"the world breaks everyone, and afterward, many are strong at the broken places."
—ERNEST HEMINGWAY

the last 7 days were full of nostalgia and rain, in Dolores, Colorado. Nostalgia is defined as a wistful affection for the past, typically for a period or place with happy personal associations. What a wonderful thing…nostalgia.

Funny, the way things work out. I had a lot of things on my 'to do' list, here. But i was tired going into the week. I was only able to see a few but they were the most important few. I visited the four corners. i went to hovenweep national monument. i went to the hot springs in ouray. i sat in a rocking chair and read, a lot.

I needed that quiet. I needed that time. There was something restorative about it. On the days that it rained I would wake, have coffee and write for a few hours. then i would take a trip to one of the 500 walmarts here and get groceries if i needed or wasp killer. there was also a weed store across the street from walmart. what else is there to do in really bad weather…walmart and the weed store. i'd be a lot happier if it was target.

during the afternoons i would read or work on photos. i read more than i have in a long time and it felt needed. the house i rented was on 10 acres and had the most incredible view. it made it a lot easier to just sit. sometimes i would stop and look up from the book i was reading and from the rocker i was sitting on and watch the birds outside on the feeders. some of them forage on the ground around the feeders, some out of the cracks in the patio and some fly into the window i sit at all day.

the silence here makes me think of an excerpt from one of my favorite books, *West with the Night* by Beryl Markham. She says, "There are all kinds of silences and each of them means a different thing. There is the silence that comes with morning in a forest, and this is different from the silence of a sleeping city. There is silence after a rainstorm, and before a rainstorm, and these are not the same. There is the silence of emptiness, the silence of fear, the silence of doubt. There is a certain silence that can emanate from a lifeless object as from a chair lately used, or from a piano with old dust upon its keys, or from anything that has answered to the need of a man, for pleasure or for work. This kind of silence can speak. Its voice may be melancholy, but it is not always so; for the chair may have been left by a laughing child or the last notes of the piano may have been raucous and gay. Whatever the mood or the circumstance, the essence of its quality may linger in the silence that follows. It is a soundless echo."

sometimes i listened to music. i had a soundtrack for these days… classical in the morning, melody gardot and nina in the afternoon, miles and hugh laurie while making dinner. just oskar and i and the prairie dogs, the elk, the birds outside and the wasps inside. I drove out to Hovenweep National Monument, which was fantastic. i was surprised i hadn't heard of that area before now. it was a really nice place to walk around and take some photos. I've learned a lot on this trip about the way i use a camera. i have learned to slow down a bit and actually see what it is I'm looking at.

the four corners…ain't that the truth?! a metaphor for my life at the moment, for life in general. take this treatment and this will happen, have this operation and this will happen, or you could take these two pills for ten years and this might happen. i went to the four corners with my mom when i was 13. i can remember moments of that day. the market stalls, the photos, the memories of being there with my mom. i remember being in a state of wonder as a young girl wandering around the stalls of colorful, crafted beaded jewelry and dreamcatchers and tomahawks! in 23 years not much has changed. it makes me sort of happy but sort of sad at the same time.

hot springs in ouray. the drive there started out as incredible, the beauty in that area of colorado is undeniable. i try to see past what is immediately in front of me to the other beauty beyond. there are snow covered mountains in the distance. i pass a dirt road called "last dollar road". sounds about right for this trip. the weather quickly changes as i get closer to telluride. i see signs warning of avalanches and avalanche blasting. it starts snowing and before i know it i cant see much. i smell hot chocolate and think how strange. i realized an hour later that it was an uneaten kit kat on the floor of my car, melting with the heat on.

while driving to the springs, i think about this whole trip and what drive did i enjoy the most. i think it has to be the drive from utah to colorado. mostly, because of the scenery but also because there were a couple of really nice moments that day. i remember thinking how alone i was on those roads. i remember being surprised by the beauty and changes in landscapes of southern utah. i remember the cows and horses. i remember the water that followed the highway. there was a moment when i looked to the right that day and saw two horses running around a pasture and it made me so happy. they looked so free.

it wasn't long after that, leaving utah, that i stopped at a scenic overlook. i was surprised when i saw what was up there at the top of that hill off the highway. there were two women making and selling jewelry. i stopped to talk to one of them and look at the earrings she was making out of cedar and black beads. i bought them for $10. i walk to the edge of the lookout and i can hear music, but i didn't remember seeing a radio. i look down and there are two guys standing on the ledge below. one was playing a guitar and one a violin. it was beautiful. i stood there in awe while they played enjoying the moment, as much as i did. they were just travelers passing through, like me.

my thoughts continue to drift off while I'm driving to the ouray hot springs. i think of where I'm going and why and how i even know of this place. in february i was given an amazing opportunity to go on an ice climbing trip through an organization called First Descents. They take young adults impacted by cancer on outdoor adventures. I have said it before but this trip changed my 'cancerful' life. They took us to the Ouray ice park, and we ice climbed for days. All of us, and we all made it to the top of those ice walls! After a day of climbing, we would always stop at those hot springs for some relief and some good talks and laughs in the hot pools. that is why i wanted to go there. to be in that moment again. to remember. And of course, a trip to ouray wouldn't be complete without a trip to the brewery and the swinging seats at the bar. nostalgia.

The next day I was supposed to go north to RMNP but with 24 hours notice my reservation was canceled due to rats and the lack of heat in the cabin. so instead of allenspark, colorado I'm in fraser, colorado. the drive here yesterday was interesting. rain, ice, snow, smartfood, sprite, repeat. up and down and around the mountains, repeat. two different worlds on either side of the mountain passes. i was up around 10,000 ft in a whiteout, for a while. The only good thing about having to drive that slow is not getting speeding tickets.

As a side note, while talking to mom the other day she says, "um, you got something in the mail..." she sounds nervous. turns out, that day that i hiked around the lake in arizona and had that awesome moment with the elk and the tire swing, cost me $450 instead of $0. Yep, two tickets, same day. they don't even have to pull you over anymore. they just watch you from the sky and send you a fine in the mail for 'excessive use of speed'. F you arizona.

anyways, i think someone must be up there laughing at me as my wrists get sore from white knuckling the steering wheel. my back is sore from straining to lean forward in a better effort to see through the snow. I'm listening to old school MJB. i wonder to myself if oskar recognizes beauty and how he feels seeing all of this or if he's just like give me another bully stick, mom. i look to the left after one of the tunnels and see a full on snowball fight happening on the side of the highway. four guys, pulled over enjoying the simple things. i needed that yesterday, that smile, that moment.

I am in Fraser, Colorado now. It's still raining and snowing on and off. I am completely content sitting here in this stunning mountain house looking out the windows and seeing nothing but snow-covered pines and mountains in the distance. I think of home, of NH. I think of how a home can be a place or a person or both.

I'm going to be here for the next week and I'm going to enjoy every moment i can of the last days of my cancercation. I'm going to sit in front of this fireplace and read and write. I'm going to think as little or as much as i want. I'm going to rest as much as i want.

i wanted to go up through Wyoming and South Dakota on the way back east next week. I wanted to see the Badlands and drive the northern route back. i have never seen that part of the country. I hope the weather lets me do this.

"Wherever you go becomes a part of you somehow."
—ANITA DESAI

xo

Ad Infinitum

November 1, 2015

**"She is clothed in strength and dignity,
and she laughs without fear of the future."**
—PROVERBS 31.25

i never met my great-grandfather, "Hep". my Mom was pregnant when he passed. but i knew my great-grandmother until she was 96 or 97 years old. i smile when i think of her. She was such a hot ticket, so he had to have been. i know my mom adored him. turns out, his passions in life were a lot like my own. he was a writer, gardener, a lover of horses and the outdoors. he was a dentist. we differ there. i wish i could have known him but his writing makes me know him.

One of my favorite things to read is a poem he wrote called *Simple Things*; what he also titled his book.

"Lord, let me do the simple things:
        The songs that touch me day by day,
A robin's throaty carolings,
        A bluebird's cheery roundelay.

I shall not find a finer air
    Than these, by nature richly penned;
No loftier tune can say I share
    The joy or sorrow of a friend.

No flights of fancy may I try,
    But on these somber, quiet wings
Shall soar within my lowly sky...
    May I do well the simple things."

—JAMES C HEPLER

Today is my great grandmother's birthday. Today is the end of breast cancer awareness month. Today I don't have a lot of words, of my own. Today it has been one year since my last radiation treatment. My cancercation is coming to an end, for now.

xo

Star Light, Star Bright…

November 13, 2015

**"imagine the deepest place where mystery and
intricate gardens of life are always evolving.
where love and passion are the strengths behind survival.
imagine…the soul of a woman."**
—AUTHOR UNKNOWN

9,000 miles, 56 days and 23 states. i am home. my cancercation is on pause for now. home is family, friends, favorite restaurants, familiarity. it is bitter sweet but more sweet right now. i look outside the window and it's raining and i can see the grass and fallen autumn leaves. i see the birds in the bush, fluffing with dampness, the squirrels running around with their tasty treats. the smells of home are the same. there is comfort for me in all of this.

i made it home on the northern route of 90 east without a flurry of snow but did have 2 days of solid rain. wyoming and south dakota were so important for me to drive through on the way back. there wasn't actually much to look at but sometimes for me that is more beautiful than anything else. i woke before sunrise, wanting to reach the badlands around that time. i know a lot of you will scold me but i skipped mt rushmore. that morning was strange and stunning at the same time.

almost running out of fuel i pulled into a very old gas station with a general store just before the park. i love these little places that remain untouched by new technology and truckers. it was so quiet there that i realized what it is like for these small outskirts to be 'off season'. before i know it, there is a huge, beautiful peacock walking around in front of me. a couple people come in and out of the market as if they don't even notice. is it normal to see a peacock in south dakota at a gas station? i was so taken back by this sight that i couldn't even reach for my camera. although looking back i should have. that would have been a fantastic photo.

i took the road through the badlands. i did not see a single other person there the entire time. i would love to go back. i have seen photos of the badlands but what i saw was unexpected. i saw it differently. I'm so happy i took the extra day to see this part of our country. had i known how the rest of that day and the next couple days were going to go on the road, i would have taken another day, driven back to colorado and driven home from there.

so i got another traffic 'citation'. Minnesota, the smelliest, most depressing state i have ever driven through. my day through there included dead deer every mile on the highway, spray painted with big orange X's and topped with bright orange cones, livestock trucks packed with poor fluffy creatures, a total lack of beautiful scenery and an emotionally unstable police officer. i don't think i will ever go back there.

what is with me and cops and why do i have this tendency to yell at them? i was pulled over, not for speeding but for something else entirely. something that was completely unavoidable and the cop knew it. when he wouldn't listen and came back to my car stating "i've issued you a citation...", i laughed, in his face and said, "whatever just give it to me." yep, i did that. he got mad and yelled. basically, this encounter ended with me yelling back at him that "just because he is a police officer does not give him the right to be rude." he put his tail between his legs and walked back to his car. i may have gotten another ticket but at least i got the last word. this situation suddenly reminds me of my 1993-94 junior high yearbook and a message from an old friend written inside to me ... "you are the type of girl that would throw stones at a cop and laugh." i guess i should be grateful i have never been arrested 😊

i sit here thinking about the last couple months, where I've been, what I've seen and i can't believe it's already over. back to doctor appointments, mri's, x-rays, pulmonary function tests, colonoscopies, pre ops, mrsa swabs. just like old times! i may be crazy but i have decided to do my own liver experiment and i am so excited to see the results. i have a mass on my liver, a big one. it is said in traditional chinese medicine that the liver is the organ of anger. i have decided to compare my liver scans from last year to the one i will have tomorrow. i want to see the dimensions and if it is smaller now. If it is i believe that will say a lot. if it isn't then i guess i need to keep traveling! Stay tuned.

i have been thinking about this blog a lot lately and if i will continue it, now that I'm home and have surgery next week. I have made the decision to get one new boob. the other one is as good as its gonna get they say. if i still hate them in 6 months then peace out to my implants. thanks for coming but your services are no longer needed. either way I'm probably going to cover my breasts/non breasts with tattoos anyways!

my cancercation is not technically over, yet. i still have a trip coming up to argentina in march to ride horses through patagonia for a couple weeks. i will be traveling with a small group of women and when we are not butchering rabbits or swimming in cold lakes or sleeping under the stars we will be writing. i have waited a lifetime for a trip like this.

the other morning i woke up early and decided to clean out some old college stuff. i came across papers i had written 15 years ago for my english lit classes. i re-read a lot of them and was surprised to find one paper i had written about goals in my life. it was amazing to read.

my goals 15 years ago were about the same as they are now. i was pretty impressed with myself looking back at all this work, all this writing over the years and research that came from libraries not computers! essays on dh lawrence, kafka, eliot. wow. i read the teacher's comments and one of them said "go further with your thoughts and ideas, represent your own voice more." "best paper of the term." yay me! so maybe i will keep writing…

so for now I'm home, surrounded by family and friends. who cares if i have a surgery next week and will be laying on the couch for a month or more. it will be a piece of cake compared to last year. and when I'm having a hard day of pain or discomfort all i need to do is look at these cancercation posts and photos and i know i will smile.

"Seeing is believing, but sometimes the most real things in the world are the things we can't see."
—CHRIS VAN ALLSBURG

xo

blog
Flight, Fight, Freeze & Metastasis

April 18, 2016

"Please believe that one single positive dream is more important than a thousand negative realities."
—ADELINE YEN MAH

My last blog was in November. So much has changed since then. I have barely written in several months. Ahh to be back in the sun of sweet New Mexico or on the endless roads of South Dakota. There is an incredible difference in the views that I have in my life currently versus then.

i started writing this blog a couple weeks ago sitting in a hotel room in boston, looking out over mass general hospital. I could see the room i stayed in less than two months ago, after having a double craniotomy to remove two brain tumors. This surgery happened less than 12 hours after I found out my breast cancer had most likely metastasized.

I hadn't been feeling well for a while. I had been struggling with the worst headache of my life from the moment i woke up to the moment i slept. everyday i was taking tylenol, advil, muscle relaxers, percocet, valium, anything i could think of or had in my medicine closet to try and make it go away. I tried heat, ice, massage, cranio sacral therapy. nothing helped. I started barfing a lot. I was blacking out. I made a lot of excuses, it's just allergies or a bug or stress from the surgery i had just had to reconstruct one of my implants, that didn't really work. i tried everything i could think of except going to the doctor.

This is the large tumor

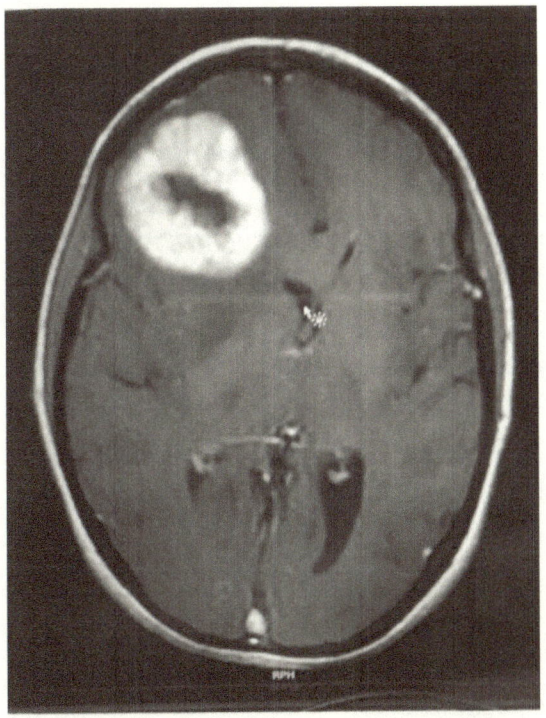

I love my primary care doctor, but I was worried he was starting to think I was a hypochondriac. Since coming home in November from my cancercation road trip, I've seen him a lot, for various 'scares' as I call them. My friend said recently, "Remember when we were healthy? Me neither." We laugh, because it's kind of true but because laughing is healing, not just a veil we can hide behind when dealing with something traumatic, something really fucking sad.

two months after the headaches, barfing and blacking out started, the end of february at this point, my mom saw me curled up in a ball on the floor. she commanded me, because let's be honest i needed that scolding, "get in the car, we're going to the emergency room." I put on my coat and walked out the door. it was time and i knew it. once i was called in the doctor ordered a ct scan to make sure i didn't have a bleed in my brain or a tumor for that matter. to be honest i felt like an asshole going to the er for a 'headache'. i was scared they would think i was a drug seeker or just wanted some attention.

after the scan i saw the doctor walking towards my room and i noticed the tone of his skin, the emotion behind his eyes and i knew. he came in, shut the door gently behind him, paused and then i really knew. he said, there's a mass, two of them". my response was, "are you fucking kidding me?" i don't always say the most appropriate things. sometimes i don't feel bad and sometimes, like this time, i felt bad. he was kind to me and i could tell this wasn't easy for him, given the past medical history he was looking at. side note – I was supposed to leave for the trip of a lifetime horseback riding through patagonia in a few days.

the er doctor paged the neurosurgeon on call who refused to come in and see me because i was not an established patient. what am i supposed to do cut out my own brain tumors? i was pissed initially about his response but i believe everything happens for a reason and i get 'policy'. i now feel grateful about this and have been told by several people who work for this hospital that "he's an asshole and I'm better off." the local hospital transported me by ambulance to mass general hospital where there was an entire neuro team waiting for me. they are gods, mini-12-year-old, pretty gods, just like grey's anatomy.

Back to the tumors, which the gods tell me need to come out asap. i knew they needed to come out but i still said, "like right now?" i was scared. I decided to name them Hannibal and Clarice while waiting to go into surgery. I have a strange sense of humor sometimes and it made the doctors and nurses laugh and my mom and i. When I first saw the images of the largest tumor in my frontal lobe, which was about the size of a lemon, there was a black space in the middle of it and my first thought was "my tumor is cannibalizing itself". i instantly thought of Hannibal, which still surprises me given my hatred for horror movies. The second tumor was small and cute and hanging out in a little space above my right ear. Clarice! I was also on a lot of pain meds aka party drugs as the anesthesiologist called them. 😊

One of my first questions for the surgeons was "do i have to cancel a trip that i leave for in a few days?" He looked at me like he wasn't sure if i was kidding. it was an obvious answer. I spent a year preparing for this trip and i had already packed! i was also going to have to cancel another trip i had been planning to colorado. i had registered to volunteer at a fundraising event for the First Descents. It also meant I was going to miss out on seeing one of my favorite people, Tig Notaro perform. F you brain tumors. couldn't you guys have waited another month, or 50 years.

after the surgery i was in the neuro icu department for a day where i barfed a lot, drank more ginger ale than any human ever and apparently kept telling my mom i wanted bacon and french fries…party drugs. the pain of having a jigsaw cut open my skull was pretty horrible. It took about 50 staples to put me back together. by the end of the first day i had two incredibly swollen black eyes. i couldn't stop looking at them. i started to realize what had just happened the night before and what it all meant. i spent the next five days on the neurology floor of mass general hospital.

my days there were filled with mri's, ct scans, bone scans, lab work, medication every four hours, insulin shots in my belly because the steroids were pushing my blood sugars too high. dilaudid, dilaudid and more dilaudid (pain meds), oncology consults with breast oncology, neuro radiation oncology, neurosurgery, physical therapy to make sure i could walk and climb stairs ok. every single person that i encountered there, that took care of me, was fantastic and kind and the best of the best.

i had a couple weeks at home before my first follow up with the surgeons and new oncology team at mass general. two weeks of having to wait for the final pathology. two weeks of trying to manage the pain of a double craniotomy. mom and i had been told by the doctors that it was very likely these brain tumors were the result of the breast cancer spreading. we were told that it's very 'unusual' for the brain to be the first stop for a breast cancer metastasis. breast cancer typically spreads to the liver, lungs and bone before the brain. my new doctor's feel as though there may be cancer lurking somewhere else, besides the brain, but isn't showing itself just yet as my body scan was clear.

follow up treatment after the surgery was ten cycles of brain radiation and a very strong conversation about me really needing to go back on the low dose daily chemo, that i have been rebelling against since last year. i will have mri's of my brain every two months and ct scans of my other organs every three to six months. the radiation treatments passed by quickly and uncomfortably. the side effects were manageable, and my hair is now falling out but only on the right side of my head. I'm used to this part although it doesn't make it any easier to be back in head scarves and hats.

in order to have the radiation i needed a custom mask made to fit my face. my face would get put in this mask and strapped down to a table where i would lay for 20 minutes of treatment. the technicians let me pick a pandora station to listen to and covered me in warm blankets as i would try my best not to have a panic attack with a little help from my friend, xanax. i can't help but feel like jason from friday the 13th with my creepy mask!

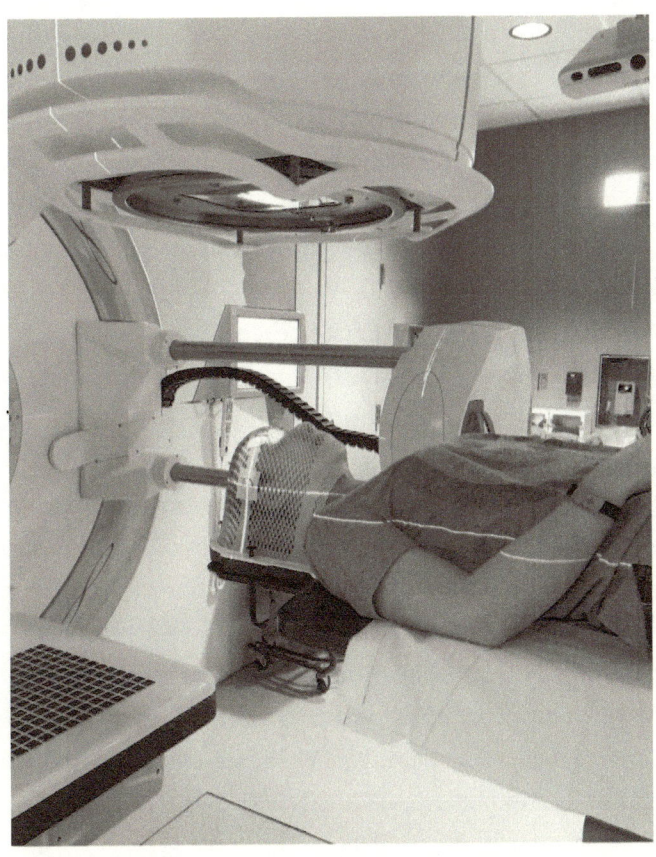

on most treatment days i actually chose to listen to whatever the patient before me had on. this started after the second day when i forgot to have the station changed. as treatment started i hear marvin gaye singing 'let's get it on'. i instantly wanted to laugh but couldn't, due to the restrictions of the mask. it made me smile and it distracted me from the laser beams being shot through my brain. the next day i mentioned it to the techs and we all had a good laugh. from that day on i listened to the motown station for every treatment. sometimes it is the little things that make all of this so much easier.

while listening to the music i would think of these other patients and wonder what they maybe thought about during these minutes. were they sad, scared, happy? i wondered what types of lives these people had before the big C. sometimes the techs would remind me to think of my favorite things which is travel, my dog, friends, family, beaches. somedays it was too hard to go to the beach in my mind. somedays i went to a darker place. my mind travels to places i never thought i would visit at 36. i think about how cancer has picked me apart little by little over the last couple years. i think about how I'm having this treatment knowing my insurance company denied it for being 'medically unnecessary'. i was just starting to live my 'new normal' life, which all of us cancerful's understand.

a lot of people have asked me about my prognosis and while i under-stand my doctor's hesitation in discussing this, the numbers are out there. this is what I've been told by the doctors as of today. they believe there is a 70-80% chance the tumors will return in my brain despite treatment. they believe there may be cancer elsewhere, but we can't see it yet. i am now considered to have an 'incurable' disease, or metastatic breast cancer or stage IV breast cancer with mets to the brain. as far as life expectancy, research shows a 20% chance of being alive in three years or a 10-14 month survival. i try not to even think about these stats right now. I'm still in the surreal feeling phase.

there has been a lot of crying, a little anger. some days pass by and I'm fine, which probably means I've stayed busy distracting my thoughts. there are some days where all it takes is a look at my dog, my beautiful munchkin and i cry. there are some days i don't do anything product- ive. there are some days i still see beauty in this world and in all the people i love. there recently came the day that i was well enough to unpack my suitcase from the trip to patagonia i cancelled. i ended up sobbing on the floor of my closet for an hour. i think it's safe to say i haven't even begun to process all of this and that coming to terms with another 'new normal' is going to be incredibly difficult.

I've been thinking a lot about a memoir i had just finished reading before my C came back. It was written by Eve Ensler, *In the Body of the World*. she writes with brutal honestly about her experience with her own cancer. it is raw but truly validating for me. i love every word, every sentence in her book, right down to the index which is so appropriately titled scans. She makes me think about why and what made this happen? the, was it this or was it that hole. was it my genes? was it the antibiotics? was it the mountain dew and mac and cheese phase i had in junior high? was it when i fake tanned before the high school prom? was it the chemo? was it the air...? Eve describes it perfectly when she says...

" Having cancer was the moment when I went as far as I could go without being gone, and it was there, dangling on the edge, that I was forced to let go of everything that didn't matter, to release the past and be burned down to essential matter. It was there I found my second wind. The second wind arrives when we think we are finished, when we can't take another step, breathe another breath. And then we do."

so, i ask myself, now what? my next brain mri is less than three weeks away. i try not to think too long about it. i will meet with my doctor that afternoon and for now just hope it's clear. my understanding is that if and when the brain tumors come back, if they're small enough, i will have more radiation. i will try the daily chemo pill again. i understand that it's only less than two months since the surgery and that it's a little early to tell how the next year will go. I do know that every day I feel better physically (now that i don't have Hannibal and Clarice and 50 staples in my head ;)). I know that i must be progressing if I'm writing. I know that i have a new mass on my liver and will have another mri later this month to figure that out. I know that this beautiful weather is coming at the perfect time.

I want to be outside. I want to feel and see the green grass. I want to go back to yoga. I want to keep traveling as much as i can. I know I have an incredible support system and people who love me, near and far. I know I'm a little scared. I know that this fear won't stop me from moving forward.

xo

Carol's Reflections
Metastasis

Metastasis. Cancer that has spread from the original site. We both always knew it was a possibility. It is not something we could prepare for or that I had even allowed myself to dwell on. We knew the statistics: an estimated 30 percent of those diagnosed with early-stage breast cancer will develop metastasis; Angela was Stage II at the time of her diagnosis. After her treatment, she always said she did not feel that she was done with cancer, but then you are never done. There is constant monitoring and follow-up after treatment is complete. Any illness raised a red flag for her primary care doctor and her oncologist. We lived with that constant question each time Angela had even a minor symptom or change in her health: Could this be cancer? Some chemotherapy may also cause other cancers to develop.

At the time Angela was diagnosed with brain metastasis, I had been working in healthcare—first as a nurse and then as a nurse practitioner—for thirty-five years. When I worked in the hospital, I did care for patients after surgery for cancer. As a nurse practitioner, I worked on the suspicious-finding side of the diagnosis: If a patient had a worrisome finding, I would obtain testing. If the tests were positive, then I would refer them to the specialists. I would not see those patients again until they had completed treatment and then returned to see me for non-cancer concerns. Although we would talk about how they were managing their cancer diagnosis and treatments, at that time, they were beyond the initial shock and grief of diagnosis.

There is a major difference between understanding and knowing something from the medical perspective and understanding and knowing it from a lived experience. As a mom and as a nurse practitioner, there was a constant struggle for me between the medical, clinical perspective and the mother, emotional perspective. Initially, I had hoped that if I tried to approach Angela's illness from the clinical perspective during appointments and when Angela had questions or we were talking, I would minimize the emotional perspective. That never worked. I am first and foremost a mother; my role as a medical professional is far down the list. I had always experienced some level of fear and worry for patients as they waited for test results; when the patient was my daughter, the fear, worry, and anxiety moved to the foreground. When Angela was diagnosed, and through the seven years of treatment, I realized how little I knew about the full spectrum of emotions—fear, grief, sadness, and still times of joy—associated with having cancer.

When Angela was initially in the hospital for her mastectomy, I became disheartened about the quality of nursing care. This was a career I had been in for more than thirty years, and the care was awful, an embarrassment. I remember apologizing to Angela.

When she was treated at Mass General, I lived in the same clothes for the entire stay. I was afraid to leave her, and I slept in a chair in the room for almost a week. I will say that her descriptions are accurate: the care was exceptional. When Angela was admitted for her second craniotomy, she insisted that I get a hotel room and leave at night to get sleep. She looked at me and said, "You know that they will take care of me here."

Before the trip to the ER, I knew Angela was having headaches, but she had not told me about the passing out or the vomiting. She later told me that when she went to her primary care doctor, she did not give him all the information either. I understood her fear.

The day I insisted on taking her to the ER, I had just talked with a coworker about my fears. I had finally said it aloud: I was afraid she had brain cancer due to the headaches. Up until that point, I had harbored the superstition that if I said it aloud, that would make it real; it would make the fear overwhelming. This was the collision of my clinical and maternal roles.

Next followed the ambulance to MGH, including twelve hours in the ER seeing neurology and neurosurgeons. Then came surgery, the waiting, eventually sitting at her bedside holding her hand—or the bucket. Listening to everything that the specialists offered, and trying to write it all down since I knew I would never remember.

Finally, home. There we realized that Angela and steroids were not a happy combination. The high dose that she needed after surgery made her extremely irritable. I learned this the day she came home and was glad her dose was being tapered.

We were given a list of instructions. One was no haircut for six weeks. The day she came home, she took scissors to her hair in her bathroom. Then she came to get me, still holding her scissors, to ask me to cut the back into the pixie she had cut the front. Fear overwhelmed me that a snippet of hair would get into the wound and cause an infection.

I did cut the back; I did not want her to try this on her own, and she was not in a state to do it. Here was Angela, as she always had done, paving her own path. I did not remind her that she was not supposed to have a haircut. It was already done. Reminding her would have increased her irritability from the steroid dose and would not have changed her risk for infection. This was the first time I cut her hair but not the last. Each time would bring me to tears.

Only once before had I ever tried to cut Angela's hair. She was a toddler, and I tried to trim her bangs. They were so bad, I took her to a stylist to have them fixed. Either Angela did not remember that episode or she chose not to remind me of the risky combination of me, hair, and scissors.

I recognized how much Angela was grieving when she wrote about lying on her closet floor crying about the missed trip. She had been so excited about that trip and had experienced so much loss already, my heart shattered. When I read about it in her blog, my heart broke again. I told Angela I would have helped her unpack, but she said she needed to do it alone.

Throughout this process of grieving for seven years—and now grieving Angela's death—I see how we often managed in a similar manner. We each felt the need to be alone with our pain, with our grief. Oftentimes, I still do.

blog
At the Next Roundabout...

July 3, 2016

"It's no heavier than the weight you give to it..."
—AUTHOR UNKNOWN

I'm behind with my writing. there are no rules that i follow for my posts in terms of timing but this one i wanted to get done a while ago. it seems like everything takes me a bit longer than i expect it to these days. as i sit writing this i am in spain, on the beautiful mediterranean coast and i can hear the water and the boats below. it feels a bit strange to be writing about iceland when I'm in spain but there are no rules here.

Iceland. a land unlike any other i have ever seen. the landscape gives off a feeling of being on another planet. the country is covered in lava and moss and people refer to it as the lava desert. at the time of our week there it was still quite cold. my mom and i arrive and rent a car and drive up the west coast towards the home we will be renting for a week. it still surprises me that i had brain surgery and radiation just a matter of weeks ago. we had been planning this trip for some time and are incredibly relieved when i get the clearance to fly.

We arrive at the beach house and are at a loss for words when trying to describe what we see. I have actually been struggling quite a bit to write about iceland. it's mysterious and majestic all at the same time. the owner, Jona, is waiting for us and welcomes us so genuinely into her home. she's an artist and shows us her workspace and i am instantly amazed at the beauty of her work. we have been corresponding now for the last 6 months about our stay and my medical condition. she gives me a gift of a necklace that's called a smiler. i am to wear it for it serves as a reminder to keep smiling. i am overwhelmed with her kindness and generosity.

mom and i relax in the mornings, have coffee and tea and look out at the water which is truly mesmerizing. we talk about the things we have seen here and the feelings we had at certain moments. there is truly a feeling of pure calm and a spiritualness that can't be adequately described by myself. i believe we are just so happy to be away from the craziness that has been the last two months of our life. we are relieved and i believe we finally feel like we can take a deep breath again. my mom and i both need this time away, to see incredible beauty and be reminded of the notion of hope and strength and will and love. as much as i am going through this cancer trip, she is as well. we both need this time to rejuvenate and rest in a place as magical as this.

I wasn't sure what to expect going into the week in terms of how i would feel and how much activity I'd be able to do. i felt really good the whole time and just that felt really good. every day we saw something new and awe inspiring. from the dramatic coast and rocky cliffs full of seagulls, to the endless number of waterfalls, to the quaint Icelandic homes and small villages, to the Icelandic horses that are everywhere as we drive, to the northern lights, to the geysers and hot springs and elf villages. it was incredible, all of it, every day. it was the perfect place for us to start moving forward, again.

Now, a blog about Iceland wouldn't be complete without talking about the northern lights. it was like pure magic to see and we were lucky enough to see them many nights. the key to seeing them is cloud coverage, reflection of light from the earth and magnetic connection. the Icelandic Vikings believed the northern lights were fires that surrounded the edge of the world. Some people believe that the lights are the souls of unmarried women dancing in the sky. you can't look away for a moment because the colors and shapes change in a matter of seconds. mom and i set our alarm for 2 am most nights, as that is the best viewing chance. it's bitterly cold and windy outside and i run in and out of the house to warm up but not wanting to miss a second of the show outside.

This trip to Iceland showed me that i can still travel, i can still see beauty on this earth despite the ugliness that sometimes fills my days. i have learned so much in the last couple years through my illness, things i may not have learned otherwise and for this i am grateful. many aspects of my life make more sense now. I'm hard on myself and sometimes hard on others. what i used to describe as running away from things in my life, i now have a different perspective of. negative times in my past, or ugly, non-beautiful moments now give me the motivation for seeking new beauty. I feel maybe i'm just trying to replace old memories that don't bring light to my life. i am trying desperately to surround myself with beauty. it's not running it's seeking change, a dramatic and beautiful change and the world is giving me this in vast quantities now.

one of my favorite authors, eve ensler, refers to herself as a 'tragedy magnet'. i understand this, i feel this some days. the more time that passes by, the more moments i have that are not tragic. i have lived a life some people envy. i have seen places many will not. i have made it through this life so far and feel as though for all the ugliness i have seen, there is more beauty in my sightline than ever before. I think about this and how incredible it is that every day i smile with something new.

i sit and reflect on all the things i always thought i wanted for my life. Love, Peace, Health. There have been times that i feel sad because what i thought i wanted wasn't occurring exactly how i imagined it. But, more so now than ever, i am beginning to look at these goals, these dreams and realize i actually have all that. maybe i'm getting everything i always wanted but in a different way. i have love in my life in the form of family and friends. i have peace in my life as i sit here on the mediterranean sea and write. i have health in that i am still here, despite my illness and i feel good today. i felt good yesterday and the day before. i can still walk and talk and dream and swim and lay in the sun and travel. i was so afraid that with the progression of my disease i wouldn't desire these things anymore.

all these feelings remind me of an email i received from a friend i met traveling last year through the southwest. he sent me an extract from his favorite poet, Robert Service. I have been fortunate enough to meet such kind people in the last year. I am a believer that everyone comes into our life for a reason no matter how long or short their stay. there is a reason he sent me this extract. i connect to it completely.

> *"Have you gazed on naked grandeur*
> *where there's nothing else to gaze on,*
> *Set pieces and drop-curtain scenes galore,*
> *Big mountains heaved to heaven, which the blinding*
> *sunsets blazon,*

Black canyons where the rapids rip and roar?
Have you swept the visioned valley
with the green stream streaking through it,
Searched the Vastness for a something you have lost?
Have you strung your soul to silence?
Then for God's sake go and do it;
Hear the challenge, learn the lesson..."

—THE CALL OF THE WILD
ROBERT SERVICE

My life has always been about change and dreams. Through cancer my dreams have changed a little from time to time but i readjust. someone asked me recently if you could trade all your life experiences, travel etc. and not have cancer, would you? i thought it was an interesting question, one i hadn't been asked before and it really made me think quite a bit about my reality. i quickly answered no. i wouldn't give it back. That is the lesson, my lesson.

"Speak your truths and let your heart be heard for even disaster is beautiful when it is pure."
—BECCA LEE

All my love,

A

Carol's Reflections
Iceland

It was a relief when Angela was allowed to fly and travel after her first craniotomy. We were a pair: she with short hair and a fresh craniotomy scar and me in an ankle boot carrying a bone stimulator for inflammation in my foot, which was originally thought to be a stress fracture, although the cause was never identified. We were of one mind: neither health issue was going to stop us from taking the trip.

Angela had been cleared to travel by her oncologist, but my orthopedic specialist, without providing a reason, said I couldn't travel. I told him the trip was not negotiable: I was going. He just looked at me and didn't say anything. In that moment, I felt like Angela, standing my ground and making the decision that was right for me. I was initially surprised that he had no interest in my comment. It reinforced for me how exceptional Angela's team was. When he left the room, I explained the situation to the physician assistant. She told me to go, wear the ankle boot, and change to a hiking boot if I expected to be in areas that were unstable or uneven.

The positive part was that because neither of us was physically in the best place, we allowed ourselves time to rest, restore, and take our time to enjoy Iceland, the people we met, the quiet time together, and the wonders of this country.

Iceland

Everything about the trip was a blessing. It occurred when we needed it; as Angela said, it gave us a chance to breathe. It was restful and peaceful. Our lives were changing and our dreams for the future were changing, but the trip was perfect. It was a week to put aside our fears and grief and just be present with each other and ourselves.

The home we rented was beautiful, and with a grocery store nearby, we were able to pick up ingredients for dinner and relax at home. The hardest part of the trip was Angela's insistence on doing all the driving. Although I did all the driving back and forth to Boston, she wanted to do it for me in Iceland—and she preferred to be the driver on the narrow, winding roads to prevent the motion sickness she usually experienced as a passenger. But you know Angela's issue with speed and tickets! She was gifted with a speeding ticket in Iceland!

Taking this trip with Angela renewed the strength I needed to go home and face the next set of scans and appointments. Today, the memories we built in Iceland still bring a smile and joy to my grieving heart. This was one of the gifts in life that I continue to hold tight.

Cyber Knives, Clarice's Baby & Champagne

August 16, 2016

**"In my everyday life, I am often consumed by
my effort to stay alive."**
—AUTHOR UNKNOWN

Today I'm sitting in my grandmother's cottage on the Ocean City, NJ beach. It is cloudy and there was rain last night. A perfect morning to wake up, write and have some coffee. This will be my last time here at my grandmother's house, a place that some people chuckle about when they hear 'the jersey shore'. This is an entirely different area of Jersey than the infamous 'Jersey Shore.' This place was an incredibly important piece of my youth, this house, this beach. I grew up on this beach, in these waves, on that boardwalk. I'm recovering from more brain radiation that I had earlier this week and I can't think of a better place to try and bounce back.

I'm reminded as I sit here having a coffee that my life is very different from others. Somedays it's easy to feel like another normalish human on this earth and then there are the days that I feel like I have a sticker on my forehead that says, "Got Cancer." The man who checks me through security yesterday, checking my documents etc., looked at my ID and remarks on how different I look than the photo. This actually happens more than I'd like it to. Maybe I should get a new photo ID. Sometimes when I'm questioned about my appearance, I just play it off, like it's not a big deal, but when airport security is giving me the questionable eye I say, "Well cancer will do that to you". He says I look wonderful and that he's sorry to hear this, to stay positive and to keep fighting. He was genuine and for once this statement about my appearance didn't make me want to punch this person in the face...oh the daily struggles of living a cancerful life.

Getting to the meaning of the title of this blog. Upon my return from Europe in July, I had a brain MRI that showed a new tumor. I have not given it a true name this time. I refer to it as 'Clarice's baby'. I was diagnosed with brain metastases from my breast cancer in February this year. I had a scan in May, and it was clear after the craniotomy and 10 treatments of radiation. This tumor is/was a very small baby tumor hiding in the back of my brain. A baby tumor so small that they actually missed it on my scan in May. Thankfully Baby Clarice has grown very slow and the required treatment this time was more radiation but a different kind, a much stronger radiation than last time. This one radiation treatment had more radiation than my last 10 treatments combined, by a lot. So much radiation in fact, that they had to partially sedate me for 3 days after because of the high risk of seizures. This treatment is referred to as cyber knife or gamma knife. The champagne is just because I've been drinking a lot of it recently!

Can you see it??

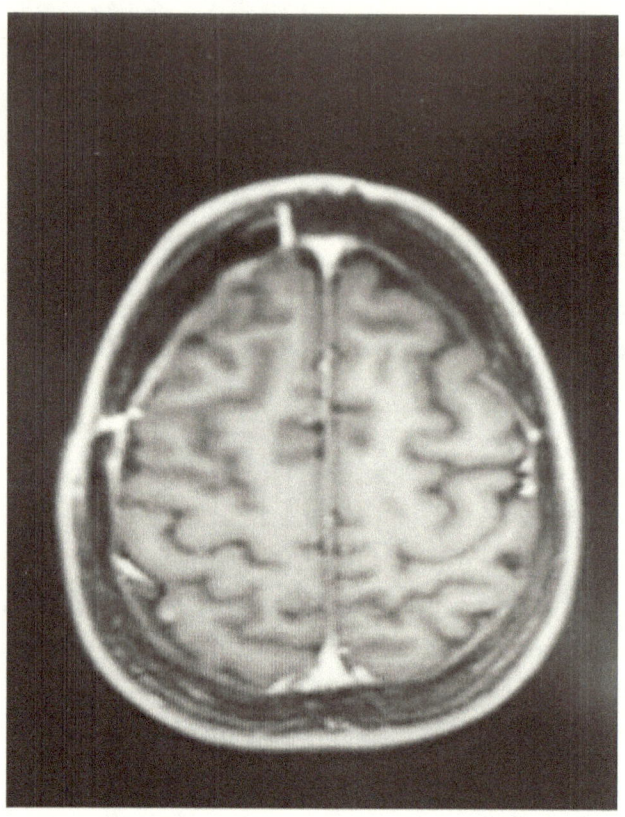

Recently I've realized how scared I actually am. The doctors say all these feelings are completely normal "given the circumstances." Before my radiation treatment I had to have a mouthpiece custom made that would secure my head in place. I thought the mask last time was bad, this was way worse. God forbid they radiate the wrong part of my brain. I had to go to a different area of the hospital than I normally do. It was in other words in the basement. The elevator opens and the first thing I see is a cancerful child, several of them, coloring at a table, playing with toys. It took my breath away. In the 3 years I've had cancer and cancer treatments I've never seen a child. I welled up with tears immediately and stood there for a second dazed.

They had beautiful bald heads and skin just like I remember. It hurt my heart. Normally I'm the youngest one in the waiting rooms.

My mom says one day recently through her tears, that the treatments are becoming more and more barbaric and that it's just not fair. Well, unfortunately or fortunately this is how we now have to manage my terminal disease. This is the cost. This is the only way at this point. The doctors refer to it as a kind of cancer maintenance. I get the idea but at the same time I want to say, 'can you not refer to me like I'm a vehicle?' So, we are 'maintaining' my disease until it becomes unmaintainable. Dr. P says it wouldn't be unlikely for there to be several new brain tumors that show up in the upcoming year.

I thought I had a clear scan two months ago but when the doctors looked back, this new tumor was actually there. They just didn't see it. The last two months and during my trip to Europe I've been on this no new tumor high, and I have felt great emotionally and physically. With this new tumor and learning that it was always there I feel like I've been knocked down by Mike Tyson or whoever punches really hard. Less than a month after my surgery it grew. I think about what my oncologists have told me since the beginning, that the first 3 MRIs are the most important and the most indicative of how the next 12 months of my disease will progress. It's reoccurring quickly but slowly. So, it's good and bad. It's 'maintainable' right now. I am devastated to be completely honest. I have been saying the whole time if I could just get like 6-12 months of clean scans, I'd be really happy, just a little more time. I am reminded that this may not be my reality, but I will still hope for it.

I feel like I've been living the last two months on a magic cancer carpet of no new tumors. Now my magical cancer carpet is coming down and I'm suddenly living in the Fault of Our Stars instead of Aladdin. I think morbid thoughts at times, like, how fast is this going to go, how much time will I have, will I get to Bali or Morocco? I think about how my life has changed since my diagnosis and the changes I've made to be a healthier me. I became a vegetarian (except I didn't give up cheese. What do you think I am, crazy?) I burned sage and whatever else people told me to burn. I meditated and practiced hot yoga consistently, I limited myself to only 2 glasses of champagne a day 😊 I've been taking alllll my pills and complying medically with everything they tell me to do now versus a year ago when I just said F off. I swallow a handful of 16 brightly colored pills at night, supplements, hormone blockers, chemo, sleep meds, anti-depressants, anti-anxiety meds for PTSD, supplements that are supposed to help me be strong and give me energy and probiotics.

What a difference 12 months make. Now, my first question for my doctors is "What's the most aggressive form of treatment I can do?" What has shifted in me to make me want to keep going with all this 'crap'? Why am I suddenly ok with all of this treatment? I feel like a hypocrite sometimes but at the same time it's my life and my decision and we all know that things change and sometimes it takes someone else to show you the path, the way, even if it's a way that last year you would've given the middle finger to. I want to keep going. I want to keep doing what I need to for me, my mom, my family and friends.

I've always said to my therapist and to my mom, that I knew my cancer was going to come back. I just didn't know when. I knew the biggest risk of recurrence was the first few years. I guess I'm right on the cancer schedule. There was actually a tiny bit of relief when it did come back. But now, there's still an element of waiting, waiting for it to come back again, waiting for it to take over my brain, waiting for it to truly affect my ability to live freely. Sometimes in my head I think F it. This effing sucks. Cancer effing sucks and I don't want it anymore. I don't have that option so educating myself about my disease and hearing other's experiences and traveling and smiling reminds me that I am still alive. I can do this. I can feel however I want to feel, good or bad. "Give yourself a break" is a sentence I hear a lot from people closest to me and from my own heart. I need to give myself permission to feel all of it or sooner or later it will all catch up to me anyway.

I'm sure I'll adjust. It's inevitable. I always typically do. I had just finished readjusting to one kind of new normal life, now it's another. Somedays are harder than others to focus on the future or daydream in the same manner I used to. There are some days when I still believe the idea of running away to an island will cure me. That, that's all it would take to find the peace in my life I've been looking for all these years. I know differently now. It doesn't matter how far I run, it's all still there/here. By 'it' I guess I mean the heaviness, the weight and sadness of my life at times, the panic that follows me around on some days. At 37 you'd think I'd learned my lesson about running. I ran to Oregon, Australia and back again. I've traveled pretty close to as far as I can go. I've seen the world by car, boat, bus, bike, plane, train and my own eyes. I wouldn't give that back.

My new oncologists told me recently that they were aware of my hesitance towards more treatment based on what they read from my medical history. I thought I was on everything I was supposed to be on chemo wise but I'm not. They're sneaky and clearly very smart. Dr. S and Dr. M said that they didn't want to 'throw the kitchen sink' at me. I understand that their motive was to ease me in gently to this new stage of my disease, to start off easy with the daily chemo again and see if I tolerate it better than last year. In actuality, there are several more things I need to be doing but they'd prefer it if I took this in baby steps, so I don't just quit like last time. ☺ So, in September along with my daily low dose chemo and everything else, I will start a monthly injection that will shut down my ovaries completely and put me into menopause. I will also have a 17th pill to take. 6 months after I begin this regimen, we will make a decision about removing my ovaries and/or doing a hysterectomy. After that I would need more long-term medications to help combat bone loss at an early age and another scan would be added to the list twice a year to monitor bone loss.

I've passed every neuro exam I've had. I know them all by heart now. I can play patty cake with my oncologists. I can follow their fingers with my own. I can squeeze their fingers using my hands. I can resist force on my legs, and I can put one foot in front of the other. The effects of brain cancer and the surgery and radiation for me are memory loss, tremors, fatigue, headaches, dizziness upon standing or bending over. Most days I keep moving forward. Somedays I lay on the couch or in bed and don't get up. I can't work so filling my days has been a struggle. I try and read a bit every day, write a bit every day, re arrange my closets and my mom's kitchen cabinets. I think I've finally gotten the cabinets perfect, even though a month later I'm still opening the wrong cabinets for my cereal bowls and coffee cups. I just started painting and that helps, even though I am a terrible painter.

Now that I can't work, I have a new struggle to work through. We attach so much importance and worth to careers and money that when that doesn't exist anymore how do we still feel worthy? Even on the days that I can't get out of bed I at least try to do an errand or cook a meal. It's incredible how just doing an errand makes me feel better.

Maybe it's a bit of just being outdoors and feeling the fresh air across my skin or maybe it's the relentless reminder of a deep need to do something, anything. That desire and need to feel useful and worthy and productive doesn't just go away.

While upset at my recent 'setback' I think about how in less than one short year I was able to experience an insane amount of cool stuff and see more beautiful places than I ever imagined. I also think about how 8 weeks after brain surgery I was walking around Iceland with my mom and having mimosas on the beach with my friend in Mexico or biking around Amsterdam or sitting on the beach in Spain. I think about the trips I have coming up this year and try not to think about the potential that I won't be able to go. Maybe I won't get to Asia or Tahiti this year like I had hoped but the travel list for 2016 is still pretty impressive and it's not over yet. I still have Hawaii and Panama to come!

I have several really important scans coming up next month and I'm not going to lie and say I'm not worried. I have a bone scan, CT of my chest, abdomen and pelvis in August. Dr. S's statement from several months ago is ringing in my ears when I think of these tests. "We are concerned that because of the rarity of breast cancer spreading to the brain as a first stop that it's somewhere in your abdomen/chest but we can't see it yet." What if next month they find something and that nothing that I'm doing will help. I can't imagine having the time left that the stats show. A year? It has already been 6 months. I can't even begin to process that potential reality, so I won't right now. Right this second that is not my reality so I just remind myself to stop it. Right now, I'm sitting in my grandmother's beach cottage and enjoying every moment and remembering her and what I had the opportunity to share with her before she passed. Right now,

I feel OK. Right now, I am doing something productive and worthy. Right now, I am happy. Right now, I am still moving forward. I won't let myself go backwards.

> **"She was beautiful, but not like those girls in the magazines. She was beautiful, for the way she thought. She was beautiful for that sparkle in her eyes when she talked about something she loved. She was beautiful for her ability to make other people smile even if she was sad. She wasn't beautiful for something as temporary as her looks. She was beautiful, deep down to her soul."**
> —AUTHOR UNKNOWN

xo

Carol's Reflections
Dealing with My Own Feelings

During the seven years Angela had cancer, I struggled to use a journal consistently. Instead, on occasion I would open my journal, write one entry, and then stop again for months or years. I kept telling—promising—myself that I needed to write, to journal my experiences, to record my view of being a mother of a daughter with metastatic cancer. I knew that it would help me to journal my feelings and experiences, but I found that it was hard to stick to it. This is one of the rare journal entries that I wrote after we received Angela's scan results on July 16, 2016.

We have just found out that Ange has another brain tumor #3. I sit in shock in that exam room. Someone has just taken a ram to my stomach. I think I will be sick as I hear these words and see the happiness Ange has been experiencing, the joy she has had in her life in the past few months just disappear. Her face contorts with pain, shock, and eyes fill with tears. Dr P hands her a box of tissues.

It has been there for 2 months, the clean MRI from 2 months ago is not clean. The breath I took two months ago was not real.

He talks about the treatment recommendation, and I am once again overwhelmed with the brutality of health care. I have been involved in health care for over 30 years and am again, as I have been for the past 2½ years, overwhelmed with a new torture device, a new way to steal a bit more dignity from my daughter.

We drive home amid bad jokes and poor humor. She again talks about moving to Oregon or VT or another state that allows medically assisted death. She knows that she is not at that point but has a plan in place. She wants 2 years. She asks for so little.

Ange writes in her journal, and we talk about the visit while sitting in traffic. She talks about wanting to wear a wedding dress.

Ange wants 2 years—how little to ask for. I want so much more!

When I finished writing this entry, I curled up in bed, sobbing. I now realize that it was a good thing and a normal response. Although I had not put a name to what I was feeling, I now recognize it as grief.

Biked, Baked & Bried

"Courage is not the absence of fear, but rather the judgment that something else is more important than fear."
—AUTHOR UNKNOWN

I have no cancer anywhere in my body, except my brain! My bone scan, CT scans of my chest, abdomen and pelvis were clear. Let's just start with that!

Before I get on with this entry though which is about the super fun topic of travel and not sometimes sad cancer, I'll fill in the rest of the lame medical stuff. So, no cancer anywhere else, yay! I have two liver tumors which we are monitoring already, a nodule in my lung which they're not worried about and a fractured rib that I totally didn't know about and that for some reason isn't healing. I wonder if the radiation caused that? I feel like I should know if I have a fractured rib.

As far as my genes go, we know about my MutS Protein Homolog 2 (MSH2) gene variance already. This gene combines with another gene to form a protein during cell development that helps "fix mistakes" in DNA. Actually, to me, the lame medical stuff is sometimes kinda not lame at all but totally fascinating. It's astonishing what happens inside the body, inside our cells & DNA, just to make a tumor. I also just found out after a test was done on Hannibal (one of my brain tumors, former) that my Fibroblast Growth Factor Receptor (FGFR1) gene is messed up too. This gene from what I've read is linked to abnormally fast cell growth and division. Hence, the three brain tumors in as many months. The mutation in this gene is quite widespread and there could be a clinical trial available. I've been referred to another new SUPER neuro oncologist and I'm very anxious for her thoughts on this.

Now that's over with, I can talk about CAMEMBERT, COFFEE, CANALS, CAVA & CANNABIS (Amsterdam & Spain)! I'm breaking all my blog rules tonight! I used B's instead of C's in the title and I just used five C's instead of three! Let's see if I actually get to the end of this entry without my OCD kicking in and changing it all back to three C's. Anyways, this entry is about my trip to Europe this past summer with my cousin and what a magical trip it was.

I had been planning this trip to Amsterdam for a year. Before I even booked my flights, I bought a ticket to see Coldplay there. The deal was made, I was off to Amsterdam. A place that has been at the top of my dream list for a very long time. Even better, I was able to use my airline miles to upgrade my seats. A private pod just for me and as much champagne and fancy snacks as I could eat and drink during the flight and I didn't feel bad about it at all.

When I arrived in Amsterdam my cousin was waiting for me and off we went to find our apartment. As we ride the bus into the city, I'm thinking about how excited I am but exhausted. I was so happy and grateful Anthony decided to come along for this trip. The flat is beautiful, in a perfect location and has two balconies! At one end of the bricked street there is Vondelpark, a grocery store, a cannabis store (which the Dutch call 'coffee shops'), a wine shop and a great cafe for morning and afternoon coffee and writing. At the other end was one of the beautiful canals. We walk to dinner on the first night and I think…I'm going to soak up everything, every moment, every sight, every 'coffee shop', every walk on the canal, every harrowing bicycle ride, every frite with mayo and every beer and museum and park. All of it.

We walked to a little pizza shop, sat and had a local beer, settling in to the away from home mode, watching the bikers pass by. I don't remember anything after that. Ha! Just kidding but what a first night out in Amsterdam. Our waitress and her roommate became true friends to us while there and brought us out for a 'few beers' after her shift. What a great way to experience Amsterdam on the first night. We walked through Vondelpark to reach the city center, and it was beautiful and dark out with the park lights creating a lighted path for us. The park opened in 1865 and is 120 acres in size. There was a foggy mist that settled in during our walk and glowed under the lights above. We talked about our lives and why we were there and their lives and their dreams. And then we reached the bars. Thankfully on the way there Evita and Diana had taught me how to order beers in Dutch. Vier biertjas, which to me sounded like fear beerchas!

The next thing I knew we were walking home at 5 in the morning watching the night turn to day with a bit of rain and a rainbow. I was more happy than I had been in a long time. The whole night we drank, we danced, we sang, we walked, we laughed, and I even got a make-up lesson somewhere in there. What beautiful people to be surrounded by my first night in this place I've dreamed of. I fell asleep at 6 am listening to the thunder and rain and my heart was happy.

I have always been drawn there. The people are kind and generous and welcoming and interested and interesting. I felt comfortable there. A once small fishing port, Amsterdam is now a thriving cultural capital of the world on 60 miles of canals. That first night made me feel a bit emotional the following day. Thankfully we slept until 3 in the afternoon, and I had the Coldplay concert to look forward to that night. I remember knowing where the emotions were coming from. It came from a place of pureness and beauty. I had such a wonderful first night and we all talked so much about life that it naturally stirred up some sadness at the same time for me.

Throughout this trip I found myself in plenty of situations where I was asked "What do you do?", in both Amsterdam and Spain. It's a natural first question. The dilemma of telling people the truth about why I'm traveling versus the desire to not make people sad or uncomfortable, which is sometimes the effect, can be a difficult place to be in for me. Sometimes I just say, "I'm taking some time off to travel." This always seems a bit wrong to me, but I know it's not technically. I'm more comfortable just getting it out there. I want people and new friends to understand me and why I'm choosing to live my life this way.

COLDPLAY! Holy shit and Lianne la Havas as an opener! I went alone and I had a horrible seat. I thought I would fall down from heat stroke, but I danced and yelled and sang and stood up the whole time. I had seen Coldplay before in Boston, but this show was different. For me there is a power in their music that opens my heart. Lianne is an amazing musician and she's beautiful and her smile and lyrics light everything up. I had tears in my eyes for most of the show and I had no shame about them or the sweat pouring down my face. "Paradise… every time she closed her eyes."

One night a friend of Anthony's that lives just outside the city center invited us to her home for dinner with her partner and their adorable two boys. A wonderful family and I felt really overwhelmed with their genuineness. To be invited into their home was such a fantastic night to be a part of. During the days we rode around the canals on our bikes, through the parks, sometimes we'd stop and lay in the sun, and I would smoke a joint because I could or sit by a fountain or visit a cheese museum. A couple nights we had a wonderful dinner in our apartment with wine and the Euro cup on TV. I loved the feeling of actually being there, in a true Dutch apartment, not a hotel room. Like I was really part of it all. I could get used to that life.

One rainy day we ended up at the Stedelijk Museum, mostly because we couldn't get into the Van Gogh Museum in any reasonable amount of time. The Stedelijk Museum holds 150 years of modern and con-temporary art and design. It holds the perfect blend of old and new. I have never been drawn much to modern or contemporary art, but I was moved by what I saw there. Room after room of 'wows'. There were pieces by Van Gogh, Kandinsky, Warhol, Picasso, furniture from the early 1900s. I read an article online yesterday and the writer described this museum and its collections as, "confusingly beautiful". I couldn't think of a better way to describe it.

Our last day in Amsterdam. I'm sad and excited. We take a bike ride, we eat frites, we have lunch at our favorite noodle bar while it sprinkled rain on us. That evening we were so graciously invited on a private cruise of the canal by a friend of a friend. He lives on a houseboat on one of the canals and has just finished renovating it. We bike to the boat and it's a gorgeous space. It takes my breath away when I see the soaking tub in the master bedroom overlooking the canal. He takes us out on his smaller boat and puts on a fantastic spread of prosecco and munchies. He takes us all over the city for over an hour. I was so happy and not just because I wasn't barfing! He points out the famous sights, even where he grew up. I may not have gone inside the Anne Frank house, but I got to see it by boat from a private tour on the canal! It really gave me a different perspective seeing it all from below, if you will. Lots of people were looking at our boat and waving and for a moment or two I think we all felt a little bit like celebrities and not tourists. I guess it's a bit appropriate given our new friends are in the film industry. As much as our first night couldn't be beat this was just as amazing and the best way to end our time in one of my new favorite places.

My cousin and I had to move on and were looking forward to the next part of our adventure, ESPANA! Evita, our new friend, accompanied us to the airport and gave me a wonderfully thoughtful gift before we left. Goodbye Evita, Dianna, Femka and all our new and old friends. Thank you for absolutely everything and I truly hope to see you all again. I was overwhelmed with pure joy when we left Amsterdam.

Spain was never a place I thought I would travel to, or it wasn't at the very top of my list. Anthony has wonderful friends whose family offered us their home to stay in. It's on the beach and has a pool and so we headed to Spain instead of Prague! His friend from his high school days lives in Torrevieja and picks us up at the airport. I know instantly that I'm going to like her and that she is going to make me laugh a lot this week, just with her smile.

Torrevieja is on the southeast coast of Spain and was originally a salt mining and fishing village. Vicky takes us to the home we will be staying in for the week and all I keep saying is 'no way'. This house is a palace on the sea, and I can't believe these wonderful people are letting us stay here and they're not even here! Every moment I was there I felt lucky and grateful. The idea of living your days as if they are your last is very real here and so are the people, I had the good fortune of meeting. They love this area. They love their lives. They love their friends and family. They're passionate and their smiles are incredibly contagious.

One hot morning I walked along the path running along the sea to the outdoor, weekly market and I felt like I was in veggie foodie heaven. There were stalls after stalls of everything and anything you would have ever needed and any kind of food you wanted. On top of everything being so fresh the prices were shockingly low. I bought enough fruit, vegetables AND CHEESE for a few days for only 14 euros! All the vendors were yelling back and forth, and the men and women were exchanging loud hellos, and some were shouting to the crowds their prices or how fresh their produce was. It was infectious and fun, and I was so happy I made the trek.

While there we were invited to a local wedding reception. I was a bit nervous at first but everyone I met the first couple minutes made that fall away. It was so loud, and everyone was shaking my hand and hugging me and kissing my cheeks and getting me drinks. It was great. We had so much fun. We had this whole little bar to ourselves and another night of dancing. One day we went jet skiing out to a tiny mountain in the sea or "the big rock" as the locals call it. The water was beautiful and so was the big rock. I was a tiny bit disappointed that our jet ski was "limited" in its speed haha but the last thing I need is another citation in another country.

Spain was a perfect choice after our week in Amsterdam. I rested up, I laid by the pool, I went swimming every day. It was a beautiful relaxing retreat. In the 6 days I was in Spain we ate paella 3 times from the same restaurant. There was an endless flow of red wine. I don't think I have consumed as much cheese in my entire life as I did on this trip. Brie, camembert, Manchego, old cheddar the options are endless. It was hard to believe that Amsterdam was everything I imagined and more. Spain was the perfect complement. The entire trip for me was magical. It was truly the trip of a lifetime. Everyone that I have had the pleasure of meeting has been so genuine and honest and beautiful in their own ways. They have all been so caring and compassionate and curious about my life. Sometimes I talk about my life and what's happening and sometimes I let it go but when I do open up, they listen and understand and praise me for living my life this way, for living my life with hope. It's a strange notion to me to be praised in this way. I feel understood now. I feel like I fit. I feel like I could live in any of these places quite happily. I feel like I have made connections and friends that I will remember always. There was never a day that went by where I didn't use the word 'magic' to describe my day or night or a moment. The last morning in Spain I sat down on the sea view terrace and looked to my left. I saw Tony meditating on the lawn overlooking the ocean and I realized that we were both where we were supposed to be at that very moment.

This year I was lucky enough to live through some pretty cancerful stuff. I have met so many special people on my travels this year and last and in all my life. I'm blessed and I know this every day. The amount of encouragement and strength I get from new friends is sometimes as equal as I get from my 'pillars'. My pillars are the people in my life that lift me up, that continue to make me smile, people that I consider family or that are family. I got this word and this meaning from a new friend in Spain, and I think from this day forward I will always use this when talking about my 'support system'.

I was made aware of the word Ubuntu this year through a fundraiser that my oldest friend held for me. A South African phrase that means human kindness. When I read about it and the history of the phrase and the sacredness of it, I can't help but feel its definition deep in my core. Desmond Tutu described the word and its meaning as, "My humanity is caught up, is inextricably bound up, in yours...A person with ubuntu is open and available to others, affirming of others, does not feel threatened that others are able and good, for he or she has a proper self-assurance that comes from knowing that he or she belongs in a greater whole..." I have so many people with ubuntu in my life. How's that for being blessed?

**"As we advance in life it becomes more and more difficult,
but in fighting the difficulties the inmost strength
of the heart is developed."**
—VINCENT VAN GOGH

See everyone after HAWAII!

xo

Pikake, Prayers and Pearls

October 7, 2016

**"Out of suffering have emerged the strongest souls;
the most massive characters are seared with scars."**
—KAHLIL GIBRAN

It's fall here in New Hampshire and the cooler air has arrived. It's late afternoon and the light against the pond has darkened already and the earlier warmth from the sun has disappeared. I look down at my hands as I write, and I see the remnants of the Hawaiian sun still on my skin.

How I wish it wouldn't leave me. My heart squeezes up when I think of this special place.

Before I get started on Kauai, I'll just announce that my brain MRI this week was CLEAR! It seems like a bit of a miracle really. I'm still having a hard time believing it but this smile on my face today feels a lot different than my smile 2 days ago. It's a quiet joy for me, an incredibly special moment in my cancer journey. We all really needed this good news and I'm going to hold onto it as tightly as possible, for as long as possible.

Just before leaving for this trip, someone that has been a constant in my life passed away after a long struggle with illness. He was special to me in the way a family member is. I'm thinking of him and remembering what he brought to my life, everyone's life and smiling with every memory that surfaces. I left NH with a heavy but grateful heart. I was on my way to spend 10 days with my Pops on the 'Garden Isle'.

After my breast cancer decided to do some traveling of its own recently, heading northbound into the state of MB, My Brain, my Dad decided we should go to Kauai. I was looking forward to us being camera nerds together and seeing the island the way he loves it. A place that has significant spiritual effects on many who visit there. I had been there a long time ago but was excited to return and see it through my new eyes and from a different perspective.

Hawaii is the most isolated inhabited land mass in the world...in the world! Seventy percent of the island of Kauai is inaccessible by foot and 97% of the land is used for conservation and agriculture. Kauai is home to one of the wettest places on earth. In a week's time I saw more than 20 waterfalls and beautiful beaches, the Grand Canyon of the pacific, Waimea and more pikake and plumeria than I could pluck from the trees.

One of the best parts of this trip was actually learning a bit more about my Dad and his past. As he told me a little about his college and summer job days, I found I was fascinated. I knew he had worked for a circus, but I didn't know the specifics. I had never heard some of these stories. He rode horses and tight rope walked and looked after elephants. He wrote a book of poetry. He was a working musician on the weekends, playing the guitar. I realized as we watched The Secret Life of Walter Mitty that we laughed at the same parts and we both have this weird cough/laugh combo.

Kauai was a reminder to me that I don't necessarily have to travel as far as I can in each direction to find beauty in our world. We have so much of it right here, in our own country. The dramatic cliffs of the Na Pali Coast, the waterfalls, the beaches, the gardens, the people, the culture, it's stunning. I saw more beaches than I can list but my favorite is crystal clear in my mind, just like the water, Lumaha'i. I left part of my heart on that beach, in those warm black tide pools, in the gentle roll of the waves and the perfect feeling of seclusion and quiet. I'd give up a toe to be able to spend more time in that place, just not my big toe!

Dad took me to a luau, and I have to admit that at first, I was worried that there would be a serious lack of authenticity and history, an awkward sort of event for me. The drumming and the dancing were fantastic and maybe it was cliche to do it, but I smiled a lot and so did my Dad. The culture of the pacific is incredibly enchanting but the staple food of cooked taro root otherwise known as poi is less enchanting. But oh, how beautiful those taro fields are amongst the lower valleys of Hanalei Bay. These luau ceremonies were once held to honor kings and gods through stories and dance and carry so much history and beautiful significance.

We spent half a day with our cameras at the McBryde Gardens on the south coast of the island. We were lucky enough to see the largest collection of Hawaiian plants that exist. It seemed as though maybe we had missed the main blooming season, but I was still in complete dragonfly and orchid heaven. These gardens were once a homesite to ancient Hawaiians, a gift to royals and is heavy in history and preservation. We even saw the rare tiger orchid in full bloom. It was YUGE! It looked like a round shrub. It was hanging casually above our heads in the mysterious shadows of the tree limb it was growing from. Pretty sweet sight.

In the mornings when I wake up and know the beautiful Poipu coast is waiting for me, I would pull back the louvered doors, breathe in and sigh it all out. There's a special feeling in the morning. It's quiet, except the roosters, but very peaceful. The ocean that my bedroom faces crashes along the rocky shore wall. I sit out on the terrace, have coffee, read, write and watch where the waves come in from both sides and meet. Sometimes I see a few brave surfers and at night the wall is lined with people, tourists, locals, all waiting for the sunset and relaxing in the moment after the day. I can actually see all of this amazingness from an oversized bathtub in my bedroom!

Some nights I would walk along the water at sunset and was able to have a completely quiet mind. I would sit on the sea wall and watch the waves and notice how the sun would reflect off the water and into my eyes. The colors in the sky change quickly from bright yellow to pink. I could sit there on that wall every night being mesmerized by those colors.

During the day I would swim, or Dad and I would head out on some adventure or shop for pearls! I met the most incredibly lovely people by the pool one afternoon. I'm so grateful for all of my new friends. I was given a beautiful gift after 5 minutes of knowing one of my new friends. I was taken back by her sweetness and her mother's and their touching and emotional story. We talk a lot about life and love and spirit, and I know I will see them again. The rowdy group invited me with open arms to their pool party that day and I'm so happy I accepted their invitation. We broke some rules, we had some wine, we had a lot of laughs, and we swam for hours in water as warm as a bathtub. It's not always about waterfalls and beaches, sometimes it's just about the people we meet on our travels that show us more beauty than any landscape could. The Hawaiians have a saying that I heard while there, "E aloha kekahi i kekahi". It means to love one another. I'm beaming as I write this from all that love. I'm beaming because I had a clear scan. I'm beaming because maybe there is something to be said for the power of prayer. I'm beaming because my heart is decidedly open.

One day Dad and I drove up the coast and stopped at one of his favorite beaches, Anini Beach. It was like something out of a picture book and for a few hours we soaked in the calm ocean water and lay in the warm sand. It's really something how therapeutic the waters around Kauai feel. We went out to a fancy dinner one night and took a walk along the beachfront after. There were a lot of honeymooners and couples of course but there was one family down by the water with a small child that made me think of a moment I had in Turks and Caicos last year. I went back to my journal from then and this is what I had written that night...

> *while lying on the beach today, looking out at the ocean that is truly magical in its color and calmness, i saw the most beautiful moment between a man and his wife. it almost brought me to tears and i almost asked them if i could photograph them. she was sitting on the sand at the water's edge and her husband was swimming in front of her in the shallow water. he swam to her slowly, watching her pregnant belly. nothing could have broken his gaze. she watched him as he came closer, and he placed the most gentle kiss on her belly full of life. i don't think anyone else saw this moment. it is a moment that has stuck with me the entire day and brings me comfort and joy and sadness at the same time but i feel privileged to have been part of their moment, maybe it was just an ordinary moment for them but for me it just added to the miracle that is love and life...*

As for my favorite parts of Kauai...I'd have to say getting to spend an extra 4 days on the North Shore of the island was a definite high of the trip, but the helicopter flight was AWESOME! Who knew?! Me of all people would love it as much as I did. And the doors were off! To tell the truth I insisted the doors be off just in case I barfed. I learned right before the flight that barfing out the door would be dumb because I would most likely suffocate. Thankfully they provided very nice barf bags. In secret I was terrified, but I knew it meant a lot to my Dad and I didn't want to be a loser wimp. For those of you who had the privilege of watching my skydiving video from a few years ago know that it wasn't my finest nor happiest moment. The first pic under this paragraph is me thinking I'm about to fall to my death and the second captures the pure joy I felt in the helicopter[5]...even though my eyes are closed 😊 Between the wind and the canyons and the coast and the taro fields and the secret beaches and the soundtrack playing Coldplay's Paradise, Moby and Iz's Somewhere over the rainbow I was in total bliss.

And then I had to come home, and you better believe there were tears. What an incredible place to make fantastic new memories with fantastic new people. I'm home now. I just found out my brain MRI was clean. I'm trying to get back to some sort of non-Hawaii life. Back to yoga, back to writing and reading and loving my dog and friends and planning my next adventure because I CAN! Over the last year I have learned so much about myself and what I want in my life and what I have to live with literally. It's easy to lose yourself in the loneliness that can be cancer and illness in general. Through people I have met who share my illness, to people I've met through traveling...I don't lose myself anymore. We should all be smiling and living the life we love as much as is possible.

This is a pretty exciting time right now for me. That feels a little strange to say but I also feel the need for some rest. I have a trip to Panama next month and also an upcoming photo project. It's a photo project of me and the different sides of my life with cancer, the light and darkness of my life. It has been something I've wanted to do since I was diagnosed almost 3 years ago. I don't believe we see enough of the 'real side' of cancer. It's also breast cancer awareness month which isn't my favorite so I'm thinking of the photo project as my way of contributing and also honoring the Cancerful.

---

5. CAROL'S NOTE: Photos from Angela's Hawaii trip can be found at www.beautyandthedark.com.

It seems I'm living another whole new life again. I get to start over, in a way. And maybe I won't get to start over completely but it's ok because right now I'm living in a no new cancer high and I'm not coming down. I mean for at least 60 days, when I have my next scan haha. I think about a passage from the Bible my new friend sent to me and how she told me it gave her father much comfort during his illness. I may not be sure about the existence of 'God' but I'm absolutely sure of something more. Faith is faith and love is love. It says,

"Therefore we do not lose heart. Though outwardly we are wasting away, yet inwardly we are being renewed day by day. For our light and momentary troubles are achieving for us an eternal glory that far outweighs them all. So we fix our eyes not on what is seen, but on what is unseen. For what is seen is temporary, but what is unseen is eternal."

—2 CORINTHIANS

xo

blog

Permanence, the Pearly Gates & Purpose

November 5, 2016

"And may you roam where roads are free
And rest where nights are fair.
Then wait a little while for me
Till I shall join you there."
—JAMES C. HEPLER

This has been one of the hardest blogs I've done. This blog has taken me longer than any before. This blog isn't about travel or a beautiful trip I've just been on. It's about a photo project I've been working on. It's about miracles and heaven and breast cancer culture and history. It's about Beauty and The Dark.

As I sit here typing, I'm listening to the pandora classical station and one of my favorite pieces by Paul Cardall comes on. It's called Life and Death. In 1973 when Paul was born, he suffered from a congenital heart defect and was given only days to live as a baby. He lived. I believe some coincidences are more signs than anything else. To me, there are signs everywhere. I'm so thankful I can see them.

As I posted in my last entry, my most recent brain scan was considered 'clean'. I remember how I felt that day, the disbelief, the joy, the renewed optimism. I found out a few days later that it actually wasn't 'clean'. There is something up there but it's too small to treat. This is a glimpse into my journal of that week:

10/4 – clean brain scan! miracle?

10/5 – day after clean brain scan. holy shit.

10/7 – the scan isn't clean. fml.

I understand that I will be in treatment for the rest of my life. I understand I will live my life in 2-month increments. A fellow cancerful friend refers to the time in between scans as 'gulps'. Sometimes my two months consist of gamma knife surgeries which leaves me with about a month of feeling like a human but actually like two weeks because then I stress for two weeks about my upcoming scan. I haven't had two months 'off' yet except for this time. Although it doesn't really feel like time off. This news has made me feel consistently sad and discouraged. To be completely honest it's a real mind F%@K actually. Yes, it's clean, no it's not, well maybe it sort of is…I guess I'll find out on December 8th.

Life is not permanent. My life is definitely impermanent. I accept this. I know that there's little chance of a 'miracle' or a cure in my lifetime. I choose to live my life the best way I can now. I wish I had done this before. Sigh…how different life would've been. I choose to try and make this whole cancerful situation mean something, to me and others. I am not afraid of my impermanence.

The photo project I have mentioned has successfully begun. This last week Part One was completed. I've decided, with a little help from my friends, that I'm titling it, Beauty and The Dark, Cancer: My Photo Memoir. This project is going to be one of the most meaningful and significant things I've ever been part of and that makes me proud. It's a project representing the different sides of my cancerful life and the different sides of cancer in general. It represents my story and many others.

I've wanted to do this since I was diagnosed and introduced to 'The SCAR Project' by David Jay. This book and documentary completely changed the way I viewed breast cancer and ultimately myself. I'm so grateful for these rare glimpses into the reality of this disease. Forbes magazine describes The SCAR Project as a "shockingly raw, yet strikingly beautiful, photo series that shows a side of breast cancer we're not used to seeing: the reality." I don't believe we see enough of the 'real side of cancer'. I want people to see it, to see how dark and light it can be. It will be three parts, and the first one represents the title in its entirety.

My photographer, Liesl Clark of Liesl Clark Photography, has been in my life for over 5 years and has become a dear friend (www.lieslclarkphotography.com). We have worked together before and this will be our third project, the most important one by far. She is so beautiful down to the very roots of her being. As grateful as she says she is for me and being involved with this project, I feel exactly the same way. I would never do this project with anyone else. I'm honored that she'll be with me for these moments.

The location for this part is saturated with incredible history. A 513-acre park is set on the eastern slope of Rattlesnake Mountain in

Chesterfield, NH. It's called the Madame Sherri Forest. The forest is named after a former owner, Madame Antoinette Sherri, originally Antoinette De Lilas. She was born in Paris in the early 1900s and eventually made her way to New York City. There, she created a life and a name for herself. She and her husband built a French-inspired chateau summer house here in NH. In the 1920s it was here that they lavishly entertained their New York City friends.

Madame Sherri's life was filled with fame, wealth, mystery and tragedy. She was described as exotic and unique. She furnished her NH home with extravagant items she bought during her travels around the world. There were a lot of rumors that filled the local towns about this Madame. With so many beautiful women always at her chateau, some believed she ran a brothel. There's a well-known story about her driving around town in her fur coat with nothing on underneath. I wish I could have known her.

In time, Madame Sherri's fortunes declined, and her castle fell to ruin and vandalism. She returned to the house in 1959 to find it in such state. She left, heartbroken, never to return again. The house ultimately burned down completely in 1963. There have been a few people who claim to have witnessed Madame Sherri walking down her grand staircase and hearing laughter and music. Her mantra was known to be "Only the best".

The main staircase, now called, "the stairway to heaven," was cut into the side of a rock ledge. The stairway still exists and stands out amongst the other ruins that surround it. It almost takes your breath away when you walk up to it. It towers up and just over the top of it is a break in the trees. The light shines down on it just like a stairway to heaven. Below the staircase are pockets of crumbled ruins and darkness and graffiti. I couldn't have dreamt up a better location, filled with significance and stories and a connection to my own life.

I have a desire to make something beautiful come from a sometimes very ugly and dark reality. It's been a struggle to accept my new self as beautiful. I want to document all the emotions I've had regarding my illness and representing them through photo has been a goal since the beginning. My need to do this now has been growing since the disease spread to my brain. I want to capture the present, my present. I want to capture beauty and the dark. I want to do this project so that I can look back, so my family and friends can look back.

I wanted to hold onto this moment of my illness. I wanted to maybe even provide some inspiration to others that may be in similar situations in life. It's incredibly difficult to pull myself up to the light some days. I'm sure this is the same for so many people, even without cancer. I like looking at the photos and thinking about how my illness has not taken my soul from me. I haven't allowed that. I feel that when some people think of terminal disease, they don't picture someone like me or many of my cancerful friends who actually don't look cancerful at all. I feel like I want to remind people that terminal doesn't always look terminal and that you never know what's underneath someone's surface.

The few people I have shown some of these photos to have had wonderful feedback. It validates this project for me. I feel understood and seen by the people closest to me. Liesl captured the very essence of me in these photos, the light and the dark. I'm proud of myself and this project. It's about my journey and adventure with my cancer. It's about my dark fairytale. It's about capturing the process of my own self-discovery through the chaos. It's about remembering who I am and being true to myself. It's about honoring others and remembering that there is beauty in the dark.

Below are the photos taken by Liesl Clark.[6]

---

6. CAROL'S NOTE: The remainder of these photos can be viewed at www.beautyandthedark.com.

While I was researching content for this blog, I wanted to learn more about heaven, how it has been described and documented over time. After doing a photoshoot on the 'stairway to heaven' I better understand it a little! I also wanted to learn more because I genuinely believe in such a place. I don't want to be scared by what lies ahead. I want to understand what may lie ahead. I found that often heaven is described as a higher place, the holiest of places, a paradise. Regardless of my belief in an actual God, or whether I just have faith in something more, heaven is there for me.

One way I educated myself was from documented near death experiences (NDE), recent and past. Many people who have opened up report meeting relatives in a dreamy, mystical, otherworldly dimension. These stories are of places with big puffy clouds and brilliant rays of light, green landscapes and butterflies and the most beautiful music one will ever hear. The most consistent and similar descriptions of heaven include, "at the center of it lies love, peace and joy, beyond human comprehension." The following passage is from the Bible.

"A river, clear as crystal, will flow from the throne of God and of the Lamb [Jesus] down the middle of the city. On each side of the river there will be a tree of life, yielding twelve kinds of fruit every month. The streets will be pure gold, like transparent glass. The walls of the city will be adorned with every kind of jewel, emerald, onyx, amethyst, topaz, etc. There will be no need for a sun or moon, and no need for a temple or church. The presence of the Lord will be its light."

I was recently given a book called *Proof of Heaven*, written by Dr. Eben Alexander. A neurosurgeon, Dr. Alexander had a near-death experience (NDE) while suffering from a very rare illness. He lay in a coma for seven days and states that during that time he met and spoke with the Divine source of the universe itself. He also describes being guided through the transition by an angelic being. His doctors describe his recovery as a medical miracle.

Before Dr. Alexander underwent this journey to the beyond, he couldn't argue scientifically that Heaven exists. Despite the number of documented NDE's and medical miracles, scientists have argued that they're impossible. This is the age-old debate between science and philosophy. Are these just fantasies that our brains are producing? Are they just a result of extreme bodily stress? Dr. Alexander now believes, "Love is without a doubt, the basis of everything... this is the reality of realities, the incomprehensibly glorious truth of truths that lives and breathes at the core of everything that exists or that ever will exist."

In Dr. Alexander's follow up to *Proof of Heaven*, he wrote *The Map of Heaven*. He starts the book by discussing Plato and Aristotle. He describes Plato as being the father of philosophy and religion and Aristotle the father of science. Throughout the book he describes how various religions and belief systems view the afterlife and the idea of Heaven. This is fascinating to me. He includes the story of Socrates's death, Plato's master. Plato describes how his master's life came to an end in a heroic and tranquil way. Dr. Alexander states that, "Socrates's supreme nonchalance in the face of death was the result of knowledge of what death really was: not an ending but a return to our truest home."

In both of his books Dr. Alexander talks about his travels through a dark and murky place before he 'arrived'. He feels that souls that are not open and ready to the idea of their death and the beyond are sometimes stuck in this place until they are ready. He says that "We end up, in the end, where we belong, and we are led by the amount of love we have in us, for love is the essence of heaven. It is what it is made of." I believe this with all my heart, always have. I also believe that this life, this 'realm' is for learning the lessons of love, compassion, forgiveness and acceptance.

Dr. Eben Alexander is referred to as a medical miracle. So are many others throughout history. A 14-year-old teenager from South Carolina lived without her heart for 118 days. A 10-year-old boy suffered internal decapitation in an automobile accident, and he lived. What about the girl that doesn't age or the 8-year-old girl that feels no pain? What is a miracle? How is it viewed by people that are lucky enough to be close to one? How do we judge if a miracle is a miracle?

By definition, a miracle is a "surprising and welcome event that is not explicable by natural or scientific laws and is therefore considered to be the work of a divine agency." Whether the subject of a 'miracle' has survived a terminal illness or escaped a life-threatening situation, who are any one of us to say "that wasn't a miracle"? Like Heaven, Miracles are dismissed by many scientific thinkers for being physically impossible. I'm not on that side.

Along with Dr. Alexander's books I was recently told to watch the movie Miracles from Heaven. This movie is based on the true story of Annabel Beam, a 10-year-old girl who had a rare and incurable disease. She also had a near death experience when she fell down into the center of a tree. It was after this accident that she was cured. In 2015, Annabel said this about her accident, "I believe that I was cured because when I went to heaven, I asked Jesus if I could stay with him and he said, No Annabel, I have plans for you on Earth that you cannot fulfill in heaven. Whenever I send you back, there will be nothing wrong with you."

During the movie Annabel had the opportunity to view a painting by Monet, Reflections of Clouds on the Waterlily Pond. She is captivated by this piece and the similarities to what she saw during her NDE. For some reason, this part turned up some serious emotions in my heart and I cried and cried. A founder of French Impressionist painting, Monet painted the Water Lily series at his home in France. Many of the works were painted while he suffered from cataracts.

Are Heaven and Miracles connected? Do they need to be? I believe in miracles, no matter how small or large. I believe miracles aren't always seen but they're happening. I believe most anything is possible. I do not believe there will be a cure for metastatic breast cancer in my lifetime. When there is, this will be a miracle. C.S. Lewis says, "Miracles are a retelling in small letters of the very same story which is written across the whole world in letters too large for some of us to see."

Before bringing this entry to an end, I want to talk a little about metastatic breast cancer. Breast cancer awareness month has just finished, and I say that with a little relief. I don't like this month to pass by without recognizing it and taking the opportunity to thank my family and friends for their unending love and support. I also like to talk a little about the statistics we don't hear about and the history we don't know about.

90% of deaths from breast cancer are due to metastases which account for 40,000 deaths annually. 10% of metastases occur in the brain. The majority of patients with brain metastases have already had a spread to their bones, liver or lungs. Not me though, I'm skipping all those parts! After lung cancer, breast cancer causes more deaths in women than any other type of cancer. Almost 100% of breast cancer deaths occur because of metastasis, and almost 100% of people whose breast cancer has metastasized will die from it.

These are the dark realities of breast cancer. Underneath these discouraging statistics lie the controversy over allocation of research funding. 30% of patients diagnosed with earlier stage breast cancer will eventually develop stage 4 breast cancer and die. I am one of those numbers.

The 'popular' fundraising movements only give on average 13% of their research funds to actually researching metastasis. Only 13%!? This is shameful, when so many will lose their lives to this disease.

These 'popular' organizations focus on prevention, which does nothing to help those of us already diagnosed. I support groups like METAVIVOR, whose goal is for cancer organizations to devote 30% of research budgets to breast cancer metastasis. Someone dies from breast cancer every 14 minutes in the US.[7] Unfortunately, this number has not decreased significantly in nearly 40 years, despite a huge movement to raise awareness and funds. Many of us know all too closely that research specifically focusing on metastasis is critical to significantly reduce the breast cancer death rate.

---

7. CAROL'S NOTE: With the passing of time, it has not been possible to locate the source of Angela's statistics. However, up-to-date statistics are included on page 252.

Maybe this is why I feel so passionately about breast cancer research and organizations that actually get it right. Maybe this is why I feel so separate from the pink ribbon frenzies. Through the documentary *Pink Ribbons Inc.*, I learned that a 68-year-old woman named Charlotte Haley created the ribbon. It wasn't pink. It was peach in color. She began this project in her dining room and with each pack of five ribbons she attached a postcard that read, "The National Cancer Institute's annual budget is $1.8 billion, only 5 percent goes for cancer prevention. Help us wake up legislators and America by wearing this ribbon."

Don't misunderstand, I do have the ability to appreciate and respect certain organizations and fundraisers and tributes. Even the pink apparel being worn in the NFL. Any help is help and kindness is kindness regardless of the disappointing facts about metastatic breast cancer research funding. I think about Charlotte and her life and what her intentions were and how genuine they were. This is what I connect to.

I am so deeply affected by this controversy. At the rate I'm going, these are my statistics:

- 6 brain MRIs per year
- 4 CTs of my chest, abdomen and pelvis
- 4 bone scans
- 2 liver MRIs
- Craniotomy and gamma knife surgeries when needed.
- Appointments every 2 months with these doctors: Radiation oncologist, Neuro oncologist, Breast oncologist
- $12,000 on average a year in medical expenses

I write about this side of cancer and my experience because maybe it will make a difference someday, even just to a few people. I write this to shed some light on the reality of health care, the costs and the emotional toll of cancer. Even though I may not be working anymore, I still want to feel worth, like I'm doing something good. And the super cool part is that this something is actually really good for me. It gives me motivation and purpose.

I hope you enjoyed this post and the first part of my cancer through photos project. I'll talk to you soon.

All my love...Angela

"Every moment of light and dark is a miracle."
—WALT WHITMAN

Panama, Private Planes
& Promiscuity

December 9, 2016

**"Sometimes life hits you in the head with a brick.
Don't lose faith."**
—STEVE JOBS

I love this quote. It's totally true. But sometimes it's a tumor or two tumors and not a brick. Either way, they both hurt. I'll get right to the Promiscuity part because clearly, I don't want to give anyone the wrong idea. Now, we already know that Hannibal and Clarice had a baby in my brain this summer. What we now know is that there were more babies. Babies that are now growing up into toddlers.

I have two more brain tumors. As my best friend said, "Clarice and Hannibal were having a lot of sex up there and now you have to take care of all their kids." We use humor so much when processing my illness. It makes everything easier to deal with. It's not denial, it's not, not taking this seriously. Trust me, I'm taking this very seriously. As I sit here, tears are falling down my face and my sweatshirt and I'm wiping my eyes so I can keep writing. This is very real.

I try very hard not to lose faith, ever again. It's hard somedays when all I feel is defeat. Sometimes it's too much work trying to hold onto hope and faith so tightly. So, the two tumors have both doubled in size in the last 60 days. I'll have another gamma knife surgery in the next 10 days. I've also decided to stop naming my tumors, they're now receiving numbers. These are tumor 4 and tumor 5.

I'm now almost 10 months out from going from remission to incurable. The stats say 10-14 months but I'm not following those rules, thankfully. Yes, I may be getting new brain tumors every two months thus far but they're "manageable", right now. Yesterday, as I asked one of my oncologists through a few tears, about my prognosis, he assured me that we are still in a completely good place. I asked him if he would tell me when he thought the shit was hitting the fan so to speak. He said absolutely.

My other neurooncologist said, if more grow after this treatment then she would like to see me in an immunotherapy clinical trial. At least there's that option as well. I'll never be 'curable'. I know never say never but the realist in me knows better. BUT I may have a lot more time than 10-14 months. I guess breaking the cancer rules is finally paying off.

This blog was supposed to be about my recent trip to Panama and California and not more brain tumors. Thankfully I wrote a lot of it before finding out about #4 and #5. I'm distracted and sad and I wrote the next bit while I was happy and warm in California last week. I just have to sneak it in here too that my ride was a private jet and not a commercial airline. I think it's pretty cool that I have terminal cancer and in the last month I've been to Panama City, Bocas del Toro, Ocean City, San Diego, Los Angeles and Desert Hot Springs. I just need to keep on moving forward the best way I know how.

My recent trip to Panama made me think of my future and this brought me to tears somedays. The tears came from the thought of my life ending sooner rather than later. "I'm not ready" is a consistent trigger. As I sat in a perfect house over the crystal-clear water, I thought to myself I'm not done seeing all the beautiful places I've always wanted to visit. Other days were a heavy combination of bliss, calm, joy, peace and an endless view of incredible beauty.

Traveling to Panama, I left with no expectations. I had read a lot about the area of Bocas del Toro off the northeast coast of the country. It seems that people are really catching on to this little piece of heaven. I was looking forward to all of it, the old, the new and the knowledge that there would probably be moments where I would be out of my comfort zone.

Several theories exist about the origin of the name "Panama". Some believe the name came from a species of tree called the Panama tree. In native language it means "many butterflies" or "abundance of fish" or "far away" which came from the Kuna Indians of Panama. In my mind, Panama means paradise.

Soaked with a volatile history, it was clear to me that there is a strong desire among the Panamanian people to maintain their independence and original character of their true heritage. Since the 1800s Panama has been tied to Spain and Columbia but is now its own nation. The United States was supportive of Panama's separation from Columbia in 1903, thus giving the USA the opportunity to take over the construction of the Panama Canal from the French. In 1999 control of the canal was transferred over to the Panamanians in its entirety.

During this time Panama remained under the control of military dictator, Manuel Noriega. The United States supported Noriega and as a result he worked closely with the CIA. The CIA were aware of Noriega's questionable activities involving drug and people smuggling, money laundering and supplying weapons to the revolutionaries in the region. In 1987 President Regan began to freeze the USA's economic and military assistance in response to Noriega's rule, despite allowing his behaviors.

Manuel Noriega was eventually accused of these trafficking crimes. Prior to his imprisonment, the United States invaded Panama, capturing Noriega and detaining him as a prisoner of war. Being described as the largest military operation since the Vietnam War, the number of deaths as a result remain a heavy topic of controversy. In 2015, Manuel Noriega apologized to his country for the offenses his regime had committed.

Writing about Panama would not be complete without mention of the canal. A 48-mile waterway connecting the Atlantic Ocean to the Pacific Ocean, it has been called one of the seven wonders of the world. The construction of the canal has made travel for ships easier, taking 6-8 hours versus sailing around the dangerous southern tip of South America.

Over the years, the canal, its construction and expansion has taken a major toll on the environment of Panama. Deforestation, water loss, pollution and the loss of biodiversity now plague areas of the country. Once a beautiful swimmable coastline, the waters surrounding Panama City are now brown, polluted and toxic due to raw sewage and industrial waste. The Panamanian government is working towards rehabilitating some of the affected areas as the wildlife is some of the most diverse in Central America and 40% of the land is jungle.

Our taxi driver in Panama City, Jose, recalls growing up there and stark difference of what the land and waters are now compared to what was during his childhood. He talks about his memories of a pristine, swimmable beach surrounding Panama City. As he drives, I see out the window an enormous difference in the view from one block to another. In between modern high rises and the city center are small areas of shanty towns, fish markets, and 'black' markets bordering the toxic mud flats. Attempts by the government to re-forest some of the country has its faults. For example, two-thirds of the trees that have been replanted are teak, which is a commodity for the country, not a natural habitat for wildlife.

Before flying to Bocas del Toro, we had a night in Panama City. We smoked a hookah for the first time and saw an incredible show at the hotel. A fusion of traditional Indian and world music, I had never heard anything like this live. It was beautiful. The hotel was located in the historic Old Town, known as Casco Viejo. Designated a World Heritage Site in 1997, Casco Viejo has a turbulent past. In 1671 the city was attacked by pirates, specifically Henry Morgan, which resulted in widespread destruction in different areas of the city. A combination of old buildings, ruins and alleys, there is a clear view of the work happening to restore dilapidated buildings.

Casco Viejo is also home to the Presidential Palace. I couldn't get too close with the heavy security guarding the entry and exit streets. The tourist police and presidential guard are on nearly every corner as well. This area of the city is the second most popular tourist destination in Panama City, ranked behind the Panama Canal. Every street holds some sort of monument of historical significance. I saw stray cats and dogs, some sleeping on the sidewalk, some scavenging for food. Graffiti marks the walls in town. I saw a big difference in the wealthy and poor.

The next day we flew to Bocas del Toro (meaning "Mouths of the Bull"), but not until the pilots could see the top of the mountain. With Costa Rica to the West and Columbia to the South, Bocas has nine main islands. Christopher Columbus explored this area in 1502 while searching for a passage to the Pacific Ocean. Originally part of Costa Rica, Colombia took control of Bocas, but in 1903 became its own province. A colorful and lively town Bocas is a hub for travelers, retirees, wanderers and surfers. I heard many people talk of visiting the area and never leaving, of getting lost there.

Bocas is going through a lot of changes right now. Like Panama City, it's a mix of old and new and the old is still ever present. A town built around mangrove swamps and beautiful private beaches, there was a mesmerizing feeling here. We rented quads one day and tore through 1400 acres of private property while listening to the howler monkeys. Riding through lush tropical rainforest and coastline we pass ruins that once held Manuel Noriega's secret drug factory. We pass landmarks like La Piscina, Blue Lagoon, Christian's Beach, Rock Beach and the Bat Caves.

During my 10 days in Bocas I spent my days on and in the water. The home I rented was built on stilts over the water. There is no land access to town so trips back and forth were by water taxis. I spent a couple days in Bocas, getting groceries, having lunch and watching the Independence Day parades and sitting in a bar drinking beers for $1.25 each. I experienced lots of offers to buy drugs, saw prostitutes, ate really bad food but it was great! Some days the rain would pour down and the winds would whip through the house. I found this atmosphere tranquilizing and meditative. When the skies were clear I'd paddle board or snorkel around the house. The reef was more impressive than I thought it would be. We saw starfish and sea urchins and brain coral and schools of brightly colored fish. What a gift to have right at my fingertips and toes.

While in Panama I was advised to take malaria medication just in case. What I hadn't remembered from my trip to Africa was the effect on dreaming these meds have. My first night in this house over the water, I dreamt of sitting on the deck overlooking the endless horizon and I saw a whale right in front of me. It breached and I saw its body slip into the water. Being someone who never remembers dreams, I looked up the meaning immediately. In most beliefs whales are a symbol of strength, spirituality and protection although they have also been interpreted as a sign of our darkness and the possibility of experiencing loss. Whales tend to appear during times of relevance when you are currently facing an issue in your life. Since whales live underwater, they can be seen as our own personal underworld. I felt that the appearance of this whale was more protection than anything. I felt comforted. I desperately long to return to this paradise whether it's just in my dreams or my real life.

So, Christmas is approaching. A holiday that has always been special to me. This year it's a bit different but still not a day goes by that I am not entirely and genuinely grateful for my life and for all the people in it. I may have skipped the decorations and tree this year but there's always next year, I pray. Pre tumor 4 and 5 I wanted to end this blog with the quote "…my cup runneth over…". Although this is very true, I think there are others more appropriate for today.

I'm wishing my family and friends and this world peace on this holiday. Hold onto your loved ones tightly and never forget to tell them how much they are loved and appreciated. Hold onto faith. Hold onto the belief that, "Everything will be ok".

xo Angela

> **"Hold onto me, cause I'm a little unsteady…"**
> **"Fight when you feel like flying…"**
> —X AMBASSADORS. UNSTEADY

blog

The Dark

December 28, 2016

"Fate rarely calls upon us at a time of our choosing."
—OPTIMUS PRIME

No, it really doesn't.

I have just finished the second part of my cancer through photos project, The Dark. I struggled a bit with the timing of this entry and when to release it. Posting it around the holidays feels a little wrong to be honest. Despite the darkness of this topic, I still love the holidays. Maybe the holidays are not always perfect, but I made it to another holiday. I lived another year. I chose the word 'lived' because I did so much more than just 'survive' another year.

Less than a month ago I found out that I have two more brain tumors. Less than a week ago I had another gamma knife surgery to treat these fast-growing newborns. The 'weight' of brain tumors #4 and #5 has thrown me quite a bit in the last few weeks. There are a lot of days recently that I have felt incredibly sad. In ten months, I have had five new brain tumors.

It is our hope that this gamma knife procedure, like last time, will shrink the tumors. Gamma rays do not remove tumors but damage the DNA of tumor cells so that they lose the ability to reproduce. Approximately 200 beams of gamma rays are aimed at these lesions. For 2-3 days after treatment my doctors use medication to partially sedate me due to the resulting risk of seizures.

There is darkness in my life at times. I have always been honest about it. This blog is representative of those times and so are these photos. Liesl Clark, of Liesl Clark Photography, is the photographer and a dear personal friend. I have envisioned this part of the project with her since my original breast cancer diagnosis almost three years ago. I've decided not to talk much about these photos as they tell this part of my story better than I could ever put into words. This time I'm going to let the photos tell my story, tell of my dark, tell of the secrets that exist in this world of cancer.

I believe we don't see this side of cancer enough. This is the side of cancer that comes up from nowhere and levels me at certain moments. These photos reveal my fear, my anger, my isolation, my defeat and my pain. In some of the photos you may notice a paper chain wrapped around my body or draped around my neck. If you look closely, these are all of my hospital bracelets, from every appointment, every surgery, every chemotherapy infusion, every radiation treatment. The robe is my original hospital gown from radiation. This is my 'weight'.

For now, I will leave you with less of my words and these photos, taken by Liesl Clark.

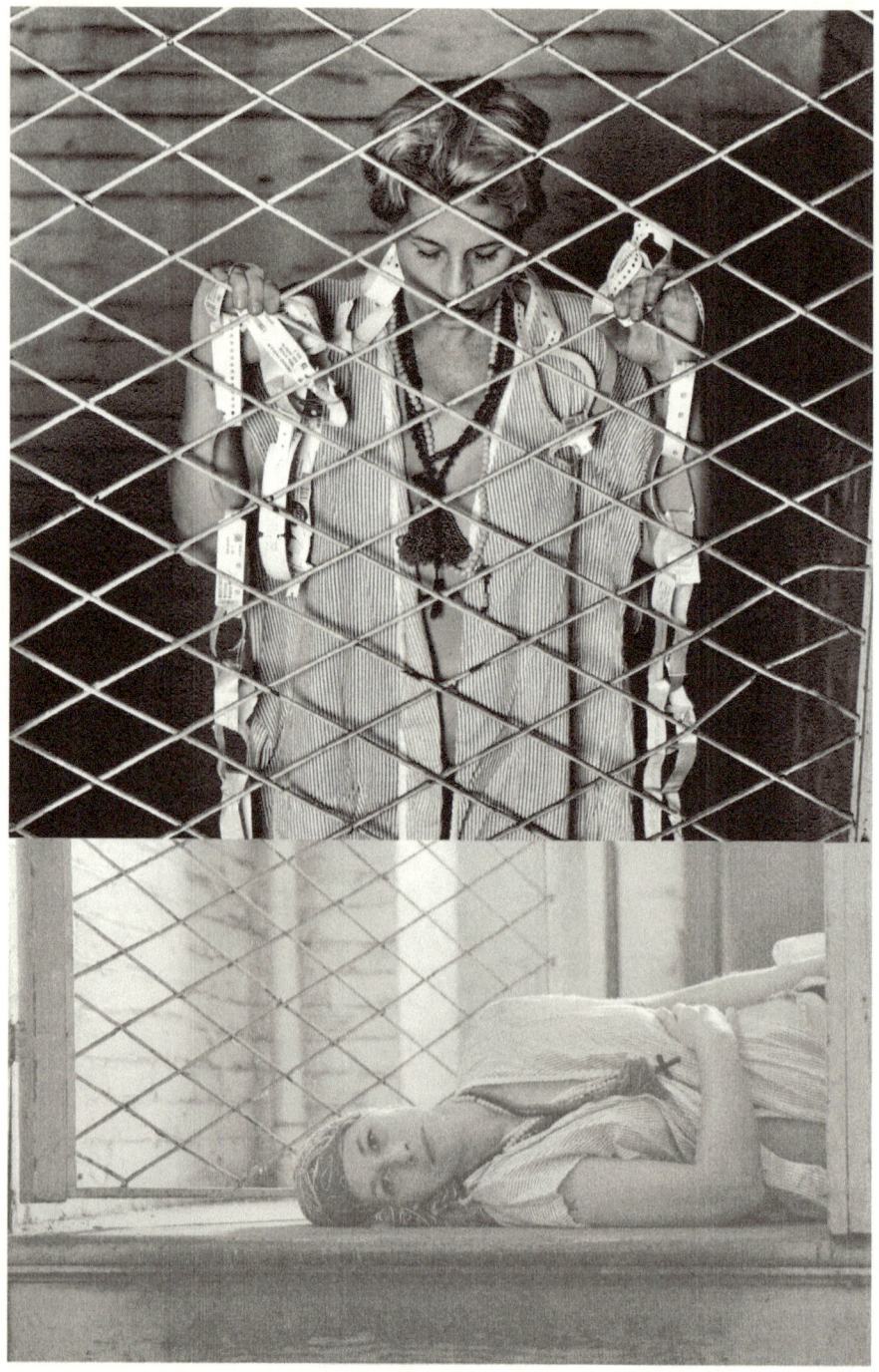

December has been an intense month. A week ago, I had another gamma knife surgery. Today, I sit posting this from Kauai. I need and want to continue my adventure. I need and want to continue to live.

To all my family and friends, I send you much love this holiday season and wish you an incredible 2017.

All my love,

Angela

> **"It is one thing to photograph people.**
> **It is another to make others care about them by revealing**
> **the core of their humanness."**
> —PAUL STRAND

Other Than That

**"Travel isn't always pretty. It isn't always comfortable.
Sometimes it hurts, it even breaks your heart. But that's
ok. The journey changes you - it should change you.
It leaves marks on your memory, on your consciousness,
on your heart, and on your body. You take something
with you...Hopefully you leave something good behind."**
—ANTHONY BOURDAIN

"How are you?"

A question I am frequently asked, as most of us are.[8] Normally, my
responses are "pretty good", "hanging in there", "not bad". This month
it has been mostly, "Meh" or "Ugh" which to me means "not awesome,
at all". This is not exactly the word I thought I'd be using to describe
the beginning of my new year. The first week of January was awesome
but everything went downhill quickly after that.

---

8. CAROL'S NOTE: I have also struggled with the why and how are you
questions, which I discuss further on pages 249 and 327.

December 26th. I had just finished another gamma knife surgery days before and I was boarding a plane to Kauai, what could go wrong? I was going to my happy place. On NYE I stood in a local Hanalei bar with my new friends, dancing, talking, listening to some good music and drinking Mai tais! I visited all my favorite spots while there and many new ones. It felt like every beach was better than the last. Moloaa and the juice bar, Haena, Tunnels, Cannons, Grandpas which I call Puddles, Hideaway, Secrets Beach and a secret spot I named Tidepools.

I wake up on my last day in Kauai and have a funny feeling in my throat that typically means sickness is upon me. Before leaving I visit with my friend Becky, and she gives me a gift. Her favorite coat that I offered her a lot of money for a few days prior and a sunrise shell. A shell that I have been searching for every trip. A shell, she happened to find on a day that was incredibly significant for her. I cannot say enough about the new friends I have made through this magical place. Thank you.

I was leaving Kauai to spend another week on a different island, the big island and one of my closest friends is flying all the way from NH to join me. I get off the plane, make my way to baggage claim and stop off at the restroom. There is one person in there and I see sneakers and I think that's her. We both walk out of our stalls at the same time, see each other and start screaming and hugging like little girls. Not soon after our reunion I say, "Dude, I am sick" and she says, "Dude, me too". It was perfect.

Despite our wretched illness for the entire week, we still managed to do some awesome stuff. Akaka Falls, Kohala coast, Mauna Kea beach, Waimea and Volcano National Park! The island of Hawaii is the largest island in the United States and is built from five separate volcanoes. Kohala, Mauna Kea (which is the world's tallest mountain and yes taller than Mount Everest), Hualalai, Mauna Loa and Kilauea. Two of these volcanoes are still active. This means that the island of Hawaii is still actually growing. Between 1983 and 2002, lava flows have added approximately 543 acres to the island.

We rented a beautiful cottage in the area of Pahoa. In 2014 this area of the island became the target of a new lava flow. 14 miles of the town were ultimately covered over by the flow. We explored the area a bit and just down the road from the cottage was the southeast coast with stunning black lava cliffs with the beautiful blue water below. A week of volcanoes and beaches and rainforests and churches and waterfalls and whiskey and so much laughing, we had the best time. Both of us leave, wishing we could stay or continue our adventure, a trip we will never forget.

Not more than a few days after arriving back to NH, I was in the hospital. I came home sick with bronchitis and a sinus infection. Not only that but a strange ugly brewing infection in my leg. I even drew a circle around the wound and the next day I woke up and said to my Mom, "I think I need to go to the hospital." The redness had extended past the lines, and I now had red streaking heading up my leg. Honestly, I was terrified, and I could barely walk it was so painful.

One morning around 5am, I'm lying in the hospital bed, I look at my phone and see the date, January 17th. This is the 3-year anniversary of my breast cancer diagnosis. I was 34. On that day 3 years ago, I was sitting in my office at work and the phone rings with caller id saying, UNAVAILABLE, and I hear, "Angela, I'm so sorry, but you have breast cancer." After two different antibiotics and the hospital doc finally just cutting into my leg to put in a drain, the infection started to clear, and I was sent home. Another 5 days at home were spent lying on my couch waiting for this to be over.

Due to this infection my January was entirely F'd up. I had to cancel a weekend in FL with my oldest friend for her birthday. I had to cancel a surgery to replace one of my breast implants gone bad. This crushed me. I have been waiting for so long to get this new boob and carved out 6 weeks of my year for recovery. Honestly, I felt even more upset because my choice is to remove them, however, finding a plastic surgeon to agree to this has been impossible thus far. Not only that, but a very close family member was in the hospital in severe heart failure, and I couldn't be there with him.

During this last month I had a moment that I don't really want to admit out loud, but I will because I want to be honest. I thought for a moment "maybe this is the beginning of the end and it's not even from cancer! What a joke." I even did something I said would never do and said, "Why?" I've tried very hard in the last three years to avoid this very thought. There doesn't need to be a reason. It just is. I have a choice on how I walk through this time in my life and sitting here asking myself "Why?" has never been something I've done or wanted to do.

As I sit currently in Yarmouth Port, MA watching the water and storm outside the window it occurs to me that just yesterday I watched a TED talk that had a lot to do with "Why me?" Janine Shepherd who titled her talk "A broken body isn't a broken person" was an athlete who was hit by a truck during a training ride skiing. She shares her story about her injuries, surgeries, emotional struggles and recovery. Her message was "You are not your body, and giving up old dreams can allow new ones to soar."

As I sat here listening to her, I welled up with tears because even though it's not exactly the same sort of injury, the emotional toll was the same. She talked openly about saying to herself "Why me?" She didn't give up at all, she became a pilot and learned how to walk again. I haven't given up either despite the challenges I have every day. Janine said this at the end of her talk, and it truly resonated with me.

> *"I was about to embark on a project, that of rebuilding a life and even though I had absolutely no idea what I was going to do, in that uncertainty came a sense of freedom. I was no longer tied to a set path. I was free. I was free to explore life's infinite possibilities, and that realization changed my life."*

So, not wanting to end January on such a low note, I did the something spontaneous. I bought a new bike. A 2017 Harley Davidson Iron 883 Sportster, the same bike I had bought myself for my 30th birthday. I was determined to turn things around while I still can.

Even if I only have it a year it will be worth it. And yes, I pulled the cancer card for a discount, and it worked! The sales guy, Sean, was a funny dude. When I told him my situation, he was a bit taken back. My best friend's husband and a great friend to me, Liam, sat next to me in his office waiting for the paperwork and Sean says, "So you must have seen The Bucket List?" Liam and I look at each other and know that as soon as we leave this office, we are going to laugh so hard.

When buying a new Harley at the dealerships there's actually quite a bit involved. And sometimes it can take a while. As I'm sitting there 4 hours later, surrounded by big men, they start saying, "You have to ring the bell!" I'm like "No way, no need, I'm good!" Liam and I realize they aren't going to let up so I walk out and see the bell on my right and grab hold of the knot at the bottom and swing it as hard as I can and keep on walking. I felt like I was ringing the bell for so many other reasons than having just bought a new bike. I was ringing it for getting through this month, for having clean body scans, for having just spent a couple of days at the ice castles with my Mom, for still being able to be "Out Living It". Thank you First Descents.

So, how am I?

I have degenerating bones in my shoulders, a fractured rib on the right, a lung nodule, a messed up implant, two very big liver tumors and terminal breast cancer with mets to my brain.

Other than that…I'm great!

"There are only two days in the year that nothing can be done. One is called yesterday and the other is called tomorrow so today is the right day to Love, Believe, Do and mostly Live."

—DALAI LAMA XIV

Game Changer

April 26, 2017

"Happiness cannot be traveled to, owned, earned, worn or consumed. Happiness is the spiritual experience of living every minute with love, grace, and gratitude."
—DENIS WAITLEY

This blog is going to be filled with the story of my 2017 so far. This blog isn't going to be filled with wonderful adventure stories and pictures from the Maldives or some other exotic location. It's a long one and I hope you stay with me. I started writing this entry over 2 months ago on a day when I was sitting at my desk, looking at a blizzard outside my window. Today the seagulls are calling, and the rain is out and I'm in flip-flops and I can't see any snow in my view, just ocean.

New years are supposed to be about new beginnings, fresh starts, new yous and better lives. That's what I was hoping for. I entered 2017 thinking this is going to be my year. I had my travel plans all figured out. I was optimistic, happy and I was starting the year off in Hawaii. Not only was I looking forward to that for selfish reasons, but for my family and friends who could use the break from my cancer too.

Since returning home from Hawaii in January, everything that could go wrong with my health has and then some, and then some more. I almost don't know how to write about it other than list things and total moments in actual time. So, I guess that's what I'll do. You can either stay with me or sit this one out. Either way, I won't be offended. "I'm not everyone's cup of tea." Julia Roberts

Time for me is strange at the moment. The last few months have felt like years, and I can't even remember yesterday. I signed up for Luminosity hoping that it will help my brain get back into shape. From the testing exercises it looks like I need work in the memory and attention categories. Shocker, I always was on the verge of ADHD and Ritalin was mentioned at a recent doctor's visit. I woke up this morning in a panic not knowing what day it was, if it was morning or night, if I was late for an appointment. This happens a lot lately after long nights of little sleep and long Cancerful days.

My cancer has spread, again, but to somewhere else, technically, even though it's still in my brain, or I guess, on my brain, or around my brain. The cancer that was confined to my brain has now spread to the dura lining. The dura is the outer membrane enclosing the brain and spinal cord. I have two new tumors inside my brain as well. I have eight new tumors that the doctors can see in my brain/dura.

Recently at my MRI results appointment my neuro radiation oncologist pauses and starts the appointment without much small talk. That's how I know. Depending on the severity of the results we either chat about travel for 5 minutes or he gets right to it. He is the same age as me, a genius in his field and I feel like I couldn't be in better hands. His smile makes me smile and the way he pushes his little round glasses up. At my first appointment with him last year I asked,

"Will you tell me when the shit is hitting the fan?" So, at my recent appointment with the news of the progression, I asked him, "Has the shit hit the fan?" He said, "Well, no, but this is a game changer." I have progressive brain metastases. But...so soon, already, huh.

We discuss my treatment options, and he gives my Mom and I his recommendation. I cry a little. He hands me a tiny box of pretty horrible tissues. Surgery and radiation are not an option. He is recommending a clinical trial using an oral chemotherapy drug called Palbociclib. There have been encouraging results in patients with breast cancer metastases to other areas of the body.

This clinical trial is focusing on brain metastases, which is new. The coolest thing about this trial is that my neuro oncology doctor designed it! I will have full body scans in 3 weeks to determine if the drug is working. If it isn't then we will move on to Plan B, which is another clinical trial using a different chemotherapy. I have been asked a lot about immunotherapy trials. After asking my doctors about them, I was told that there has been little proven benefit for breast cancer patients, so we have crossed this treatment off the options list.

I am in the 'dark' place. I'm sad, more sad and angry than I have been in a long time. I went to the doctor that day expecting him to say ok, there are a couple more spots that we'll treat with radiation blah blah, piece of cake. I made a mistake having expectations of my cancer or at all. As I'm writing this I'm getting upset and mad and I'm pausing and rubbing my forehead. I'm fidgeting a lot, re-reading and taking deep breaths. This is hard. I'm not comfortable with this at all. It is incredibly difficult to be positive sometimes. It is incredibly difficult to talk about the decline of my health and the progression of my disease.

So, instead of sitting on a beach in the Maldives at this very moment, or dune buggying or camel riding in Dubai, I'm sitting here in Maine waiting for my daily chemo alarm to go off. It has taken me a long time to finish this entry. So much has happened that I haven't even covered at all. I have had to rewrite this entry several times. I've been thinking a lot about all the things cancer has taken from me so quickly this year and from the last 3 years. The peace that I had found last year with my cancer feels so far away from me now.

It feels like it was just yesterday that I was having that conversation with my doctor about my cancer being in a good place, that I didn't need to worry yet. It may not have been yesterday, but it was only 3 short months ago. How quickly things change, without warning even. When cancer progresses, it's like sitting on a boat, all alone facing a rogue cancer wave. It can be an unpredictable terrifying Cancerful event. I felt safe three months ago. I don't feel safe now. I'm on a life raft in the Sea of Cancer, hoping for rescue but there isn't any in sight.

From January until now this is how I have spent a lot of my time:

- 12 appointments locally totaling approximately 19 hours
- 7 appointments in Boston totaling approximately 39 hours
- 4 days at the local hospital for IV antibiotics every 5-8 hours
- 5 weeks of oral antibiotics while being bedridden for two subsequent infections in my body
- 2 medical procedures to surgically open and put in drains for infections
- 2 brain MRIs
- 1 bone scan
- 2 CTs of my chest, abdomen, pelvis
- 4 EKGs
- 1 spinal tap which resulted in bed rest and heavy pain medication for over a week for a spinal headache
- 2 new hormonal treatments which has induced immediate menopause. One treatment is an injection once a month and the other, a pill every day.
- 1 oral chemotherapy for a new clinical trial
- Labs every 2 weeks, which this week has been 3 out of 5 days due to being neutropenic. (Neutropenic means that I have an abnormally low level of neutrophils. Neutrophils are a type of white blood cell. In order to continue on the clinical trial my neutrophils need to be at a minimum level of 1,000. Two weeks ago, my neut's dropped to 330 and my chemotherapy was cancelled until my counts improved. I have just this week restarted chemotherapy)

Now onto the fun topic of the financial side of cancer! Yay! If anyone knows me at all you know I have a big voice when it comes to the medical insurance system. Without inserting an excel spreadsheet I broke down the numbers and this is how bad it has been for me, and I know many others. My only income is social security/disability. I'm unable to work and haven't exactly found something in my life at this point to make money doing. I've exhausted any money I had from the sale of my house, savings, retirement funds and a fundraiser put on by my oldest friend. Since being diagnosed with breast cancer just over 3 years ago I have spent over $35,000 on medical bills, premiums and other medical expenses. As of now 80% of my monthly disability income goes towards medical bills, health insurance premiums, medications etc. This leaves me with less than $200 a month to live on. I'm managing. I live with my mother. I have a wonderful space here and Oskar can be here with me. Up until now, I traveled on points from years of piling up medical bills on 5 different credit cards.

I pay my $500 a month health insurance premium and a monthly minimum payment towards my hospital balances but that's all I do. I will most likely be making payments towards medical bills for the rest of my life. I have been advised by the billing department at MGH that I will be sent to collections, small claims court etc. due to not paying these balances in full within 18 months. That would mean I would have to pay $666.67 per month towards my medical bills. What am I supposed to do? I have bigger things to worry about like the fact that I'm fucking dying, and I have other bills, other responsibilities, like making sure I have a will and what I want for the end of my life, and a car and dog food and chemo and prosecco.

So, sorry to all of the medical organizations I owe money to but I'm literally doing the best I can and the best I honestly would want to do for you. I'm also sorry to tell you that you're not going to get your $12,000 right now or most likely ever. I finally get it after 8 years of being a medical practice manager and a billing manager. I finally understand all those emotional breakdowns over the phone with patients struggling financially, as I sat in my big comfy office, probably enjoying a venti latte (j/k I don't even like those, coffee black please). That time feels like so long ago. I think that's what we call irony. I was also just notified that my insurance plan changed November 1st last year and my deductible was increased by $3,000 so I owe them even more money. Is this even legal? Turns out…it is.

In 2016, I was receiving a government subsidy for my health insurance due to my projected low income. The government was paying $100 towards my monthly health insurance premium, which was fantastic! When my projected income for 2017 changed to ZERO due to my illness, the marketplace determined I was no longer eligible for a marketplace plan or the deductible discounts because I qualified for NH Medicaid. I apply to NH Medicaid and find out they won't cover out of state medical care (makes sense I guess). However, when I went to SNH ER the neurology doctor on call refused me as a patient… something about protocol, don't get me started. The local hospital sent me by ambulance in the middle of the night to Mass General Hospital in Boston. So, I have to keep a private health insurance plan to allow me to continue my care at MGH. Just as an extra F*%K you the government requires me to pay back the subsidy. So SORRY, but I didn't exactly plan financially from birth to be 'disabled' and dealing with a terminal illness at the age of 38. My mistake. My bad.[9]

---

9. CAROL'S NOTE: Further information on finances can be found on page 261.

"The American Heath Care System's dysfunction matches its brilliance."

—BJ MILLER

As I've said before, one cannot underestimate the benefits of having a good therapist. She listens to my rants about the system some days, other days she just lets me be quiet or cry. There is rarely a happy medium to my moods in there. She's got my back. At a recent appointment I was telling her how confused I was about everything happening to me. She just said one word that made everything make sense. "Your body is in turmoil." We talk a lot about time. Or I talk a lot about time, about having too much time, too little time. We talk about the connection between time and freedom. There is such a thing as feeling trapped in time with too much freedom. We talk about feeling lost within time and the panic that can accompany it. We talk about the exhaustion of being strong and weak over and over again. We talk about my writing, which she reads and says all the time, "needs to reach a larger audience." The idea of me doing discussions at the hospital for the doctors has been mentioned and I'm actually open to the idea. The anxiety that accompanies time for me has been made worse by my desire to turn all of this into a book. I fear that I won't have enough time, especially when I go radio silent for almost three months.

Time for me is also especially now, connected with loss. Loss can be in any form, loss in travel and loss in the form of people or pets or things. I've been part of a new club, The Cancerfuls (anyone who has/had cancer) for three years now. It is inevitable that we experience the loss of each other. For some of us we move forward towards remission and for some of us we move toward a progression in our disease.

Last year I lost Argentina and Patagonia. This year I lost the Maldives, Panama, Florida, Colorado and Hawaii so far. It's been a rough start. A year ago, I was having an emotional breakdown in my closet unpacking from a trip I never went on. Almost a year to the day I'm doing the same thing minus the breakdown. Now, I'm just pissed. I should have known better. Nothing like cancer to smack you around a bit, making it clear that some serious reprioritizing needs to happen. Cancer and the clinical trial come first for now. I need to accept that, if I want to stay in this trial. I'm just tired of losing, of having to readjust to things being worse than they were. I'm never readjusting to a new great thing in my life. Recently I was looking through a journal from February I found a couple of interesting entries. I never said I was an artist.

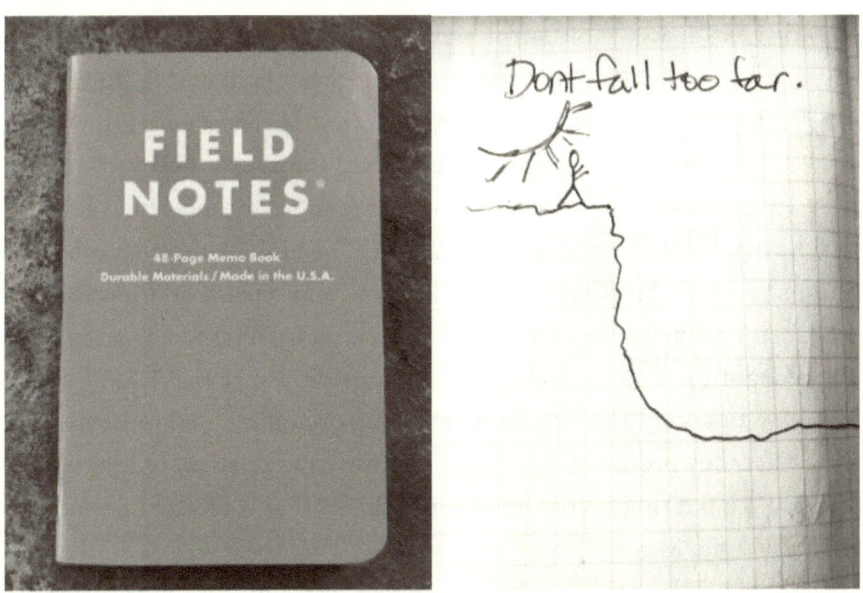

> Dear God,
> It's me, Angela.
> Can you please help me?..

I'm not much of a pray-er and I would never normally write anything like that, so I was a bit surprised at myself. Lately, there have been important people in my life talking to me about God and faith. I listen, carefully and genuinely, despite my own beliefs. You never know what you will connect to and I have an open ear for almost every opinion. I grew up finding comfort and faith in other things besides the Lord and that hasn't changed now that I'm an adult. I heard a word this weekend and I already forget where. I didn't know what it meant or if it was a real word, so I looked it up. Omnism. According to Wikipedia, omnism is the recognition and respect of all religions. It also says, "it can be seen as a way to accept the existence of various religions without believing in all that they profess to teach. Many omnists say that all religions contain truths, but that no one religion offers all that is truth." I connect to this, big time. Maybe I'm an omnist.

It occurred to me over the last few months to maybe try reading the bible or other religious writings recommended or sent to me. As I sit here writing this I look up over the computer, at my feet resting on the coffee table and I see a big stack of books that I've just recently finished or are reading currently. All of these books have been incredibly inspirational. *Breast Left Unsaid* by Jude Callirgos is a memoir of her battle with breast cancer. This book and her language and tone are eerily similar to mine. *Alone in Antarctica* by Felicity Aston is a memoir of her solo ski voyage across the Antarctica. *It's What I Do* by Lynsey Addario is a memoir about life as a young American photojournalist in war torn countries across the world. This book and the way she writes her story had me hooked from the first page and is by far one of my new favorites. Today I started reading *Maiden Voyage* by Tania Aebi, a memoir about her 2 ½ year adventure sailing around the world by herself at the young age of 18. I'll save the Bible for later, I think.

There's a screaming theme when I read these titles. I connect to what these women struggle with emotionally and it gives me some peace as I spend time reading their stories of strength and bravery. I think that's why I love them so much. It lifts me up. I'm going through a challenge and a struggle just as they have. In some place in the back of my mind I feel we are the same on some level. Reading about real independent women who need a change in their lives or have a calling or desire for adventure, soothes me. I'm living through their stories with them as I read.

Their solitude and terror of being alone but courage and determination are more than inspiring to me. I understand feeling the need to change your life. I understand the true desire for adventure or spiritual quests. I understand the need to be taken seriously. I understand some of their fear and loneliness. I understand some of their physical challenges. I understand being vulnerable. In the end these women succeeded in their journey. They found love along the way and most importantly themselves.

I believe if I didn't have terminal cancer, I would try an adventure of my own. I mean definitely not in Antarctica, but maybe the PCT or move around the South Pacific or just work my way around the world. Felicity Aston who skied across Antarctica said in her memoir, "...there is a part of my desire for adventure that I can't attribute to parental influence. Much of it is simply an integral part of who I am, as tangible and intrinsic as my height or the color of my eyes. From the start I couldn't help but see the growing possibility for adventure wherever I happened to be." I too have also felt this way during almost all of my travels.

I met with my PCP for a follow up last month and he knows I'm sad and I him. I normally have some travels to tell him about but this time I don't. He has known me for a long time. His nurse and I also have a special connection. We go way back, and she goes way back with my Mom. She cries, hugs me and tells me she loves me. She tells me as she walks out the door, "You have a light. You have a thousand angels watching over you."

I'm so grateful for moments like these, pure human kindness, compassion and empathy. You will never be a good doctor or nurse or any healthcare provider or any human being if you don't care for people. My PCP knows how disappointed I am at all of this SH%T happening. He steps out of the room for a moment and comes back in with his favorite guitar.

His case is covered in stickers from his earlier days, and he tells me about some of their stories. He takes the guitar out and I can see his face light up. This is his thing, like travel is mine! He plays and I instantly well up with tears because he's playing one of my most favorite songs, Blackbird.[10]

Wouldn't Cancerland be so much more fun if we had relationships like this with all our medical providers? I'm not naive however and understand that this sort of appointment is not the norm. I appreciated it though and it made for a special moment between patient and provider and a special moment for me in an otherwise regular Cancerful day. I see so many different doctors in different specialties and have a different relationship with each one of them. I wonder about their own lives, their families. I have so much respect and admiration for the care they have shown me. I have and do continue to put my life in their hands.

> **"Take these broken wings and learn to fly."**
> —PAUL McCARTNEY

These feelings I have about provider and patient relationships is the theme to a Ted Talk by BJ Miller I recently listened to "What really matters at the end of life". BJ is a hospice and palliative physician who lost three limbs when hit with an electrical current. His talk and his life's passion are end of life issues for his patients. He discusses the importance of making sure he builds a graceful end for his patients. He talks about how there needs to be a better understanding of patient needs. Everything can change so quickly and addressing a potential change in a patient's priorities is of the utmost significance. "…another great thing about necessary suffering is that it is the very

---

10. CAROL'S NOTE: A video of Paul McCartney singing "Blackbird" can be found at https://www.youtube.com/watch?v=JiL5JpUtjqY.

thing that unites caregiver and care receiver - human beings. This, we are finally realizing, is where healing happens." BJ Miller

These relationships that I have had with my caregivers have ultimately made me reevaluate relationships of my own at times. At times there seems to be a constant coming and going of people in my life. This can be difficult for me. There's nothing like feeling rejected because you have terminal cancer. I do understand the extreme of emotions that can occur within illness and friends and family, but it hurts me incredibly when this happens in my own life. I wish I could say that I've never felt the sting of the disappearance of someone from my life because of my cancer.[11] Sometimes I really love meeting new people and forming new connections traveling. Some of the closest relation-ships I now have are from traveling.

Sometimes it seems there is a fascination for me by the new people I meet. "BUT you don't look sick!!!" There ultimately seems to be more attention paid to my illness than my actual character. How bout I just sit here behind these bars, like a zoo animal, and let you ooo and awww about my cancer? The constant "How are yous?" and my lack of decent responses. Someone asked me recently after I responded to their "How are you?" with "Not well", whether it was emotional or physical. I immediately responded with "One equals the other." I'm generally a lot friendlier but between being chemically forced into instant menopause and being taken off medications I've been on for a long time because they're not trial compliant, I'm a little fragile, a little "mouthy" and clearly a lot moody.

---

11. CAROL'S NOTE: Further reflections on people disappearing from your life can be found on page 329.

My recent intolerance or impatience with awkward cancer conversations isn't exactly new, honestly. I'm sick. I know it's hard. I know it's hard to accept. I know it's not right or fair. I know that you are all sad and so am I. What I don't need to hear anymore is how much people can't believe this is happening. It's happening, I've accepted it, now please do yourself a favor and accept it too, so we can get back to just being you and me, because I miss that. Please don't make me have to be your therapist for this wonderful lunch we are having. I ask myself if this is too harsh but convince myself I'm allowed to feel this way. But I mean, let's face it, I've always been sort of a B&*%H some would probably say. As a child my Mom or some adult was always calling me "fresh" or threatening me with a bar of soap.

My freshness seems to be amplified at times during long waits in waiting rooms. We are all Cancerful in Cancerland. We all belong to this place. Yet it's a strange universe where no one talks to each other. We barely look at each other and people whisper. This has always bothered me. At my last appointment a woman approaches me in the waiting room as I'm walking out of the lab and asks me if I can let her into an exam room because her relative is in there. I was very confused and then I realized she thought I worked there. I saw several people looking at the exchange and I responded to her, "I'm sorry, I'm a patient." As if it wasn't clear enough already from the bandage wrapping my arm from that lab draw, I just had, for the second time because they forgot something and the big white patient bracelet I'm wearing.

Weird things happen every time I'm at the hospital for an appointment. This most recent time my Mom and I were sitting, waiting in the neuro oncology unit and I excused myself to walk the hall. The unit is on the 9th floor and has a wall of windows looking out over the Boston skyline. It's beautiful. As I was waiting for my name to be called looking out at the view I hear Blackbird. I turned instantly and there was a man sitting there just playing his guitar, a volunteer I'm guessing. MGH does this in some departments and I can't praise these efforts enough. For me, music, especially someone volunteering his or her time to provide us comfort, calms me immediately and reminds me of human goodness.

While I was in the hallway, a gentleman sitting across from my Mom and I in the waiting room says to her, "Boy she looks anxious." My Mom explains that we'd just received some disappointing news on my last scan. He exclaims, "My wife has been terminal for 19 years!" I'm sorry but is that supposed to make my Mom or myself feel better, cause it doesn't, but thanks. I'm sure it was his immediate reaction and his intention to help us feel better but sometimes things are better left UN said. I'm sensitive right now and so is she, understandably. Either way, it's a good thing I wasn't sitting there because there's a good chance I would've been 'fresh'.

To add insult to injury (I think that's the phrase) I was in the lab this week and witnessed a young guy being evil. He was lucky I was so fragile at the time because I would have close lined him on the way out. I was wearing a mask like a good girl because I'm neutropenic (basically means I'm not allowed to get sick at all) and out of the corner of my left eye saw him snap a picture of me with his gigantic cell phone. I was so taken aback by this that I couldn't even move, let alone respond. I wasn't even sure if that's what happened but what else could it have been? So, I did this (see pic below) for the next time, except I'm not going to use permanent marker again. Not the most brilliant idea I've had.

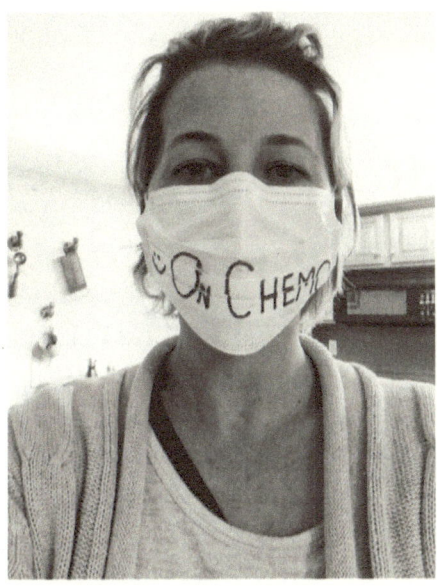

If you have made it this far in the blog, thank you. Thank you for caring that much. I do apologize for the delay in an update of my health. As of today, I'm actively taking my chemotherapy every day. The doctors have reduced my dose in hopes of preventing another round of neutropenia. I'm doing the best I can. I can't say that every day I even get that far. It's been tough to enjoy life during these times. We'll find out in a few weeks if the drug is working and whether I will continue on this clinical trial. I have no feeling about whether the drug is working or not. I can only hope that all the prayers being said for me and my own hopes and faith are enough to provide me with some more time and a bit more freedom.

> **"Prayer is an act of love; words are not needed.**
> **Even if sickness distracts from thoughts,**
> **all that is needed is the will to love."**
> —SAINT TERESA OF AVILA

Holy Moly Magical Moments, Holy Moly Menopause, Holy Moly Hanalei, Holy Moly Long Blog

August 9, 2017

**"There is a crack, a crack in everything
That's how the light gets in."**
—LEONARD COHEN, "ANTHEM"

I've been holding off on this entry for several months. Why do I feel like I've said that before? When living a life in two-month increments, things can change quickly. As I look back at my life since December, SH%T has been crazy to say the least and not in a good way. As I write this though, happy to be writing again I'm listening to the seagulls fly above the cottage up in Maine.

Since May, I've had two rounds of full body scans. Likely due to my slightly pessimistic nature and not wanting to jinx anything, I withheld the results until now. As of May 18th, I had, for the first time since my cancer spread to my brain, a stable scan. Not just a stable scan but a

16% reduction in tumor sizes. After just 5 weeks on the clinical trial chemotherapy, Palbociclib (Ibrance), provided by Pfizer, there was a 16% reduction. This is worth repeating! I remember driving home that day with Mom, texting and calling my closest friends and family about the results. I remember it was also quiet in the car. It was quieter than I expected. I was reminded about not having expectations in Cancerland. Even a stable scan can bring up some heavy issues.

Everyone kept telling me to celebrate but I was remembering that it was this time last year that there were brain tumors that were missed. I felt a quiet joy. I felt confused. I felt exhausted. I felt a little bit of anger actually. I felt the bitterness of my life. I felt the cancer roller-coaster. This is not the normal ride that we expect from an amusement park. The closest I can come up with for a comparison is the ride that just spins around in circles over and over again, taking away your breath. The cancer version of this ride is a little more extreme. When it stops spinning like a roulette table it's not red or black, you're either dying or living. As of July 20th, I had a second set of stable scans. The clinical trial is working and working really effing well. I have been asking in my silent prayers for more functional time, and I'm being given that by taking this drug.

Let me explain a little more because I'm not sure that it's as clear as it is in my tumor filled brain. Back in March when I received the news of the further spread and when the clinical trial began, I was scared beyond what I've been thus far in this journey. Words like hospice, lawyers, wills, decisions, palliative care, were being mentioned. Life wasn't looking so good, or the near future and I wasn't even close to ready for that. I'm still not. From one day to the next, sometimes my head just spins with the constant thoughts of "yes, you're going to die" or "no, you're not dying yet."

That weekend with my hands in my garden and a good motorcycle ride in the sun, I finally felt it. I felt happy. I felt the relief. I felt my breathing change. I felt the excitement. I believed the doctors and I believed in the results and I believed in the trial. On the way out of the neuro oncology unit that day at Mass General Hospital, I stopped in to see my two favorite vampires (phlebotomists haha). I wanted to share the news with them. They see me so often but yet rarely hear the results, let alone good ones. Ann who follows my blog and makes me smile with her kindness and funny Irish family stories in Boston. Lin, who stuffs my pockets with Swedish Fish because she knows I love them and there are never any left in the candy bowl. Come to find out, the Swedish Fish are actually brought in by a fellow patient. I think I will bring more for the supply. Those hard round candies taste like crap.

While in the lab sharing my good news, I met a woman with stage IV ovarian cancer, who also received good news that day. She and her husband travel from Washington DC to be part of a different clinical trial here at Mass General with the same neuro oncologist. She has also just found out that she has had a 16% reduction. We celebrated together in the lab and offered each other hugs and smiles and congratulations. These are the moments that are permanent happy memories for me in Cancerland and moments I recognize don't happen often around here. Maybe I should play roulette number 16!

In the last year, but really the last 6 months, I've learned so much about myself and made sense of so much, specifically my past. You know, those dark moments we like to forget and always wonder why we made those decisions or dated that guy. I'm getting closer to moving forward towards my future instead of partially staying stuck in the past with these sad memories, accepting the space that is me and accepting my past. I'm coming out strong. The emotional side effects of cancer are forcing me to look back and make peace with non-peaceful events. I can feel myself evolving and I'm running with it.

It's amazing what happens when my brain relaxes and when I open my heart. I'm having huge moments and realizations. Through talk therapy I learned the significance of the word Safe. I learned what this word has meant to me my entire life and now. From a very early age I had to be strong. Yes, it may be a bit cryptic but I'm a bit cryptic and some of these sad moments I refer to are just for me. Now more than ever I have the need and desire to be true to myself alone. It took a bit longer than I hoped but I'm here now.

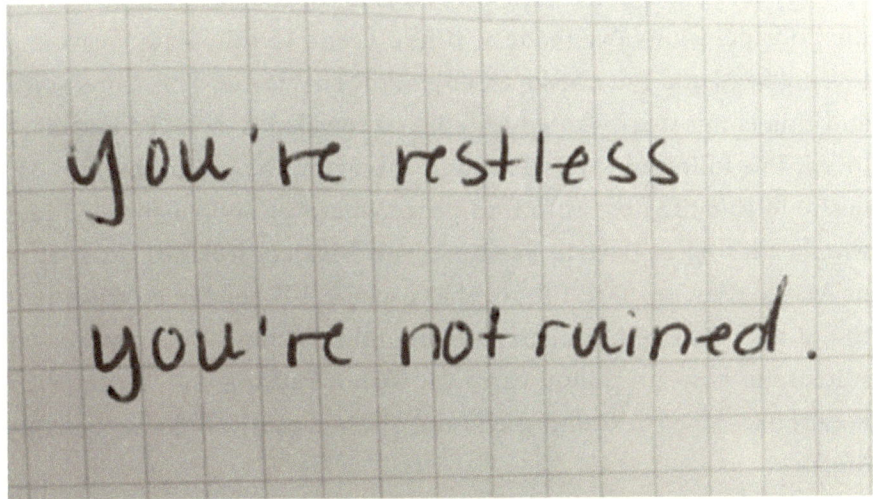

Those chapters come and go, and pages turn. But it's definitely time for some of those chapters to be closed. My therapist says I'm not coming unglued; I'm piecing things back together, that sometimes a story needs to be changed just like the ending. Earlier this year I was experiencing Fight Flight Freeze once again, a common reaction to living with PTSD. I was frozen, for a while. I'm de-thawing now… unless I get bad news in two months haha. Recently, I read a not so happy story of a very young girl [Athena Orchard] who was diagnosed with cancer. She took her life and left this note for her family behind a mirror in her bedroom. A portion of the note read: "Happiness depends upon ourselves. Maybe it's not about the happy ending, maybe it's about the story. The purpose of life is a life of purpose…" I hear you and I'm listening, with a lump in my throat. You should still be here. This is a note for all of humankind, especially now. For a very young girl, she left an incredibly brilliant and beautiful note that we should all hear and listen to.

I finally feel like I don't have to apologize for the path I've chosen or the poor decisions I've made at times. I tend to follow my heart and less my head and I'm not sorry, anymore. This is me. This is my spirit and this is my story. I'm educated. I'm traveled. I've loved and been loved. I've followed love all around the world. Now I follow me. My desire in this life now, is to find peace wherever and whenever I can, whether it's here, Hawaii, Panama, New Mexico, Iceland, Costa Rica or Maine, that's where I'll go, that's where I'll be. My suitcase isn't full of the crap I've been carrying around my whole life anymore. My suitcase is now a 4 pound carry on with a bathing suit, a camera, a notebook, some rocks and shells and all the beautiful moments of my life, now.

I'm holding on to some pieces of who I used to be though, the better pieces. I'm coming back together and some days my puzzle pieces lay still on the table and that's OK too. With an open heart and an honest relationship with a healer in my life I've been rewarded with clarity, understanding and acceptance. I've felt the deep need lately to revisit my past. I guess when living with a terminal illness at this age and time in my life, I felt the need to reevaluate past situations or traumatic events that have had influence over my person and my character. It amazes me sometimes how little but yet how much I've changed over the course of my life but more specifically in the last couple years. I think the parts that remain the same; the core of me, the center of my being and where I continue to receive inspiration are exactly the same and I like that. I'm keeping the best of me and burning the sad moments that never made sense until now, just like a phoenix.

I feel euphoric some days, liberated, liberated from myself, from my past. This is happening because I made the decision to go there and say I'm figuring this shit out and making sense of it and moving on. It was a choice I made. I tell my healer/therapist how grateful I am for her presence in my life, for being the sounding board for my personal evolvement, for providing the safety in talking about my saddest times. I think it's important to tell people how much you value them. I don't take that relationship or what she does for a living for granted, ever. With her encouragement and motivation, I push through the tough stuff and wow it has been worth it! The feeling in this change is that I haven't necessarily forgiven those who have hurt me in one way or another, I'm just not angry about it anymore and that's huge for me. One step at a time. I'm acknowledging and accepting the life I've had, the choices I've made, the people who have caused me pain and it's freeing.

Back in June, my family got together and had a big party in New Jersey. On the drive down with my Mom a sad thought occurred to me. I made a list of all my female relatives in my family that I know of. The current statistic of breast cancer diagnoses is 1 in 8 people will be diagnosed, men and women, don't forget. Unfortunately, this statistic has not dropped. Of the 60 approximate women in my family including aunts, cousins etc., about 8 could potentially develop breast cancer in their lifetime based on these current statistics. This isn't OK with me!!! I don't want this to happen to anyone I love and cherish.

I worried about putting this part in here but it's a real issue and I have absolutely no intent to scare my family or friends but to educate everyone about the dangers of this illness. I have a book I leave on my coffee table, and I use as a source of answers, called *A Guide for the Advanced Soul* by Susan Hayward. When thinking on this topic and the inclusion of this, per instruction on the back of the book, I opened to a random page and this was the thought to my concern, written by Gita Belli, "Everything I do and say with anyone makes a difference." There was my answer.

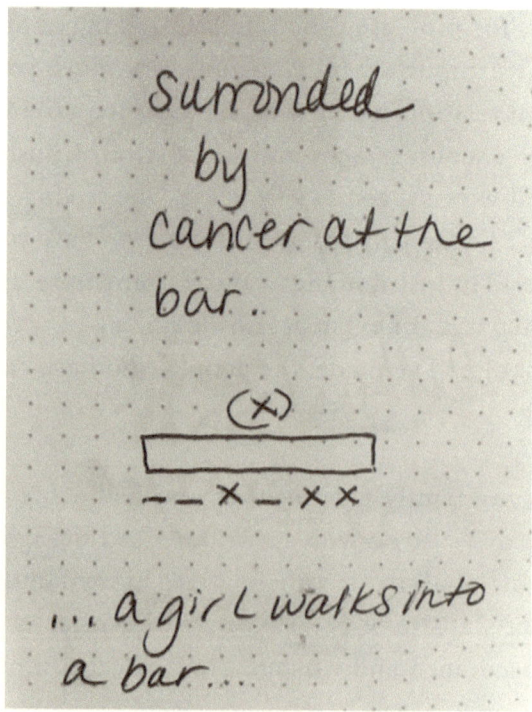

This is why that statement is true. This is a drawing, not really but you get it, of a restaurant that I stopped at recently to have a drink. Walking in, there was a woman sitting there with a scarf on her head. About 15 minutes later, well into my glass of champagne, I felt a tap on my shoulder and heard my name and I realized I knew her. We used to work together; I just didn't recognize her. She has breast cancer and is just starting her treatment. Another friend was there, whose mother has breast cancer, there was me and then another woman on my right I spoke to because I recognized her from the garden center. She also has breast cancer. Please make it stop. I guess Mondays are the day for us Breast Cancerful's to have or need a drink.

Traveling to NJ the following weekend to visit family was intense in a beautiful way. I realized that weekend that I need to accept my own limitations and have respect for my health. On the day my Mom and I arrived, we had tickets to see Sigur Ros in Philadelphia, an Icelandic band we have both grown to love since our trip there. I was tired and I took a few minutes to figure out if I should go or stay and rest but also have more time with my family. We decided to miss the show. The deciding factor for me was the fine print on the ticket that said, "laser light show". My 8+ brain tumors don't need a laser light show. Disappointing people is hard and making decisions to take care of myself sometimes means missing things and losing money haha. It has become very important for me to have this balance in my life.

That whole family weekend was full of reconnecting and love and for me so much more. Most of my cousins have now gone on to have their own children, mostly girls but a few adorable boys. There's a new generation of our family. I was reminded that weekend that my line will end. There's will keep going. There were so many moments when sitting on the side of my aunt's pool, just observing, that I felt the surrealness and beauty of it all. I was watching us as kids only now we are the adults. I realized that growing up in NH vs. PA/NJ gave me a different relationship with the entire family. I accept that now. It's difficult sometimes but family is family, and I love each one of them with my entire heart.

After the family party I heard and realized that because of the distance many family members were concerned about how I would look, being as sick as I am. I got a lot of "You look so goods", which I appreciated and understood. It makes me think about change in life, in a person, in me. I am still the same despite cancer, careers, passions, lifestyles, tattoos haha. Distance is hard and especially even more difficult during hard times, like illness. Most of my family never saw me sick, sick. I think about the preconceptions and stigma humankind has about illness. It makes me kind of happy to show my family, to show the world, that terminal disease doesn't always look 'terminal'.

On the drive home my Mom and I discussed this topic and whether or not it was the right decision to stay in NH when I was little. We decided it was. I'm grateful that my Mom was so brave during a time when returning to a 'safe' place would've been comforting. I think about my Mom and our relationship and our similarities and at times it's kind of laughable. The same thing happens when I spend time with my Dad. I see the similarities. I also see the differences and I like that too.[12]

Through talk therapy, private thought, social interactions, getting older, learning and evolving, I've realized a lot. I think this has to

---

12. CAROL'S NOTE: Angela originally included "our high school portraits," which can be viewed at www.beautyandthedark.com.

do with the tiny bit of pressure I feel to "figure it all out" and fast. I discovered I may be an emotional introvert and complex at times but there's a good reason. I'm not shy. I listen and observe life. I'm sensitive, caring, dedicated, generous, curious, giving, compassionate, strong-minded and fresh. I have faults just like everyone else. I've been called a paradox, which I totally can understand. Per Conde Nast Traveler I may have 'vagabond neurosis' which since the year 2000 has become a legitimate disorder. The definition states: "sufferers have an abnormal impulse to travel: they are prepared to spend beyond their means, sacrifice jobs, lovers, and security in their lust for new experiences." Sounds about right. I've been doing that since the age of 18, I believe.

I learned to love traveling when I was a young girl. Although I didn't necessarily learn to love traveling, I just did. Love of travel runs deep in my family, on both sides. My parents and Grandparents provided the influence for my vagabond neurosis. Growing up I visited Germany and the Caribbean, Italy, the west USA. In my adult and Cancerful years I've seen Turks and Caicos, Iceland, Mexico, Spain, Amsterdam, Panama, Costa Rica, Hawaii 5 times and Africa. I've driven across the US three times, taken a train across once and have seen every state except Alaska and North Dakota. I have speeding tickets in more than 5 states and in more than one country;). I've lived in Oregon, NH, PA and Australia where I ultimately received my bachelor's degree.

I don't want to survive cancer and life. I want to live. I was taught early on by a fellow Cancerful and a very good friend that we need to try and just cure moments or an hour or maybe even a day. I get so much inspiration from people I've met that are also going through this experience or have. These people inspire me to live an authentic life. Many of the Cancerful young adults that I've had the blessed opportunity to meet are choosing to change their lives and do something better, something more selfless and self-fulfilling. For many of us, cancer gives us the motivation to reach for those dreams we've always had, just a little faster.

Quality of life for me means being able to travel and living out my dreams the best I can. My dreams always included the rest of the world and being part of it. About two years ago I decided to leave my job. A job I had been at for 8 years or more. The people I worked with became family quickly and leaving was not an easy decision. I took a leap of faith that everything would be all right. On a yoga retreat in Costa Rica later that month I realized I had made the right decision. This was my first step towards my authentic life. I was in remission. I sold my home. I broke even. I wanted to live smaller, lighter. I just needed to figure out where and I was being called to New Mexico.

Six months later and less than a year in remission, my cancer spread. I left my job because I knew underneath it all that I wasn't done with cancer. Try explaining that to your boss, who is also a doctor and someone that was like family. I don't think he necessarily understood why I left but I just knew it was the right thing. I left my job because I knew I needed more, and I knew my time could be a lot shorter than I once thought. In my non-Cancerful dream life I would've loved to be a photojournalist for National Geographic or the NY Times or something like that.

Dreams... Maybe what I'm trying to attempt with this blog is a sort of photojournalist project in some ways, just about me instead of war-torn countries or wild mustangs in the West or birds of the Galapagos. Oh, and I might as well tell you at one point before I decided to go to college, I interviewed with the Marines. I had a desire for military for some reason or to be a police officer, but I think I'm pretty happy with the path I took.

I've had the great luck of meeting so many wonderful people on my travels, many of whom I still keep in touch with and many of whom I have special relationships with. At this point in time finances make living the life I have come to love difficult. I've been reevaluating my dream destination list. For six months this year cancer stopped me from doing what I love but it didn't save me any money. I still have a trip list, don't get me wrong, but instead of French Polynesia there's the Maldives and instead of Vietnam or Bali there's the Canadian Rockies and Kauai as much as possible and Alaska and North Dakota, my last 2 US states to see. I just need my cancer to give me about another 12 months to get it all done!

So, how do I feel now, with two sets of stable scans behind me? I feel pretty wonderful. My body is in rough shape from so many months of inactivity and so many months of chemotherapy every day. I'm getting past the worst of menopause with the help of acupuncture, massage, reiki, yoga, chiro, supplements and I'm finally back to New Hampshire Power Yoga! Recently, one of my breast oncologists gave me a beautiful gift and I wear it almost every day to remind me of the kindness I have found along the way in this world of cancer. These healers, all of them, are helping me get through every day. They're helping me live and they respect how I want to live my life. I have found the balance between eastern and western therapies finally and see only progress from here.

"...And the day came when the risk to remain tight in a bud was more painful than the risk it took to blossom."

—ANAIS NIN

PICTURE TAKEN BY LIESL CLARK
OF LIESL CLARK PHOTOGRAPHY.

Now onto Kauai, the 1st trip I have taken in 6 months. I needed it to be here. I needed to restore my soul and my body. I arrived onto the island around 8:30pm and as I walked off the plane amidst a swarm of tourists, into the open air, the humidity hit me in the face, and I smiled. To know that warmth and sunshine are waiting for me is the perfect beginning to the second half of my year. After the first morning, my first coffee, reading and writing for a bit, I felt myself coming out of the freeze. The last five months have been some of the toughest months of my life and when my doctors told me I could take a trip I wasn't surprised that I went running back to Kauai as fast as I could.

I have connections there. I've had a connection there since 1995. For a long time growing up I believed all I wanted was to work with animals. I believed I wanted to go to a university in Hawaii. My father has been to Hawaii 18 times. My Mom took me when I was 16 and we spent an amazing couple of weeks together going from island to island, taking tours of the schools. After deciding not to go to college right away and moving to Oregon to begin college a little over a year later, Mom and I took a trip to Maui. This trip happened after a terrible and horrendous family tragedy.

This is what happened after that trip in a very shortened summary. We took a snorkeling trip one day, 17 years ago in Maui. At the end of the day (that I spent hanging over the railing trying not to barf) the employees passed out internship applications for the Pacific Whale Foundation. The options were internships in Hawaii researching the dolphins and Australia researching the humpback whales. I couldn't believe this was happening and as soon as I returned to Oregon, I filled that baby out for the Hawaii options, and I didn't care about the cost.

This is where the story turns in an unexpected direction, literally across the world direction. I didn't get accepted for Hawaii. I got accepted for Australia. I ended up moving to Australia immediately after that. Love may or may not have had something to do with that. I lived there for three years, in Hervey Bay, Queensland, bought an old home a street from the beach, renovated it, had dogs, chickens, parrots, snakes, spiders and went to the University of Southern Queensland. I had an amazing life there and the people that became my family I will never forget, and I will love forever.

I did not return to Kauai until just last year. I feel like in a full circle kinda way I may be going back to where I belonged. It was on this recent trip I realized how many connections I have to the island. I won't list them all but there are a lot and I'm a huge believer of signs. I see kindness around almost every corner in Kauai. I have been completely accepted. I'm not a tourist anymore there but I'm not a local. I'm a locust haha or lourist. On this trip someone born and raised on this island, which is rare, said to me, "you can't be here if you're not strong in spirit". I believe this whole-heartedly. Everyone I've met there is strong in spirit and so am I.

Why do I keep going back to Kauai? Because, I've had more consistently cured moments and time there than anywhere else in the world besides New Mexico and Costa Rica. I recognize and respect this pull, this effect. I recognize the full circle and the connections through people here even. This island makes me believe that there is something to be said for fate and destiny.

From every corner of Kauai, I have a connection and it's not going unnoticed.

There seems to be a parallel between the people I have met and who have come to stay. There's no judgment. People are always laughing and hugging and sharing their lives with each other. I had the privilege on this trip of meeting two women that are descendants from the oldest and most royal Kauai families. My cheeks hurt from laughing after talking with one of them. Turns out we share a cancer connection. I felt honored and blessed to be included in this celebration. People who I've met there tend to have had tragedy in their life at one time or another. They've healed here in this place. Maybe this is part of my connection to this magical island. I understand the intensity in which the people living here cling to their land and to their customs and to each other.

Kauai is the oldest of the Hawaiian Islands and volcanic in its birth. It's the 21st largest island in the USA. Legend states that the island's name came from a Polynesian navigator and that the word means "around the neck", as in how a father would carry his favorite child. Kauai has quite the volatile history. Kaumuali'i originally ruled Kauai and the island of Niihau. He resisted takeover by King Kamehameha for a long time but in 1810 agreed to join with the other Hawaiian Islands. In 1815, Kaumuali'i led secret talks with the Russian American Company in order to gain Russia's support against the King. These discussions with the Russians ultimately failed. The United States took over Hawaii in 1893. Also, a little-known fact is that the U.S. Navy's "Barking Sands" Pacific Missile Range Facility is located here. Based on current world news this is probably a good thing.

Prior to all of this instability in rule, the infamous Captain James Cook landed in Kauai in the late 1700s. At first the relationship between the Hawaiians and Cook was peaceful. After a long story about Cook interrupting a Hawaiian ceremony and taking advantage of the natives, they were discovered as liars. Due to the interruption in the ceremony the Hawaiians believed Cook and his crew were immortals. Once found out, Cook was killed by local Hawaiians after a chief was shot and killed. Oh man I hope I got that all right or even close to right!

Speaking of volatility and frustration I want to vent about something as a traveler and as a woman very quickly. Hell, this blog has gone on long enough why not a bit longer! Now don't forget after reading this that I'm an independent woman who was raised by an independent woman and who does not need assistance but would at least like to be asked. I have noticed during my travels over the last couple years that no one helps each other anymore or very rarely do I see it. I help people whenever I see someone struggle. A flight attendant has even thanked me for being so nice. WTH is wrong with people? Although this is not a question I necessarily need the answer to. It's an answer I already know. I didn't experience anyone helping me as I struggled with an effed up ankle, shoulder, hip, knee, neck and back, oh and terminal cancer but I get it, I look fine. I could've asked for this man's help sure, but he should've just gotten off his bleep ass and helped a female. So, after I awkwardly almost dropped my suitcase on his head and my face flushed with frustration and secretly wanting to drop it, I looked at him and said, "Thanks for your help." I'm still fresh. Which was confirmed a few days ago when I yelled at a man driving like a lunatic in the mall parking lot. I saw him once inside and said hey, you should drive a little slower or you're gonna hurt someone and he looked shocked and actually apologized. Holy moly menopause. I'm not even going to talk about how brutal chemically induced menopause is, but I will say that acupuncture has made going through it tolerable and so that I don't close line people in the neck that make me upset. Don't even get me started on the body shattering, mind numbing hot flashes. Any of you watch Sex and the City and remember the part where Samantha is on stage giving a breast cancer speech and has a hot flash and tears off her wig?...yeah it's that bad.

Back to Kauai. On the surface it doesn't look like it but there is a dark side to the island, as I believe there is everywhere. In the words of a friend who lives on the island, "Stupid tourists do stupid things on sacred land." Due to the remoteness of Kauai and the landscape, Kauai doesn't always make it "easy to get to know her." During time and time again of attempted colonization, the introduction of diseases, weapons and STDs, entire villages were at times wiped out. There is a "rooted distrust" of outsiders for some. As a local living on the island, there is a constant battle to survive here. Land prices have escalated to the extent that the people on the island have a difficult time reaching financially. Down every street there is property after property that sit empty or for sale. Imagine the bitterness for the people who live here to have to see these enormous empty homes day after day or end up leaving their home here, their island, for the mainland. With the sugar and farming industry declining, some of the best jobs on the island are in the tourism industry. "Paradise isn't always pretty." Author unknown

Now, Kauai may have a little bit of a dark side but don't we all? Kauai is also one of the most spiritual places I've felt. The Dalai Lama talks about two areas on Kauai called Anahola and Polihale that he wanted to visit on his 1994 trip. Apparently, he told his guides that in the ancient Tibetan tablets, Anahola is where souls enter the earth and Polihale as the place where souls leave. The original spelling of

Anahola was "Anehola". 'Ane' means the breath of life, and Hola means the hour. The two words together translate as 'birth.'

Over 20 years ago, when my Mom first brought me to Hawaii, she had a ring made for me with my Hawaiian name, Aulani. In Hawaiian we were told this name means the messenger of a chief or a place that speaks with great messages. There is another interesting translation of the word Aloha. Aloha in Polynesian means to share breath. It's not just a word for hello and goodbye. It's also a word that can symbolize love, compassion, mercy and kindness. The people who live here and have grown a spiritual connection to the land believe in balance and harmony. That is what Kauai is about for me…balance, healing, connection.

What I've found during my travels there is that, especially on the North Shore, there is a small-town vibe, despite the overwhelming number of tourists. Everyone helps everyone and everyone knows everyone (the coconut express haha). There is always laughter and physical connection. While there, a new friend called me Sister. I didn't say anything at the time, but I felt this might have had a deeper meaning. The next day I asked my other friend about it. Her response was, "She called you Sister?" I said yes as I secretly was shaking in my flip-flops about the meaning. It's a good thing; it's a good thing to be called "Sister". It means acceptance. I cried a little when I learned that.

This trip back to Kauai was magical. Anyone who is familiar with the weather in Kauai knows that 10 straight days of sunshine on the north shore was a gift from above. Every day was perfect. Every day I went to a different beach, saw friends, had good conversations and laughed a lot. I celebrated the 4th of July at Anini Beach. While at the party I slipped away alone and walked the beach, with a glass of champagne in my hand, reflecting on the last few months, reflecting on my choice to be here vs. anywhere else, reflecting on the peace that this island gives to me over and over again.[13]

Walking the beaches and just mopeding down the road, I am encircled by beauty. I think about my illness and being ill and living the best I can, when I can. I think about my oncology team and how they have worked with me to give me this freedom. They understand my goals and my dreams and how important quality is for me. I reflect on a TED talk that I recently listened to. I always try to reference these talks because there are so many people in this world that are able to put things into perspective in a brilliant way through story.

A TED talk given by Luci Kalanithi in 2016, called "What makes life worth living in the face of death", accomplished this for me, the perspective piece. She tells the story of her husband Paul, a neurosurgeon who was diagnosed with stage IV lung cancer. After his diagnosis, he turned to writing. I wish I could just put her whole talk in here but the biggest quotes I took away were these:

> "...watching him reshape his identity during his illness, learning to witness and accept his pain, talking together through his choices, those experiences taught me that resilience does not mean bouncing back to where you were before, or pretending that the hard stuff isn't hard. It is so hard. It's painful, messy stuff. But it's the stuff and we get to decide what success looks like."

_____

13. **CAROL'S NOTE**: Photos from Angela's trip to Kauai can be found at www.beautyandthedark.com.

From the perspective of a loved one she said, "it was almost like there is peace in the passing because the illness can be so torturous". This talk made me feel better about the "messy stuff" and how we get through it. Everyone's different. She validated how crucial it is to be honest about the emotional and physical suffering we experience. She provided an outside perspective, which made me think about the pillars in my life, going through this journey with me and their perspective. To all my pillars, friends, family, thank you, thank you for being here with me for this journey. I know it's not an easy position to be in and I know that you are all being incredibly strong for me. Your strength gives me strength.

So, now with a successful trip to Kauai completed and some good stable scans, I'm feeling really good. I'm still taking chemotherapy every day and some days really suck but most days are good. My Dad and I have just booked a trip to Yellowstone and the Grand Tetons and my Mom and I are talking about a trip to Alaska next summer! So as long as Pablo keeps working (the name my chemo has been given haha) I'll make it to these places and back to Kauai as soon as I can. Happy summer and thank you for reading! XO

> **"That you are here—**
> **that life exists, and identity:**
> **That the powerful play goes on,**
> **and you may contribute a verse."**
> —O ME! O LIFE! WALT WHITMAN

The Dirty Dozen

April 11, 2018.

"Death commences too early—almost before you're half-acquainted with life—you meet the other."
—CAT ON A HOT TIN ROOF

"If you have been brutally broken, but still have the courage to be gentle to others then you deserve a love deeper than the ocean itself."
—NIKITA GILL

This blog was originally going to be a very lengthy read and still may be, actually it will be, considering the amount of time that has passed and the events. This is my first blog since August 2017, and I apologize for that to you and to myself. As pages and pages and new titles were written over the months, I decided to trash it all. I may be a little all over the place but stick with me, there is so much to talk about. Since I have last posted, there has been a relentless attack on the labyrinth of my brain. I ended the already extremely difficult year with brain surgery #2 and the loss of someone dear to me. It was a loss that shook me to my core and still does some days. The stability of my disease last year is far-gone and I'm on another new clinical trial drug that began the first week of January. It's called Pembrolizumab (aka Keytruda) and it's an immunotherapy drug.

In order to be eligible for this new trial the neurosurgeon had to leave one tumor behind during surgery at the end of November. In one month of being off treatment after the surgery and radiation in November-December, I grew 12 more tumors in my brain. Yep, 12. It makes me realize how lucky I am to be so 'well', so 'high functioning', considering. We will see what happens with this new drug. I have zero expectations. I learned the harsh lesson last year when one week I was stable and the next I'm being kicked off a clinical trial for several reasons and having my brain cut open again. One-week pneumonia, next week brain surgery. Nbd.

To be honest, I've been in a funk for about 6 months and have been unable to travel like I had hoped for last year. Cancer is taking my passions from me slowly. Cancer keeps taking little pieces of me, my mother says, picking me apart piece by piece. I was having a difficult time maintaining my positivity, optimism, and perspective (notice the past tense J). I reread my last blog recently after my last Kauai trip in the summer of 2017 and wow what a high I was on. I was approaching the 'hilltop hour' at full speed but had no idea what was to come, medically and personally. Soon after returning home, it was clear that my lifelong connection to Kauai, the island of displaced misfits (I've heard it was called), was over. I know when it's my time to move on from a situation or place or person. I learned all I could learn there.

Last summer I was feeling really good and that I was living a cancer-ful life of purpose with this blog, my photography and the people I was surrounded by. In the last six months I've had trouble with what my purpose is and feeling sometimes like, "Why am I here?" I've been trying to figure out some heavy stuff and the tone of happiness and peace was lost for a while. I'm working really hard to get my spirit back. I don't want to lose the desire for all the things I've loved about my life. Due to the lack of consistent content here, because of this gap in time, I considered just letting this blog go, deleting it and then I started writing again.

Here is a list of all the blog titles I've had since last September:

- Another Day Another Struggle
- I do not like cancer here or there I do not like cancer anywhere
- The Clink
- Cocktails, Clone Wars & Cancerjail
- Clarice's Christmas Crap
- Dema Chaos
- The Quintuplets
- F U Quints
- Déjà vu
- Cancer made me broke
- Cancer made me fat
- The Hilltop Hour
- No one is perfect
- "Enough about me, what do you think about me?"
- Worst. Year. Ever.
- #canceremmy
- Hair? Are you there? It's me Angela…
- Wtf humanity?
- Then I got pneumonia
- Red man syndrome
- The pain ain't cheap

- War of my life
- Brain surgery #2
- Blinded by the light
- Bombogenesis
- World meet Dema – demogorgon
- 'Ain't that a kick in the head'?
- Endoscopies, colonoscopies, endometrial biopsies & fu oscopies
- Back in the Saddle Again
- Triumph

There's been more cancer than traveling this last year. Even bigger than both of those things was the loss of one of my pillars, my people. He was a bright and shiny light who was an incredibly special person to me. Cancer took him from us. He was my cancer mentor, my kindred spirit, and he fought harder than anyone I know. Everything else I'd been writing about before his passing seemed so insignificant all the sudden. This blog should be a dedication to him and the life we shared and all of the things I'm so proud of him for.

Kindred Spirits are defined as two people that make a special connection by sharing a bond that has joined them on a higher level of consciousness. His name was Charles (Chad) Phillip Peacock Jr., and this is how he came into my life. February 23, 2015, a newbie cancerful and about to walk through the door of a mountain house in Ouray, Colorado for a trip that would change my life forever. Behind that door would be 10 other Cancerfuls, personal chefs, mountain guides and medical staff all waiting to give us the ice climbing adventure of a lifetime!

The organization that I know I've talked a lot about before and heard about through one of my pillars, is called First Descents. This organization is "a recognized leader in outdoor experiential programming. Through outdoor adventures, skills development, and local adventure communities, FD improves the long-term survivorship of young adults impacted by cancer. Our participants experience free outdoor adventure programs that empower them to climb, paddle, and surf beyond their diagnosis, reclaim their lives, and connect with others doing the same." Let me also state that I applied for the surfing trip but was placed in the ice climbing program. The founder of this organization, Brad Ludden was CNN's Hero of the Year in 2016.

On our first night there we were fitted for gear, helmets, crampons and everything else we were going to need for the week. I fell asleep pretty terrified and intimidated about the prospect of climbing up a gigantic, freezing cold piece of ice with axes. I was also panicking that I wouldn't connect with anyone. In the morning as we were preparing for our adventure, I sat back in a big comfy recliner looking out at the snow-covered mountains, while everyone was eating breakfast. There was an empty seat next to mine and as I relaxed there, writing, Chad came and sat down. He didn't talk to me; he just sat there writing like me.

Eventually, we spoke, and the conversation quickly led to introductions that led to him finding out my last name. AMOROSO! Anyone from the Philadelphia area knows this name and what it's associated with…BREAD. Not just any bread but the bread used all over PA and NJ for the famous Philly cheesesteaks. His eyes lit up like it was Christmas, but I disappointed him, telling him unfortunately I'm not part of 'that' family.

Over the course of the week, our conversations grew longer. At first, I said to my roommate who's that guy that's kind of arrogant?

Ultimately, he became my closest person there and man did he make me laugh about Cancer. Finally, I felt so relieved to be in this tribe of people my age who were like me! The vibe of arrogance I had at first wasn't arrogance but knowledge and strength in his character and in his relationship with his own disease. He knew how to live with Cancer and succeed in life and still find joy everywhere despite going on 6 years of being an 'Incurable'. He taught me how to cure a moment or a day. That was what he tried to do every day in his own life, and he wanted to show others how to do it also.

We spent the week at camp talking with everyone, laughing non-stop and pairing off as others did during the week. We may not all keep in touch as much as we would like to but during that week we became a family. Chad and I were the two who snuck off and hid some wine and an electric cigarette and giggled at cancer jokes. Recently a cancer camp miracle happened when two campers fell in love and married which makes my heart explode with happiness.

At the end of the week, we had a ceremony under the stars in candlelit snow. All of our guides, medical staff and volunteers gathered with us that last night, leading us through a cancer camp parting ritual. We each held a candle and placed them in the water before us while we dedicated that moment to anyone we had lost from this disease. Friends and family were honored. We honored each other. We were each given a piece of string by our guides and directed to tie it around someone else's wrist from camp. Chad and I turned towards each other and tied the knots. I wore that string bracelet for over a year and when it broke, I kept the knot and keep it in a special place.

Later, as our last night wound down, we all stayed up and talked about our life, our struggles, our blessings and our curses. We laughed, cried, promised to stay in touch and the next day we said goodbye as everyone made their way home. I hugged Chad and he whispered in my ear, "I'm sorry I have brain cancer." I replied, "I'm sorry I have breast cancer." I watched him fly west and I flew east knowing my life would be forever changed, because of this beautiful soul and because of this whole inspiring experience. I had no idea that for the next years we would cure so many moments.

When the cancer spread to my brain a couple years later, there was almost this sense of relief that we were finally both part of the 'incurable club'. There began a game of one-upping each other in brain cancer land. He was jealous when I had gamma knife surgery because he hadn't yet. I was jealous when he had brain laser surgery instead of a full craniotomy. I mean, who wants 20+ staples in their head?

During his Cancerful years he endured and triumphed through 6 brain surgeries and trial after trial. He not only had brain cancer, but GLIOBLASTOMA. He was fascinated with medicine, the brain itself and any and all clinical trials he could get into. I think the best trial was the one with magnets. He was supplied with magnets that would attach to his head with a battery backup carried in a backpack. When he sent me a picture of his head with the magnets, I was shocked. He had this huge grin on his face. What made that trial more manageable for him was actually giving the device a name, Toby. Toby was temperamental sometimes. Toby didn't like the heat and would sound alarm if he got too hot. Chad was religious about wearing Toby. That was one of the coolest trials for him! After talking with his doctors about why he kept referring to 'the device' as 'Toby' the company holding the trial considered implementing that into the protocol (naming the device).

Chad passed away unexpectedly due to complications from a seizure and resulting surgery. They did surgery and he never woke up. I didn't get to say goodbye. I knew something was wrong. It has taken me quite a while to make any sort of peace with his passing and him being gone. I'm starting to cry less and see the signs he is giving others and me and that makes me happy. He's ok and as a recent psychic medium said to me during a reading, he wanted me to know that "I've got a lot of power up here now." Without question, that was him and his family agreed.

During one of his services on the East coast, we sat for a traditional Quaker service. People stood to tell stories, read poems, laugh about something he did in the past. It was more personal than our typical ritual funerals. There were times of complete silence. His passing brings up a lot for my mom and I and the feelings of sadness overwhelm us sitting there. This was his favorite poem, which he read at his Grandfather's funeral and was read at his as well:

Funeral Blues by WH Auden

"Stop all the clocks, cut off the telephone,
Prevent the dog from barking with a juicy bone,
Silence the pianos and the muffled drum
Bring out the coffin, let the mourners come.
Let aeroplanes circle moaning overhead
Scribbling on the sky the message 'He is Dead'.
Put crepe bows round the white necks of the public doves,
Let the traffic policeman wear black cotton gloves.
He was my North, my South, my East and West,
My working week and my Sunday rest,
My noon, my midnight, my talk, my song;
I thought that love would last forever: I was wrong.

The stars are not wanted now; put out every one,
Pack up the moon and dismantle the sun,
Pour away the ocean and sweep up the wood;
For nothing now can ever come to any good."

In one of his last blog entries, I had a weird feeling that something was different. I think he recognized the progression of his disease, and he wrote this:

"Oh, you got a new Hyundai? Well guess what, I had deadly tumor cells removed from my brain...With LASERS! And before breakfast!"

I am particularly eager to brag about this with my dear Cancerful friend who recently had the one super cool brain cancer procedure that I have not yet done, called Cyber Knife (which uses radiation beams— pretty cool, but not as cool as LASERS!!) This particular friend also writes a blog about her Cancerful experiences, and it is extraordinarily beautiful, just like her. I highly recommend you check it out, since if you're reading this you obviously have a taste for cancer blogs. And hers is a really good one. Hers also has extremely beautiful photography, which mine lacks. But Mine has more jokes. And I am having LASER brain surgery 😊 *Here is the link to her blog, I hope you'll check it out: http://beautyandthedark.com*

I was so honored and surprised by this. I looked up to him in so many ways. From the way he lived his life to his writing. I remember reading his blog one day and he was talking about feeling alone with cancer. He was explaining this, saying that even if you were lying in bed with the love of your life, you'd still be alone with your cancer, unless the love of your life has cancer too. This touched my soul, because it's true. Not only was he a writer and a screenwriter but also founded the organization called The Cancerful Foundation and he had a blog for many years at https://thebrainchancery.com. He wrote a screenplay for a movie that was in the works when he passed called, **Cancer!** (The Musical!). I hope to see this completed someday.[14]

He said, "Since there is no cure for what I have, I have learned to cure myself— to give myself moments where having cancer doesn't matter. By laughing, by jogging through a National Park, by smelling ridiculous amounts of roses, I have learned to make my moments and my days not just about dying of cancer, but about being alive, and happy. And I'm succeeding. That is what this movie is about. It is about having cancer, but more so it is about LIVING with cancer. Just writing this movie cured me in unbelievable ways, and I know in my heart that it can and will cure a lot more Cancerful people."

In a text exchange with him from last fall he said, "I'm gonna just keep rocking it as hard as I can! Which today means organizing my pill bottles." My anger since his passing and how I make peace with it and still remain positive about my own future is a tough place to be in. I'm doing this new trial because of him, because he would have told me to. This disease can bring people together in a magical way and rip them apart at the same time. Some days I am exhausted from the constant loss and a disease that always seems to win.

"Cancer isn't for light weights." Mom says recently.

---

14. CAROL'S NOTE: Photos from their adventures over the years can be found at www.beautyandthedark.com.

I have found that lately during this long swim back to the surface that I have very little patience for people who are not kind and I'm easily reactive. I have been slammed again and again by disappointment it seems this past year, not just by cancer but also by people. Some days what's happening in our world is as heavy for me as this disease. I've also had a dramatic shift in my personal relationships. There is something to be said for "suffering in silence." I have no more room for toxic people in my life. I have control over my own shit, therefore, "your presence has to feel better than my solitude". Khalil Gibran said, "People ruin beautiful things." They sure can.

After reading my last blog, one of my healers left this comment:

Dear Angela,

I am so grateful that you have come into my life and that you have allowed me to be part of your journey. Thank you for the kind words and for the amazing courage you bring to our work together. Witnessing you process the narrative in your life, claiming your original identity and shedding what has never belonged to you has been an affirmation of the power of the human spirit. Sharing it with the world via your gift for writing is a purposeful, healing call for all of us to live more deeply, to love more generously and to believe that evolution wants us to fulfill the uniqueness that is our birthright. I look forward to our next meeting, as always.

I was a sobbing mess when I read that because it's true and I never would have been able to describe this shift I'm going through, like that. In one paragraph she summed up everything I've been trying to say in allll of these pages and it made total sense. My entire life

I've been carrying around these stories and these events that never belonged to me. I have been carrying around words, memories and the constant flux of people in and out of my life. There's been a lack of stability, of safety, of dependence, which isn't necessarily a negative thing but it's not a great way to learn life's harsh lessons. I grew up too early and too fast. I was forced to become an adult entirely too early. Finally, at age 39, I am actually figuring it out. I have wanted this clarity my entire life. I believe this is part of the reason I've had a huge shift in my life in the last two months and part of the reason I'm so dedicated to evolving and growing in this particular life I've been given. Sitting still is a dangerous place for me to be.

I wonder sometimes, was illness my fate? Maybe it was. Maybe it wasn't. But I'm not going to leave this earth without making it mean something to myself and to my pillars, something besides a cool extended travel story. When I talk about the failure of personal relationships so much it's because, as a decent human being, I become very upset by someone who is not. I've had to accept that some relationships will never be more than a disappointment. There will be people in our lives that consistently lift us up and some that will consistently push us down, without us necessarily even knowing. There will always be negative people who pass us by. We just need to keep walking.

Even though we may desperately want those people to be the ones lifting us up, that might just not be their path in our lives. Cancer has kept people away. At the end of it all, I just believe it comes down to not just me being brave, but others as well and I have seen more cowardice in my life this year than any other. I have let people go, which is not easy. Not only am I fighting for my life every day, I'm also sometimes fighting to keep people in my life. Cryptic...everyone is different, and everyone should be different, and everyone should also be his or her authentic, original self. Sometimes those versions are not compatible with our selves anymore and that's ok. A quote from one of my yoga teachers this week resonated with me and describes the last couple paragraphs, "Don't fight battles that don't lie between you and your destiny." The fact of the matter is that it's not my job or my responsibility to spend my time and energy trying to figure out their souls and their cracks that need healing.

A friend said to me recently, "Sometimes you gotta rip shit up to make room for new possibilities." This makes complete sense. I might have burned it all down in a gigantic forest fire but the seeds for something new and different are there. The dust will settle and eventually the seeds will sprout. "Sometimes you just have to remove people without warning. We are getting too old to be explaining what they already know they're doing wrong." [Author Unknown]

I read this next quote somewhere and wrote it down. "Never apologize to others for their misunderstanding of who you are. Never regret being a good person to the wrong person. Your behavior says everything about you, and their behavior says enough about them." [Author Unknown]

"Man has the power to act as his own destroyer – and that is the way he has acted through most of his history." Atlas Shrugged. [Ayn Rand]

As a side note about that quote actually, I thought I'd throw out this little bit of information I learned about the progress of breast cancer research. My mother, who is a nurse practitioner attended a conference over the winter for primary care and heard about this drug that has the potential to save thousands of lives. I'm losing my life every day because this drug wasn't available for me 4 years ago and it existed. Turns out, people have been talking about the use of this drug pre breast cancer surgery and lung cancer surgery for YEARS! This drug is given during pre-op for breast cancer AND lung cancer and can provide an immediate reduction in recurrence in the first 2 years. Its name is Toradol (Ketorolac).

This drug has the potential to save 10,000 lives annually; maybe it could have saved mine! How have I not heard of this?! It's only $5 million; in comparison to what is funded annually that's not much! I read more about this drug and the discussion on this topic through Global Cures. Global Cures is a "non-profit medical research organization dedicated to curing patients with cancer and other diseases by rapidly promoting clinical research on scientifically promising, readily available and cost-effective treatments. Our strategy is to repurpose existing drugs, currently being overlooked for cancer use, due to lack of profitability. Global Cures is about affordable medical innovation." They posted these statistics...a recent study found that in patients undergoing mastectomies for breast cancer receiving a pre-surgical dose of the drug Ketorolac, the recurrence rate in the first two years dropped from approximately 17% to 6%, a difference maintained over subsequent years. End rant.

It seems sort of inappropriate and insignificant in the grand scheme to talk shop about travel stuff like national park history etc. when I have just lost someone so important in my life and also 2 family members in the last month. I did a lot of research for these trips and for the blog but instead I'm just going to include some photos of where I have traveled to since last September.[15]

---

15. CAROL'S NOTE: Photos can be viewed at www.beautyandthedark.com.

- YELLOWSTONE & THE GRAND TETONS
- TURKS & CAICOS
- ICE CASTLES, NH

Last summer after returning from Hawaii I started hiking again. It felt incredible. However, cancer caught up with me and so did pneumonia shortly after. There are 48 4,000+ footers in NH. I completed only 2 last year, during my short season, Mt. Pierce and Mt. Jackson. I succeeded though and I am going to keep working on that list this year. I gained so much self-confidence and peace out there on those mountains. 2 down 46 to go. Hopefully I can have this year off from brain surgery so that I can reach my goal of one 4,000-footer each month at least.

In her memoir, *Climbing Free*, Lynn Hill wrote:

> *"While resting at the belay, I looked across the valley at the face of Middle Cathedral. On its mottled wall I noticed a play of shadows for the shape of a heart. I have always noticed the symbols around me, and this heart on stone reminded me of the values that have always been most important in my life."*

Traveling and being surrounded by beauty in nature and in culture makes me remember this passage Chad wrote:

> *"She's a beautiful lady, Life. She's gorgeous, in fact. With one of the most beautiful faces-and the biggest heart – I've ever seen. So caring, Life! She walks beside us day after day, holding our hand even when we don't realize she's doing it. Even if we tried to let go of her hand, we couldn't. Because she holds onto us, Life. And it is only when SHE is ready to send us on our way that she finally releases her careful, caring grip. And there is no need to fear that moment, because Life will take every ounce*

of us with her-she will carry us with her! - as she goes along on
her beautiful, merry way. We are an inextricable part of Her,
and Her us, and it will always be that way."

In the months ahead I have a lot of plans, and I really need to have a couple more stable scans to get it all done. If that doesn't happen, then treatment will have to wait. This year is too important to me. I want to Triumph this year. I've recently been participating in a program through my yoga studio called 40 Days to Transformation, a program designed by Baron Baptiste. I've been surprised how dedicated I've been to myself and to this class. In the last several weeks I've felt an amazing shift in my practice, in my relationships, my perspective and I'm the one who is making that happen.

Someone asked me recently what my plans are for the big 4-0. My response was to make it to the big 4-0. But before I even worry about the 4-0 I have some travel plans. Spain in June, Tahiti in July and Hawaii in October. Recently on the train to Brooklyn I started reading *Across Siberia Alone* by Mrs. John Clarence Lee in 1913. It begins with this quote by Josephine Peabody, and it made my heart beat a little faster.

"Out of your cage!
Come out of your cage
And take your soul
On a pilgrimage!"

I believe this is what I'm doing currently, and it feels so good to finally feel good. I'm enjoying this newfound dedication to self, and I feel stronger by the day physically and emotionally. I wish I could take a leave of absence from cancer, but I can't. So, in the days moving forward I will fight for my life every day, fight for self-peace, fight for joy, fight for kindness and fight for others. If you've reached the end thank you for staying with me and I hope to share some adventures with you soon. XO

"A match is lit, Our life is struck.
And the way that flame twists
Is all we've got.
But the smoke that is generated,
Whispering away into air...
That will speak of us.
And the gleam that our light leaves
In the other's eye, as they pass by,
So do we go to them.
And if, by chance, our flame might ignite another,
Then we alight, together"

—CHAD PEACOCK

Vino, Vino, Vino, Viva Cancer!

July 22, 2018

"Death is not fearful, suffering is."
—BJ MILLER

This blog comes at an awkward and sad, yet joyous time of my life. Having just received some incredibly disappointing scan results, I'm finding it difficult to focus on what this blog was originally going to capture. I was supposed to be writing about an amazing trip to Spain, but my thoughts are with The Dirty Dozen. I can literally feel them re organizing for their next war, as I squint through a tumor headache, swallow a pain pill and attempt to see Spain through the Cancer.

Spain was incredible. Spain was beautiful around every turn. Spain was historically complex. Spain was delicious. Spain was sunny and vast and full of love and spirit and faith. Spain was a celebration of life every day we were there. Spain was a celebration of the merging of love, friendship old and new and of course more vino and tapas than I could imagine!

We started in Malaga, Spain the southernmost city in Europe on the Coast of the Sun, 80 miles north of Africa. This is where Picasso was born and raised and where it is not uncommon to see Antonio Banderas having a drink downstairs from his apartment, right inside the historical center. Muslim rule continued here until 1487 when it was retaken by Christian forces. The clear combination of Muslim and Christian rule shines through in the architecture the most.

After a couple days in Malaga, we took the train to meet up with my longest, closest friend and her new husband and friends. Let the wedding celebrations begin in one of my favorite places I've been, Córdoba, Spain. We rented an adorable apartment steps from the historic center and the largest Mosque in the entire world. We celebrated on the rooftops with wine and (pineapple juice ;)) and platters of hummus and other Spanish dishes! We laughed and hugged and celebrated this new union overlooking one of the most beautiful places in the world.

Córdoba was a Roman settlement but then colonized by Muslim armies in the 8th century. Córdoba consisted of hundreds of workshops creating goods like silk. There were libraries in addition to the many medical schools and universities. Córdoba had a prosperous economy with its "skilled artisans and agricultural infrastructure". Recaptured by Christian forces in 1236, this historic center was named a UNESCO World Heritage Site. After the Christians recaptured the city, the mosque was converted into a large Catholic cathedral. Córdoba was known as a spot of "peaceful coexistence of three different cultures: Jews, Muslims and Christians". There is also a popular saying that the prettiest women of Spain are natives of Córdoba!

One day we decided upon the urging of others to go see the Alhambra, a Moorish palace in Granada. Located at the foot of the Sierra Nevada Mountains, the landscape includes olive groves as far as the eye can see. This area is based at the bottom of these majestic mountains where there is a combining of 4 rivers. What an incredible short road trip from the historic center of Córdoba. Our tour of the site began in the gardens of the Alhambra, a stunning and colorful view laid before the palaces made of stucco against the bright blue of the sky and the backdrop of the green and snowcapped Sierra Nevada Mountains.

The Alhambra, "The Red One or Female", is a 35 acre palace and fortress complex built in AD 889. It remained ignored until the ruins were covered with a new royal palace in 1333. The Alhambra is a "palace city" that was declared a World Heritage Site by UNESCO in 1984. It consists of a walled city, a defensive area, residential palaces, gardens and orchards. The Alhambra is a testament to Moorish culture in Spain and the skills of Muslim, Jewish, and Christian artisans and craftsmen. Poets have described it as "a pearl set in emeralds".

The palace complex garden was designed with endless rows of – have to stop and smell every blooming rose-kind of garden. The wildflowers, myrtles and fountains blew my already exploding Cancerful mind. I was panicking trying to capture everything in the photo but at times dropped the camera for my own eyes. As I stop to see and listen there is a mystical and captivating sound of water everywhere with all the fountains, cascades and long sun-lit reflecting pools. The majority of the palace buildings are quadrangular with all the rooms opening to central courts. As each new ruler came through the palace, new sections were added, covering the old and following the "paradise on earth" theme. It was here in 1492 Christopher Columbus requested a royal endorsement for his westward expedition.

During our last couple days in this magical old town we settled in at our favorite vino/tapas bar, walked around the mosque and saw it lit up against the dark of the night, sat on our deck, took a long walk to the cathedral with a nun who liked to rub my head and hold onto me real tight and sat on our deck taking in the view of old Córdoba and saying goodbye to friends venturing on to new places. Before we knew it, it was our time to move on to Seville.

Seville is the capital, and its Old Town contains 3 UNESCO World Heritage Sites. We were lucky enough to visit 2 of these sites and many others. Seville was originally a Roman City then conquered by Muslims and again by the Christians. Seville became one of the most important ports for trans-oceanic trade and it was here that the first circumnavigation of the Earth departed in 1519. Many people even travel here to visit film sites for movies like Lawrence of Arabia, Star Wars and most recently Game of Thrones.

Seville is also known as the birthplace of Tapas, a term meaning 'to cover' or 'top', the cuisine that originated as thin slices of bread and meat consumed with small glasses of sherry. Surprisingly I actually lost weight on this trip. I think moving here should be considered. Seville is approximately 2,200 years old. Along with tapas comes the birthplace of Flamenco. What an amazing dance to witness. The dance began in the gypsy culture, as an expression of the poor and marginalized. Today, there are more flamenco dancers in Seville than anywhere else.

The official motto of Seville is "NO8DO". It is believed to mean, "No me ha dejado", or "It [Seville] has not abandoned me". The eight in the middle represents a skein of wool. Legend states that the title was given by a former King to the city and is now the emblem on the municipal flag and on city property such as manhole covers. It is also imprinted on Christopher Columbus's tomb, located in the Seville

Cathedral. With such mysteries as these, one of the most popular Spanish cultural sites in Seville is the Plaza de Toros de la Maestranza which we received permission to tour.

This bullring in Seville is considered to be one of the best in Spain and one of the oldest in the world. Although many of the younger generations in Spain loathe the sport, new regulations have been slow to come around to protect the animals but also to maintain a balance in cultural events. The Seville Plaza dates back to the 1760s and can seat 10,000 people still today. On the tour of the ring, we visited a small museum, seeing memorabilia like costumes, posters and bull-heads. We were also able to visit the actual ring, which was incredibly intimidating and heavy with sadness, especially for me who could never witness such an act.

During the fighting season, around 20 fights will be scheduled here. The building is in the shape of a 16-sided hexadecagon. According to one expert, Alexander Fiske-Harrison, author of *Into The Arena: The World of the Spanish Bullfight*, "Bullfighting festivals have existed for around 300 years, although the fighting of bulls dates back to Roman times. The first bullfights were on horseback to celebrate special occasions such as royal weddings and military victories." The regulations on bullfighting define in exacting detail the structure and procedure of bullfighting in Spain. Rarely, when a bull shows exceptional skill, the animal is pardoned and, rather than being killed and sent to slaughter, lives on the ranch where it was raised.

Seville was the perfect city to end our adventure. Spain, a special place and home to a saturated history, beautiful food, architecture and people. I couldn't have envisioned a better trip. It felt important to me to witness these sites, traditions and cultures and to learn the history. Not only a final resting place for Christopher Columbus, but also a city soaked in picturesque churches and buildings. This has been my 2nd trip to Spain, and I hope it's not my last. How I would love to go back to Córdoba for a month to read, write, wonder the streets, eat and laugh and forget about the rest of my real life.

Coming home, back to NH was nice but the immediate news of my spreading disease wanted to send me packing back to the quiet life in Spain with tapas and flamenco and all of it. I've had a hard time with this blog because of that but also because of the amount of content I deleted due to my lack of motivation since the "news". In my mind plays, "EXTRA EXTRA READ ALL ABOUT IT: CANCER SPREADS!" This makes me think of an article in the paper recently that referenced the clinical trial I WAS on before The Dirty Dozen grew up into adult children while I was enjoying myself in Spain.

This recent article in the paper was quoting breast cancer stats for the clinical trial drug that I was on at $150,000 per year. A drug that makes $14 billion in combined sales with another drug. They also spend $500 million in ads. These numbers frustrate me for a bunch of different reasons but more so because THIS drug didn't do shit for my disease as it turns out. My cancer got a few months nap, but I didn't. When it woke up, I lost my clinical trial and a big dose of HOPE.[16]

---

16. **CAROL'S NOTE:** I have not been able to locate this article or verify the financial information provided. Per the Keytruda website, cost without insurance is $11,795.44 every three weeks. Merck's financial report listed 2024 sales of $29.5 billion.

"Cancer's purpose is to destroy life.
Cancer is therefore, the purest definition of evil..."
—AUTHOR UNKNOWN

These recent results have forced me to reach out in other directions, towards other treatments. There's not much to offer me at this point of the Star Wars in my Brain movie besides the same slice it open and radiate the s@%!* outa my head skit. I have been researching alternative therapies, located domestically and internationally. I wonder if Pfizer or Merck would like to contribute to the 3-month program I was accepted into for the low cost of $58,000 per cycle bill? I have about $500. Looks like that's not gonna work. So, for now, I'll just keep researching and carrying around anti-seizure meds and opioids then. So, if anyone is with me and I start having a seizure, just stuff a bunch of the toxic pills in the shell case in my pocket into my mouth.

"Inhale I am not my past, Exhale I am not my future..." my insanely smart yoga teacher guiding us in a meditation.

Recently I was interviewed by Jen Morabito, the creator of The Self Stories (theselfstories.wordpress.com), for a feature article for her website. for a feature article for her website. I was in shock that the owner of my yoga studio thought that highly of me to give Jen my number. After that, I realized Jen was also an instructor at New Hampshire Power Yoga, I had just never attended one of her classes. In such a short amount of time I fell in love with this person who is so full of life and ambition and love and who is already doing remarkable things at such a young age. I feel like I should be writing a story on her as her story and zest for adventure reminds me so much of myself at that age.

We met a few times for coffee or a picnic in the park or some nearby trails for the photos included in her article. I am in awe of her and so grateful she wrote this feature on me. She is a beautiful writer and photographer and soul, and I can't wait to see what she does in the next couple years. Please check out the link below to read the story about my history with yoga and how it has enriched my life for the better over the years.

https://theselfstories.wordpress.com/publications/

In other Cancerful news, NH Medicaid dropped me due to an error on their part and they are now coming after me for 2 years of any bills they paid on my behalf. Apparently, I make too much on social security. Unbelievable. Is there such thing?! I will be hiring a lawyer, and I will never pay them a cent…ironic how things have turned out sometimes. Never have I ever thought I would be on or need state assistance and now that I do there is none to be found for me. I struggle with the fairness of this and how at 39 with metastatic breast cancer over 75% of my social security every month is allotted to medical bills. Am I the only one who believes this is right? I can't work, obviously. Times are tough but I am grateful to those practitioners who offer me kindness and their own generosity.

Another well-deserved headline, for the end of this blog, should read, "4 DAYS UNTIL TAHITI LANDING." My Mother of the Year is taking me on my dream trip of French Polynesia. It may not be a convenient time medically, but we are going, and we are going to live every moment of it. Thank God she's also a nurse! Be sure to be on the lookout for that entry and photography.

To end this blog entry I want to express my gratitude to New Hampshire Power Yoga, to Jen Morabito of *The Self Stories*, to my few very close friends that keep me laughing, to my family whom I hold dear always, to my doctors that keep me alive, for my legs that keep taking me up these mountains, to Oskar who keeps me on my toes, to all the people that make me smile and lift me up on dark days and for giving me reasons to take adventures in Spain! XO

blog

Tahiti & Cancer...
Beyond the Postcard

October 17, 2018

"Strength of character lies in performing the drama of life with courage and confidence, practicing self-reflection. And self-control under any circumstances."
—DAISAKU IKEDA

"Twenty years from now you will be more disappointed by the things that you didn't do. So throw off the bowlines. Sail away from the safe harbor. Catch the trade winds in your sails. Explore. Dream. Discover."
—MARK TWAIN

Where to begin...let's get the fun stuff done first! TAHITI! Mom and I, we went, we saw, we conquered! We lived in a dream for over a week. For as long as I can remember I have wanted to travel there but never believed it would ever be possible. As the days in my calendar turned, I came to the week of departure, and saw this written there, "I can't believe I'm writing Tahiti in my calendar." As our flight out of Boston took off, I had no idea what to expect, except beauty and adventure. Bring it on FP.

French Polynesia is a beautiful combination of Polynesian culture, historic ceremonial sites, azure water, thriving reefs and tiny islands. French Polynesia is made up of 118 scattered islands and atolls covering an area about the size of Europe and is divided into groups of islands: the Society Islands Archipelago, Windward Islands, Leeward Islands, the Tuamotu Archipelago, the Gambier Islands, the Marquesas Islands and the Austral Islands. Among 118 islands and atolls only 67 are inhabited.

On this National Geographic expedition, we visited these islands/atolls/motus: Rangiroa, Fakarava (lots of jokes about the pronunciation of this island), Makatea (I thought this was a made-up place from the movie *Six Days, Seven Nights!*), Huahine, Bora Bora, Raiatea, Taha'a and Papeete. French Polynesia was one of the last places on earth to be settled by humans and European explorers. The first island to be settled was the Marquesas Islands around 200 BC and in 1769, the British explorer, James Cook arrived.

In 1803 the King of Tahiti was forced out of Mo'orea. In 1812, many Polynesians were converted to Protestantism and the French Catholic missionaries arrived in 1834. In 1842 the French took over the islands and the Marquesas Islands. The first official name for the colony was the Establishments in Oceania. It wasn't until 1888 that Tahiti became a true colony after the Leewards War. In 1940, French Polynesia recognized the Free French Forces and many Polynesians served in World War II.

The French and the Polynesians were unaware of Japan's motive to make the islands Japanese possessions. In the end French Polynesia remained free from Japanese invasions and in 1946 Polynesians were granted the right to vote. In 1962, France chose the Moruroa atoll in the Tuamotu Archipelago as the new nuclear testing site. Tests were conducted underground after 1974. In September of 1995, France stirred up widespread protests by resuming nuclear testing. The last test was in 1996 and during the same year that France announced its intention to comply with the Comprehensive Test Ban Treaty and no longer test nuclear weapons.

INTERMISSION

On our first day in French Polynesia, we arrived onto the Rangiroa atoll, meaning "Vast Sky". Rangiroa is one of the largest atolls in the world. An atoll is described as "a ring-shaped island or reef formed from coral." As we flew to the atoll, Mom and I were mesmerized by what we were seeing from above. We have never seen anything like this. It was on this last leg of a very long journey from Boston that I realized how special this trip would be for us.

After boarding our expedition vessel, the ship Orion, we set out for the first snorkeling trip on the biggest atoll in the world. It's on this very first adventure that I would swim (definitely not on purpose) with black tip reef sharks. I was only sort of freaked out but surprisingly kept my cool. We saw manta rays, turtles, nurse sharks and just a magical underwater world of life. Within five hours of arriving, we were already snorkeling in the Pacific Ocean and with sharks!

Later that day at our first briefing by Expedition Leader, Jimmy White, he reminded all 87 of us that, "This is not a cruise. This is an expedition." After only a couple days we realized what he meant. Don't get me wrong, it was one of the most amazing times of my life and it was still luxurious and comfortable and fun and joyful! It's so impressive when the staff remembers your name, knows your food allergies and what drink you like. Within a couple days, we had all made friends and were enjoying every single moment with each other and the crew.

Mom and I were so impressed with the entire crew. There is not one single thing I would have changed bout this trip, except the really bad tour of Papeete on the last day. They work so hard every day for long hours, for generally several months at a time. Some of the crew are from the Philippines and work 8 months on at a time. Despite their schedule there wasn't a single day that we were not greeted with complete and genuine happiness. Miss you Eddie With and Eddie Without (waiters who share the name Eddie but distinguish themselves by hair and no hair haha). They referred to us for the remainder of the journey as Mom Carol and Lady Angela.

The next morning, we wake up in Rangiroa and on our itinerary for the day is a hike through the mesmerizing Blue Lagoon, visiting a local coconut processing area and an island search for the ever-elusive Blue Lorikeet, which unfortunately I only heard and didn't see. We walked and chatted and laughed and learned about our fellow passengers. The Blue Lagoon is one of the most absurd places I've ever seen, meaning good. Now, the zodiac ride back to the ship that afternoon gave us all a glimpse of what the word 'Expedition" means. That day on the way back to the ship in our zodiac we experienced that word. There was a lot of very rough chop on the way back. Holding on for our lives getting pounded by waves over and over. Out of the corner of my eye I watched as the driver grinned at us. We must have been a sight!

"Security is mostly a superstition. It does not exist in nature, nor do the children of men as a whole experience it. Avoiding danger is no safer in the long run than outright exposure. Life is either a daring adventure, or nothing." Helen Keller

That afternoon after our adventure we were treated to a photo presentation and lecture by National Geographic Photographer, Jay Dickman, titled "The Importance of Photography in our Lives." Jay is a Pulitzer-Prize Winner and has been working in photojournalism for 30 years. He has been present for and photographed events such as Super Bowls, the 40th Anniversary of the bombing of Hiroshima, the war in El Salvador and national political conventions. He has also co-authored guidebooks on photography. During his lecture I was emotionally spellbound as he went through his slides of his prize-winning photos and told the stories behind them. His photos touched my heart and soul as he has captured some of the most intimate moments during these events. Even more impressive was the genuine enjoyment he received from helping the passengers with their cameras and shots. We were so appreciative for his guidance and his moving talks.

For the next two days we explored the Tuamotu Archipelago. This Archipelago includes approximately 80 islands and atolls. There is a small village located on Teamanu, which was once the capital. The first church, built in 1874, is located on this island. While visiting here we had a couple bikes, so we did some self-exploring of the island. We went to visit the church, the old lighthouse that looks more like a Mexican ruin and we had the opportunity to pet and feed a couple of beautifully gentle nurse sharks. Every day they come to shore to feed from the locals. Fakarava is one of the largest atolls in French Polynesia and part of the UNESCO Biosphere Reserve for rare species.

Makatea was our next stop; the island I thought was made up. Makatea is one of three coral islands that were known for its large phosphate deposits. Hundreds of people and miners flooded the island. Eventually, the mining stopped and Makatea was left in poor shape. To mine the phosphate, 75ft deep circular holes were dug and drilled into the limestone, making the island very dangerous to walk around. The school and other places were leveled to the ground. The vines and jungle took over the island eventually and abandoned buildings and forgotten mining equipment scattered the coast. As a result, the population of the island is now very small. Ultimately in 1909, a ship wrecked on the reef and a bent rod stopped the engines and the current carried the ship onto the reef.

So, the day on Makatea started with an amazing personal experience at a cave grotto for my Mom and I only. The day before the leader and the physician on board called me in for a meeting about my health. There were decisions I had to make, and I needed to fill them in on where I am in terms of my disease, medications and my wishes. In preparation for this I filled in the doc and Jimmy, that I am a DNR and DNI. This was the first time someone mentioned DNI so I was unaware of what it meant. It means do not intubate. If I was to have a seizure in the water, they would intubate me but the doc explained he could do this, but the ship did not have the facilities to keep me intubated as long as may be necessary. All of this makes complete sense given the situation we would be in and the risks.

To start off our private excursion through the grotto, we left the ship before the other passengers and went over to the island of Makatea.

This was a dream come true for me. This kind of career path was everything I always wanted. They brought me over early to help set up the site prior to the actual excursion. As I climbed further down into the darkness of the grotto, placing tea lights along the path, I looked up and down and realized how beautiful this setting was, especially after placing the lights under the water. It was then that two of the crew guided my Mom and I through the cave, snorkeling through the tunnels and seeing the magnificent cave. I look up to take a breath and we are in the middle of an incredible place. It was out of a movie, like Pirates of the Caribbean. We had the place all to ourselves. They gave me a magical and once in a lifetime experience and for that I will be forever grateful. The crew truly cares and wants to make sure people like me really enjoy the trip by doing these special things for us. We were blessed on this trip.

I think it was around this day that we experienced rough seas on the Orion in the early evening on our way to the next stop, Huahine. Mom and I watched from the enclosed library on the top deck at the passengers on the front of the ship holding on and getting smashed with waves. However, they did get the best view of the pod of dolphins swimming and jumping through the waves at the front of the ship. Walking back from dinner that evening I finally understood the need for the seasickness bags at every corner of the ship. After returning home I saw video footage of the next expedition's experience with a day of rough seas, and I was so grateful we didn't experience that.

Huahine is actually two islands connected by a bridge, Huahine Nui (big) and Huahine Iti (small). Known for its lack of mass tourism and sacred blue-eyed eels, this island was originally home to Tahitian royalty. Referred to as The Garden Island or the Garden of Eden, the beautiful vanilla orchid exists only here. The highest density of ancient marae exists here. The marae are known as communal and sacred places. They generally consist of an area of cleared land rectangular in shape and bordered by large flat stones. Many of the marae have been destroyed or abandoned with the arrival of Christianity in the 19th century.

Many Polynesians believe the marae are, "portals between Po, the world of the gods and darkness, and the Ao, the everyday world of people and light, so that people could communicate with their ancestors." In 1994 archeologists working to repair a marae on Raiatea discovered human and pig bones. This led historians and archaeologists to the idea that it was actually possible that these bones were a result of human sacrifices, specifically to the Polynesian god Oro. Oro in Polynesian history was known as the "God of War" but also the god of many other things.

Huahine is not just known for its marae. A tropical jungle hides coconut plantations, banana trees, breadfruit trees, watermelon fields and ancient temples. The name Huahine comes from the Tahitian word, which means woman. On Huahine there is a mountain resembling the outline of a pregnant woman. In the afternoon we spent some time at Bourayne Bay. Mom and I took out the stand-up paddle boards and paddled around the curve of the island. I gazed at the landscape around me, and I was in complete awe. The water was beautifully clear and incredibly warm. I could see the stunning reef below. It was a perfect day for both of us and I was super proud of my Mom for killing it on the paddle board. I could have stayed there all week. A couple other notes about Huahine is that it's known for some of the best surf in the South Pacific and each October the biggest outrigger canoe race begins here.

That evening on board the ship we were treated to a very special Polynesian event including a buffet dinner along with a show of hidden talents put on by the crew. This was one of my favorite nights aboard the Orion. Many of us danced until late in the night to the music performed by the crew. We learned later that this talent show is a very serious event for the crew. They practice every day and hold auditions. The bartender Eric makes the cuts. The different groups come out in hilarious costumes (YMCA/Hula Girls) and play some great live music for us. I don't have any photos from that evening because I was having too much fun!

On to Bora Bora! Surrounded by a crystal-clear lagoon and reef, Bora Bora is also home to the extinct Mount Otemanu and Mount Pahia. In ancient times the island was called "Pora mai te pora", meaning, "created by the gods" or "first born". Historically, Bora Bora was an independent kingdom until 1888 when its last queen, Teriimaevarua III was forced to resign to the French. During World War II, the United States used Bora Bora as a South Pacific military supply base, including an oil depot, airstrip and a seaplane base. Known as "Operation Bobcat", the base provided a supply force of nine ships, 20,000 tons of equipment and nearly 7,000 men and at least 8, 7/45 caliber guns. At the time these guns were considered to be the largest weapon with rapid fire that one man could handle. These weapons were set up at calculated points to protect the island against potential military attack. However, the island saw no combat as the American presence on Bora Bora went unchallenged over the course of the war. The base was officially closed in 1946.

The day before our Bora Bora expedition I was talking to one of the cultural specialists, Isa and I mentioned that I'd love to have a day or morning just being on a beach, feel the sand in my toes. The next morning when I was walking to breakfast, I saw Isa and she had tears in her eyes. She looked at me, hugged me hard and said, "Jimmy is giving you your Bora Bora beach day." Jimmy and some of the other crew arranged to take my Mom and I to a private motu called Tapu. We took the zodiac before the other passengers set off for their day and he dropped us off on our own private island for the whole morning. There is a caretaker of the island who lives there, and he acknowledged he would keep watch and changed into his SECURITY t-shirt and insisted on showing us his home on stilts.

After returning to the ship, I told Isa about the tour of his home, and she laughed and told me he really wants a wife and that he did the same thing with her, but she was "too old" haha. Mom and I spent the morning walking around the motu, swimming, laying in the sun and collecting shells. In broken English he asked about my tattoos and showed me his most recent one, a very beautiful custom Polynesian tattoo. I took this photo of him before we left.[17] This picture also made it into the last night's slide show of photos from the week. I was trying to capture a 'Moment' photo, which I did well. I am grateful to Jay Dickman for his explanation of this type of photo and for his guidance.

After we spent an incredible day on Bora Bora we sailed on to Raiatea and Taha'a. These islands share a lagoon and reef. Most people believe this was originally one island that split in two. Raiatea is one of the most important cultural sites of French Polynesia because of the Marae Taputapuatea, a ceremony and memorial center. This center was referred to as the "Polynesian Triangle" and includes New Zealand, Hawaii and Easter Island. Historians believe this center dates back to

17. CAROL'S NOTE: This photo can be seen at www.beautyandthedark.com.

1000AD. Polynesian seafarer and priests gathered here, and it's also known as a site of human and animal sacrifices made to the gods.

Known as the "Vanilla Island", Taha'a produces outstanding pearls and vanilla beans. Taha'a produces 70-80% of all French Polynesia's vanilla. As this was technically our last afternoon, Mom and I chose to snorkel at Motu Mahaea and it just so happened to be the best snorkeling of the whole week! I couldn't believe how healthy the small reef was and how many varieties of fish we saw. These are definitely some of the best photos of the week!

Now, a blog about French Polynesia would not be complete without a little background on the legendary over the water bungalows! The story of the overwater bungalow begins on the Tahitian island of Raiātea but it's also documented that they began in Moorea. A trio of American expats was running one of the country's earliest hotels. Jay Carlisle was one of them and was quoted in an interview with Conde Nast Traveler, "We were trying to get publicity for the island—it doesn't have any beaches, but we were right on the reef, so we wanted to put in something different." The ex-pats likely gathered their inspiration from the locals and their over the water fishing shacks.

Our last day, Papeete. What a sad day including a pretty sad/bad tour of the island before heading back to our real world. Papeete is the capital of Tahiti. During WWI, German vessels caused significant loss of life and damage to the island. Eventually the decision was made to move a nuclear weapon test site to two atolls almost 1,000 miles to the east of Tahiti. In 1983, The Church of Jesus Christ of Latter-day Saints built a temple here because of the large number of members in the region. In 1995 the government conducted the first of the last series of nuclear test detonations off the shores of Moruroa. Rioting in Papeete began after this and resulted in a large number of injuries and significant damage to the capital.

Another sight definitely worth mentioning on Papeete is the former home of James Norman Hall, the co-author of *Mutiny on the Bounty*, published in 1932. The novel was based on a mutiny against a commanding officer in 1789. Hall died in Tahiti in 1951. The novel has been made into several films and a musical and is cherished as one of the most gripping sea adventures ever told. To be able to see his home and all of the items he had throughout was inspiring and beautiful to me. I had chills when I saw his desk with his typewriter. If only I could move to a place like this, I'm sure my writing would significantly improve. After all, not even half the islands are inhabited so...but unfortunately, I have a non-friend called Cancer that I have re-named, "The Baker's Dozen" and not "The Dirty Dozen", due to one more tumor that was born this summer. Even though you're not here physically Clarice, I hope you and Hannibal burned violently in hell and I hope someday all your little bitch offspring will as well. It's inevitable anyway; I'm being cremated ha!

I know this is a very long blog so I've inserted Intermissions where it might be a good time to rest and take a break or take a tour of Tahiti through my eyes and through my lens. I was inspired to do this after watching *The Sound of Music* a handful of times recently and that movie is 3 hr. 44 min! This next part is about my cancer, my prognosis and everything that goes along with that. Here are some of my Garden of Eden photos.[18]

INTERMISSION

———————————

18. **Carol's note:** The photos can be seen at www.beautyandthedark.com.

**"She is a beautiful piece of broken pottery,
put back together by her own hand.
And a critical world judges her cracks while missing
the beauty of how she made herself whole again."**
—JM STORM

Even after an intermission, it still feels heavy to jump right from magic Tahiti land to CANCERland. I have a lot of cancerful updates this time, mostly not of the celebratory kind. I don't want to depress everyone since I was just writing from such a positive place. But this is my life and anyone who knows me knows that I have high highs and low lows in terms of my disease. This part will have a little of both. It's also Breast Cancer Awareness month and you all know how I feel about that. However, I'm trying to come from a different perspective this year and not be so negative about the pink crap blah blah…I hope my cancer will help researchers save just one person from having to be a passenger along this ride, that you really have very little control of. I am, on the other hand, no pun intended, wearing my teal green METAVIVOR - Don't Ignore Stage IV bracelet. Choose them, donate to them. This is an organization doing the work that other foundations aren't and SHOULD BE. After all, 2 out of 5 people will develop cancer in their lifetime and 90% of us will die due to cancer metastases.

After returning home from French Polynesia in August, I had scans right away. Once again, these scans showed another progression in the size of my tumors. So, once again I am kicked off another clinical trial and now on to "last resort treatments". These options include craniotomy #3, whole brain radiation and a very toxic chemotherapy called Xeloda. I chose the chemo but I'm regretting that decision as I sit here in Hawaii sick, not able to walk very well and feeling like I am being poisoned as the skin on my hands and feet is dying, my nose is full of sores, my fingertips and toes are numb and painful from increasing neuropathy, unending fatigue with very little sleep, heart irregularities, muscle, joint and bone pain, dizziness, skin changes all of which I have, rapid weight gain (13 pounds FU), dehydration symptoms and a lot of other shit I don't need to explain. About 3 weeks into starting this chemotherapy the oncologists had to reduce my dose. There are three toxicity grades when it comes to chemo and side effects. Obviously, you don't want to be graded any of these, let alone a three. Within three weeks I was at a toxicity grade 2.

"Xeloda is a recently developed drug. It's a type of medicine called an antimetabolite that interferes with the metabolism and growth of cells. Capecitabine is an unusual anti-cancer drug in that it is most active in cancer cells; normal cells are exposed to far lower concentrations of the drug. Cancer cells convert capecitabine into another anti-cancer drug called 5-fluorouracil. This substance prevents cells from growing and reproducing. The U.S. Food and Drug Administration have approved Capecitabine for the treatment of metastasized breast cancer that is resistant to standard chemo-therapy."[19] The silver lining...I may die anyway or decide to quit treatment because of the quality of my life at the low cost of $350 per month out of pocket. Obviously, this is a joke. Thanks for the help, Medicare. Middle finger up.

Now, all this "last resort" talk has me really questioning everything. I decided I needed to have a conversation with my team about my prognosis. So, about a month ago I had a come to J talk with the

---

19. CAROL'S NOTE: I was unable to identify the original source of this quote.

oncologist I trust the most. I told her what I wanted to talk about, and her response was, "Are you sure you want to talk about this?" At this point I feel the need to have some idea about what they're thinking time wise. I'm a numbers girl, that's why I ended up as a practice manager at a medical facility and not a nurse! She said, "I would be surprised if you made it to next Thanksgiving." I didn't have words and there was no hesitation from her. At my next appointment with my 2nd breast oncologist (MGH), we discussed this conversation, and she said there might be some truth to that. So, the 15 months I was given is now 12-13...what do I do with that? She also stated that they (the MGH team) didn't anticipate I would survive as long as I have.

Several months ago, through social media, I saw a video that made me incredibly emotional. This was the last letter written by Holly Ann Butcher. She passed away the day after she wrote this letter that I've included [a part of] below. Holly was a beautiful, 26-year young woman from Australia, diagnosed with stage IV Ewing Sarcoma.

"It's a strange thing to realize and accept your mortality at 26 years young. It's just one of those things you ignore...

That's the thing about life; it's fragile, precious and unpredictable and each day is a gift, not a given right...

I haven't started this 'note before I die' so that death is feared - I like the fact that we are mostly ignorant to its inevitability. Except when I want to talk about it and it is treated as a 'taboo' topic that will never happen to any of us... that we all have the same fate after all so do what you can to make your time feel worthy and great, minus the bullshit...

…Be grateful for your minor issue and get over it…

…I'm watching my body waste away right before my eyes with nothing I can do about it and all I wish for now is that I could have just one more Birthday or Christmas with my family, or just one more day with my partner and dog…

…Friend or not…be ruthless for your own well-being…

Give, give, give. It is true that you gain more happiness doing things for others than doing them for yourself. I wish I did this more. Since I have been sick I have met the most incredibly giving and kind people and been the receiver of the most thoughtful loving words and support… I will never forget this and will be forever grateful to all of these people…

…Have the guts to change. You don't know how much time you have on this earth so don't waste it being miserable…

…Till we meet again."

I don't feel I need to spend much time writing about this letter. Holly wrote everything we Cancerful's think at one point or another. Her words are words to remember and take seriously because after all, "This is your life and it's ending one minute at a time."

I recently listened to a TED TALK on How Cancer Cells Communicate & How We Can Slow Them Down, by Hasini Jayatilaka. I try to stay educated about cancer and especially when there may be new treatments available. I appreciate these incredible figures trying their very best to do anything that would make a difference for those of us in Cancerland.

"Cancer is a battle the human race has been fighting for centuries."

"Hasini Jayatilaka discovered a mechanism that causes cancer cells to break away from tumors and metastasize. Jayatilaka is currently conducting research on understanding the complex pathways that govern metastasis, the spread of cancer, which is responsible for 90% of cancer-related deaths. She recently discovered a new signaling pathway that controls metastasis and showed that by blocking the pathway, the spread of cancer can be slowed down. When cancer cells are closely packed together in a tumor, they're able to communicate with each other and coordinate their movement throughout the body."

"Using different drug cocktails we can stop the communication between cancer cells and slow down the spread of cancer."

In talking about her research and the beginning of her career and the challenges she faced she said, "Let's face it, cancer cells in our bodies aren't stuck to plastic dishes." Hasini is a brilliant and comedic woman who is leading the way towards crucial cancer treatment discoveries. She discussed how she and her team, "...discovered a new signaling pathway that controls how cancer cells communicate with each other and move based on their cell density (now named the Hasini Effect). Our researched drug cocktail found that they had no effect on tumor growth BUT DIRECTLY TARGETED METASTASES. This was a significant finding because currently there are no FDA approved therapeutics that directly target the spread of cancer." She received an overwhelming positive response to her hypothesis from the medical community and patients.

She stated, "My team is currently using the Hasini Effect to develop combination therapies that will effectively target tumor growth and metastases. We are also working on lowering drug toxicity and reducing drug resistance. Collaboration is my favorite superhuman power." Watch out cancer world the Hasini Effect is coming through!

While on topic of brilliant researchers it is necessary to announce to those of you who haven't heard the news that The Nobel Prize in Physiology or Medicine has been awarded to two cancer immunotherapy researchers, James Allison of the USA and Tasuku Honjo of Japan. Their research involves using our own body's immune system to attack cancer. A statement from the Nobel Committee saluted their accomplishments as launching, "an entirely new principle for cancer therapy." The drugs that have been released as immunotherapy treatment can put people into remission but also have their own set of side effects. The last trial I was on was an Immunotherapy trial. These drugs don't work for everyone and can be costly. The other downside that researchers are working on is how to prevent the immune system from attacking the body in the process. This trial ultimately didn't work for me, but numbers show that it is working which gives us hope.

INTERMISSION

Over the past couple years, I've made connections with people I meet during my travels or at my yoga community. We keep in touch and these incredible men and women give me hope, support and love. I received an email from a wonderful woman I met in NY relaying a story she had read in the NY Times magazine.[20] This excerpt is from an article on love and loss. The wife lost her husband. The husband gave his wife instructions on how he wanted to live the rest of his life: "I just want you to know that I am not going to do the dying part… We are only going to do the living part."

My friend told me this article resonated with her and made her think of me. She told me, "I know that you have a core of positivity and strength. I am thinking that you want to just keep living until you can't. That's all any of us can do. I know it may be of no consolation to you, but we are all dying, me too. None of our fates are guaranteed. Hoping you can keep moving forward, until you can't. Hoping for another blog post. You are a very good writer. Often good writers tell their stories by not "spelling everything out" for the reader. Often what is not said is more powerful than what is. Use your writing to enrich others through your life-affirming activities and joy of life. We all die. Nothing new there. But we don't all "live". You do." It seems like the universe knows when to send me messages like this. It serves as motivation and optimism that I still need in this life. We may not be the best of friends or even live in the same state. This woman I hardly know keeps in touch and is always sending me messages of hope. You all should be celebrated for keeping my head above the Ocean of Cancer and for those of you that have different motives…

"I will not let anyone walk through my mind with dirty feet."
—MAHATMA GANDHI

---

20. CAROL'S NOTE: The article, by Susan Dominus, is listed in Angela's bibliography at the end of this book.

A couple weeks ago a friend I met through my yoga community at New Hampshire Power Yoga sent me this via text. The timing was interesting given I was having a bad day. She can always sense my emotions. It's a very powerful gift. Her text read, "You have so much shit to shovel all you can do is the best you can at the moment you are in as events unfold and you have to make sure not to hold yourself to the same standards on bad days that you do on better days or you will go nuts/it takes too much effort to re-train your thinking when your mind is overwrought and your body adjusting itself on a daily basis, so sometimes it's helpful to just ignore your own self/don't look at your time away from yoga, hiking etc. as a limitation, but as an opportunity to do something else you enjoy!/you still have shit to do here. Admit it. You're not like the others, and that's not just OK, it's F-ING beautiful..."

Speaking of hiking, unfortunately I wasn't able to complete one 4,000-footer hike per month this summer. But on July 22nd I hiked Mount Avalon, Mount Field and Mount Tom all in one day. It was such a beautiful day; perfect conditions and I had this amazing stamina and determination to do this. At the end of the day these were my fit bit stats: 25,267 steps, 259 flights of stairs, 10.71 miles, I burned 2,925 calories and was active for over 260 minutes.

Now I would call that pretty darn impressive for a chick with terminal cancer.[21]

---

21. CAROL'S NOTE: Photos from Angela's hike can be found at www.beautyandthedark.com.

"I cannot believe how sensitive I am to the smells of cut vegetation, of the flowers…of the forest. It is as if my nerve endings are plugged into an amplifier. The green fields, the pink and orange roadside flowers, practically vibrate with color. I am awash in stimuli."
—STEVEN CALLAHAN

In ending the potentially longest blog I have written, I won't write much. But I will tell you this; in the last month I have not grown any new tumors. Something is happening, whether it's my current chemo or lasting effects of the immunotherapy trial, I'll take the extra 2 months and sprint away with it. In the next month I will be traveling Hawaii for two weeks and then Tokyo with one of my closest friends and California in December to celebrate the life of Chad Peacock. I still miss you every day.

"Start over, my darling. Be brave enough to find the life you want and courageous enough to chase it. Then start over and love yourself the way you were always meant to." Madalyn Beck

Recently I heard this quote from a TV show about a young woman with breast cancer, "I did everything I was supposed to do and I still got cancer. I'm not playing by the rules anymore." At this point in time, I think I'm going to follow her lead. Until next time.

Angela xo

blog
I Made It Through Another Year

February 4, 2019

**"Move, as far as you can, as much as you can.
Across the ocean, or simply the river. Walk in someone
else's shoes or at least eat their food.
Open your mind, get up off the couch, move."**
—ANTHONY BOURDAIN

I've been writing this blog for a few months. I decided after being so overwhelmed with the content I scrapped the whole piece. A lot has occurred over the last few months and instead of talking about the good and bad I will leave you with photos from the last few months of travels.[22]

*2018 TRIPS

- TURKS AND CAICOS
- ICE CASTLES OF NH
- BROOKLYN X 4
- 40 DAYS BAPTISTE COURSE

---

22. **CAROL'S NOTE:** Photos can be viewed at www.beautyandthedark.com.

- SPAIN
- TAHITI
- HIKED: MT. TOM, MT. AVALON, MT. FIELD, MT. HALE, MT. TECUMSEH!
- MEXICO
- MAINE X5
- JOSHUA TREE NATIONAL PARK

"The world is a book, and those who do not travel read only a page."
—SAINT AUGUSTINE

HAWAII

"That it will never come again is what makes life sweet."

—EMILY DICKINSON

"For once you have tasted flight you will walk the earth with your eyes turned skywards, for there you have been and there you will long to return."
—LEONARDO DA VINCI

JAPAN

"The best thing to hold onto in life is each other."

—AUDREY HEPBURN

"One of the most beautiful gifts in the world is the gift
of encouragement. When someone encourages you, that
person helps you over a threshold you might otherwise
never have crossed on your own."
—JOHN O'DONOHUE

LONDON

"The life you have led doesn't have to be
the only life you have."

—ANNA QUINDLEN

"We wander for distraction, but we travel for fulfillment."
—HILAIRE BELLOC

*CALIFORNIA DESERT HOT SPRINGS/JOSHUA TREE
NATIONAL PARK

"Grief never ends, but it changes. It's a passage not a place
to stay. Grief is not a sign of weakness, not a lack of faith.
It is the price of love."
—AUTHOR UNKNOWN

"If ever there is a tomorrow when we're not together...
there is something you should always remember. You
are braver than you believe, stronger than you seem and
stronger than you think. But the most important thing is
even if we're apart...I'll always be with you."
—WINNIE THE POOH

After all the pages of beauty I guess I should update you all on my status in Cancerland. I'm so tired of cancer and the aftermath that it leaves behind. A few months ago, I walked into an appointment with one of my oncologists when it came time to switch chemos, again, "I don't want to do this anymore." With a little bit of a push, I reluctantly started the medication and within 2 weeks the doctors took me off due to the toxicity in my body. I've been on the chemo since and guess what, IT'S WORKING! However, I have this annoying lil new baby in my brain that brings me to craniotomy #3, coming 1st week of May. Can't wait...I also have an immense of swelling in my brain that I need to start IV medication for.

One last update on my broken back situation. I broke my back in 4 places while traveling in Hawaii in October. I had spinal surgery at the end of November and have been prepared for a 6-month recovery and a constant rotation of fentanyl, oxycodone and muscle relaxers. It's not that I don't want to live, I don't want to live like this. I'm trying to stick with it to buy me some more time. But living in this state is not what I wanted for my life. The poem ["Wild Geese" by Mary Oliver] was given to me by someone special and I feel it needs to be included here.[23]

All the best to my friends, family and supporters. xo

---

23. CAROL'S NOTE: A lovely reading of this poem, narrated by Helena Bonham Carter, appears here: https://www.youtube.com/watch?v=RgBEli4h1Mo.

Carol's Reflections
2019 and 2020

"Constant struggle good and bad, beauty and gloom,
deep breath vs shallow ones, weak to strong and back
again, heaviness of starting over."
—ANGELA AMOROSO

"…saying you have had enough is not failure.
It is just as brave and OK to say "Enough," and to "fight"
no more. Death is not a failure. It is not a test:
we don't succeed or fail at it."
—KRIS HALLENGA

Angela's last blog post was written just over two years prior to her death. Later, I went through her papers hoping that I might find a partially written blog, but I did not. Photos from that period were also scarce. Similarly, Angela rarely took out her camera. At the time, I recognized this as the physical, emotional, and spiritual fatigue that travels with cancer. She was losing joy in the activities that gave her life meaning—activities that brought her happiness, a sense of purpose.

I have reread her blog many times, both while Angela was still living and since her death. I am aware that her last blog post includes a few quotes about death. I had noticed those when her blog was first posted, but I did not ask. I remember wondering if she was aware of the changes and had a thought that the life she had been living was drawing to a close. She was also having thoughts about stopping treatment.

Brain cancer robs people, including Angela, of their dignity. For the seven years she lived with cancer, I always worked to help her maintain her dignity.

I have created this section to fill readers in on some of our experiences during those last two years. As you will see, I have chosen to focus primarily on the good times—the light we experienced in the darkness—omitting some personal details to maintain Angela's dignity and highlight how she'd want to be remembered.

I have Angela's calendar for 2019, and I know the trips she was planning, but I do not remember which ones she took. According to her calendar, planned trips included Key West, Costa Rica, New York, Mexico, and the Pacific Northwest. I found a few photos of all but the Key West trip.

Angela wanted to have another family party, this one in Ocean City, NJ. We started planning and ended up scheduling it for her fortieth birthday, April 5, 2019. It was planned for a weekend with the hope that all her family would be able to attend for at least part of the weekend, and they did. We rented a large condo with an elevator so Gramps could join us and so people traveling from out of town (and even locally) could stay. Unfortunately, Gramps passed away a few months prior to the weekend. His presence was missed, but we were still able to enjoy the gathering. Angela felt so blessed that some family traveled over a thousand miles to spend time with us.

Angela was doing well that weekend, and everyone enjoyed themselves. For most of her family, that would be the last time they spent
with Angela—a weekend full of wonderful memories that we are all
able to hold onto.

Throughout 2019 and 2020, Angela and I were both aware that she
was exhausting her treatment options. We had been informed that
most people with brain metastasis don't survive as long as Angela
did. As she had done since diagnosis, Angela had paved her own path

with her disease. Any time that we were provided with a prognosis, it was always with that caveat. Angela had a way of breaking the rules, for which I was grateful. I was not certain how I would ever come to peace with the lack of treatment options.

Medically, Angela continued to have stereotactic radiation for tumors. Unfortunately, her anxiety about the treatment escalated and could not be managed with Ativan. Sedation was needed, which meant longer days and recovery. At one point, she had a brain bleed due to the medication intended to reduce swelling. Luckily, it resolved without long-term effects. Another challenge was that Angela's ovaries decided to make a return visit. Despite five years of chemo, which was still ongoing, they decided to start pumping out estrogen again, which fed the tumors. Another medication was needed to put them back into retirement.

2020 started with Angela and I returning to Joshua Tree and the spa we both enjoyed in Desert Springs. We enjoyed ourselves, escaped cancer for a week, spent time on light hikes, wandered antique shops in Joshua Tree, and returned with many items I now have in our home. We also enjoyed spa treatments, although Angela's CBD massage left her feeling a bit dizzy for a day. We ate oranges picked fresh from the trees and remembered time spent there just over a year ago.

After the trip, we found that Angela needed another craniotomy, scheduled for the end of January, followed by another two weeks of radiation.

Then Covid hit, and all travel plans were off. The Ireland trip she was planning for the spring was put on hold, along with our plan for Acadia in the fall.

In March, another tumor made its appearance. Time for craniotomy #4, this done amidst the initial surge of Covid. This was the first time that I was not allowed to be in the hospital with her. I had to leave her at the door and drive home, in tears. I spent thirty-six hours anxiously waiting until I could pick her up. During that time, Angela called me frequently for reassurance and answers to questions. Surgery always left her with an immediate worsening of her memory, and it was heartbreaking not to be there to provide comfort along with the answers she wanted. I had to rely on phone reports from the surgeon to know the outcome of the surgery and her status.

Angela recovered, a new chemo was started, and the trips she had been planning to Ireland and Acadia moved from delayed to cancelled.

After both procedures, we spent time recovering in Maine. Although we had to quarantine for two weeks during each of our visits, it was not an issue. We could still take walks and enjoy the beach, and we took everything we needed with us. Pizza could be delivered and left on the porch. Spending time in Maine was about being on the beach, relaxing, and enjoying our home. Even before COVID, we spent most of our time at home or on the beach.

The new chemo was a struggle for Angela. It required frequent dose reductions; she continued to take it with difficulty. This was another time when the question of stopping treatments arose, but she persevered. Angela was receiving palliative care, and we had multiple discussions about hospice with her oncologists.

Cancer was clearly taking its toll. Angela developed seizures and lost her ability to drive. Cognitive effects progressed, and she experienced frequent falls from her medications, which necessitated the use of a wheelchair to go out and take a walk; this also meant we could no longer walk on the beach. To compensate, we would drive down and sit and listen to the waves and the gulls.

More support was needed to manage her complex medication schedule. Treatment options were nearly exhausted. Come Fall, she needed further radiation. The cancer had spread in a way that was not amenable to surgery, and the chemo was not working. Again, I was not allowed to be with her for her treatment, which concerned me. As she had done for past sessions in Boston, she stayed in a hotel each week—something we used to do together—and returned home on weekends. Staying in a hotel was more of a challenge for her now because restaurants were closed. We packed food that she could microwave; she could also pick up a meal at the hospital cafeteria to take to her room or walk to Whole Foods to get something. Even so, these were not simple or straightforward solutions, because the worry associated with the risk of COVID exposure was always present. We had talked about COVID when it first started, and Angela and I were both concerned that with her compromised immune system, she would not survive exposure. She was also concerned that she would not be given a ventilator if needed due to cancer. Angela looked at me once and said that she was going to be angry if COVID ended her life and got her before cancer!

As the Fall progressed, the radiation did its trick, and in the end, we had a wonderful holiday. Although we did not say it—some things are too hard to say out loud—we both knew that this would probably be her last holiday. Most of December was wonderful. Her energy was good, she was managing things well, and she was excited about the holiday.

Even so, we both experienced deep heartbreak in December. Oskar, one of Angela's pillars, passed away. Angela had always said her goal was to outlive Oskar, which she did. But neither of us was ready to lose him, and we certainly were not ready for the grief of Oskar's passing, added to the grief we were already experiencing with Angela's disease progression. Up to that point, my days had been scheduled around Angela's needs, while Angela's days had been scheduled around Oskar's needs. Oskar was her constant. With Oskar gone, Angela's daily structure/routine was gone.

With that in mind, we remained determined to enjoy the holidays as best we could. Angela wanted her grandparents' spaghetti for Christmas dinner, so on Christmas Eve, a big pot of sauce with meat-balls and lamb simmered on the stove all day. As we always did when preparing this meal, we kept a baguette on the counter. According to our family tradition, the only way to know if additional spices are needed is to soak a chunk of bread in the sauce, add Romano cheese, and taste! For that reason, we always cook it a day ahead; by the time it is done and we've adjusted the spices all day with multiple chunks of bread, we are never hungry!

As the new year approached, I realized that despite the medical chal-lenges of 2020—two craniotomies, radiation, a new chemo, and the pandemic—we had still been able to enjoy living, although different-ly. All days were not bad. There were a lot of good moments, good days, beauty during a time that would seem so dark, so bleak: quiet time together, sitting and talking, time in Maine, hours wandering the nursery, many more hours in the gardens, and visits from her friends, who would sit outside with her with masks on. These are the good memories during the challenging times that hold me up most days.

In January 2021 Angela had a repeat MRI. The oncologist had recommended that we wait until after the holiday to repeat it, a delay of
a few weeks only. I took that as a sign that they wanted us to enjoy
that holiday and not deal with the emotions that would arise if there
was disease progression. I am grateful for that kindness and sensitiv-
ity. January showed progression in areas of the brain not previously
treated. It felt to me that cancer was running and hiding, getting away
from the treated areas to a safe place.

So, back to Boston for two weeks of radiation. This time I was allowed
to accompany Angela. They felt that she should not be in Boston
alone—and they were correct. Angela needed a wheelchair to get from
the hotel to the hospital due to the effects of cancer and medications.

Again, hospice was discussed multiple times with her oncology team
and between us. Over the years, Angela had, at times, said she was
ready to stop treatment. In each of those cases, new options had been
offered, and she had decided to continue. Her friends told me that she
had talked with them about being ready to stop care. This was one
of those issues she did not talk with me about outside of the medical
office. I was glad to hear that she had her friends available to her.

I am not certain how you can make the decision to stop treatment.
We had always talked about the balance of quality vs. longevity. It is a
narrow beam to walk without a right or wrong answer. Quality always
won out. The question was always this: Would the new treatment give
her quality?

At the time, Angela was hesitant to have this last treatment. She
asked her prognosis: one or two months without treatment, and
possibly six with treatment. She said she was not ready to die. I

couldn't breathe. Hospice was again discussed. Angela decided to have the treatment, and as a follow-up she requested an MRI to be scheduled for April so that she would know if the treatment had worked. At that time, she would enter hospice. In the meantime, she continued with palliative care.

In these last six months, they also found some spots of cancer in her cervical and thoracic spine. Treatment would be radiation; the recommendation was to monitor. These spots were not causing any symptoms at the time. I read "between the lines" that they were not certain she would survive long enough to develop symptoms.

This is cancer. It robs people of little bits of themselves until it grabs you with both hands. Cancer now had my daughter with both hands. I saw my independent, fierce daughter needing help with daily activities, in a wheelchair to get to appointments and when I took her for walks. Those cancer hands were crushing both of us. The emotional strain of being Angela's caregiver is without words.

I had previously helped care for my grandmother, mom, and dad. I had always viewed this as a gift that I was able to give them. I was not always certain I would be able to do that for my daughter. Yet I did—and I was able to help her maintain her dignity, the loss of which she was afraid of. That is the gift of love that I was able to give my daughter.

Blog Post Written by Carol Hordis[24]

– To Do Before –

July 19, 2021

"When you die, it does not mean that you lose to cancer. You beat cancer by how you live, why you live, and in the manner in which you live."
—STUART SCOTT

I was recently sitting at Angela's desk looking for something and found one of her many lists. Ange had been making lists for years to help with the effects of treatment. This one was titled:

– *To Do Before* –

I was hit with my initial sense of panic and questioned if I wanted to read this. After closing my eyes, deep breathing to relax, and talking out loud to Ange, my answer was yes. I don't know when she made

---

24. CAROL'S NOTE: I posted this entry on Angela blog. She did not want her followers wondering what happened to her. She had asked a friend to write it, thinking that would be better, but her friend was having as much trouble writing the blog post as I did.

this list but believe it may have been the past year. She had also asked me to make a list of things I wanted her to do.

The first item on the list was: Laugh.

I was struck by that. I wonder if she may have written this as a reminder to herself. She struggled in the past year with significant health challenges and changes; physical, emotional, and spiritual. This may have been her reminder to continue to find joy in those small moments. A reminder that in those joyful moments, as we both believed and she had learned, Angela was cured of cancer.

I wonder if it was also meant for those of us whose lives Angela touched, to find time to laugh amidst our grief.

Laughter was an important part of Angela's life, finding joy in life both before and after cancer. She laughed often with joy during good times throughout her life. Angela's laugh has always brought me joy, and laughing together would fill my heart.

Laughter is also how we got through the harder times. Often during our drives home from Boston, after receiving news we didn't want to hear, the humor would turn dark, but we would laugh. Laughter could be more helpful than tears, sadness, anger, frustration, and a sense of being overwhelmed. Although there was plenty of that, there was still and always laughter. Angela was often told by people reading her blog that they would laugh and cry at the same time. I remember some chuckles as I sat by her bedside with a few of her friends, holding her hand and sharing happy, fun-filled memories. As Angela has said, "Laughter is healing."

One afternoon, I was sitting in Angela's rocker on her patio, writing in my journal about the list. It was one of those beautiful, peaceful afternoons: baby robins chirping as mama fed them, birds singing, and critters scampering in the woods. The first dragonfly of the season landed on the table next to me and just sat on the edge watching me. Then a female cardinal arrived on the fence and sat watching me. I spoke to both of them and asked if I should make this a blog post. I felt Angela's big hug around me, giving her approval to blog about her list and laughter.

There were many other items on her list. The ones you would expect: lawyer, Life Ceremony, items to gift, tattoos she still wanted, and others. But the first item was laugh.

It has been two years since Angela's last blog. She started many but was never able to finish. Writing, which Angela loved, had become a struggle because of the effects of cancer and treatments. She would never post anything unless she was 100% happy with the result.

As an "observer" over the past seven years Angela lived with cancer, one of the hardest things to watch is how the disease steals little bits of a person, making everyday tasks and enjoyable activities more of a challenge. We spoke of this often. However, being Angela, she always found a way around the lost fragments to something better—but could not find a way around writing.

Angela is sending little, subtle messages and big bold, mischievous reminders that she is still with us and still laughing. Through our collective grief, there is comfort in that. With an open heart, Angela and Oskar will always be with us and she will always be laughing.

Angela Amoroso 4/5/79 – 3/21/21

Blog Post Written by Carol Hordis [25]
The End, Legacy

March 16, 2023

"A project representing the different side of my cancerful life and the different sides of cancer. It represents my story and many others."
—ANGELA AMOROSO

"I don't believe we see enough of the 'real' side of cancer. I want people to see it, to see how light and dark it can be."
—ANGELA AMOROSO.

Those who knew Angela personally or through her blog know that she was working on a three-part Photo Essay on cancer. The first two parts, Beauty and The Dark, are part of her blog. Part 3 she referred to as The End, although I think of it as Legacy.

Unfortunately, Angela was not able to complete the third part. She had completed an interview, and her friends, after her death, completed a song and music video as part of her project, which I will link to shortly.

---

25. **CAROL'S NOTE:** I added this post to Angela's blog in 2023—both to highlight her legacy and to complete her photo essay.

I believe that we all learned different things from Angela, from how she lived her life, her writing, photos, conversations, and what she shared with us.

It is my belief that her legacy is personal, individual to each of us with a general theme. It is about everything we learned from her that has become part of who we are and how we choose to live our life.

Angela's legacy, for me, is about living. She lived with grief daily: loss of friends and family, living with a terminal illness, loss of independence, body image struggles, and uncounted challenges in her daily life. After spending many of the seven years bald, she once told me that she missed her hair. Angela also, despite the dark times, the challenges, acknowledged the blessings she found in living with cancer. To see only the darkness, you miss beauty around and surrounding you.

Angela wrote openly and honestly about how she would be down at times, going to her dark place. Despite those dark times, she always found a way to continue to embrace the beauty in life and to find a way to live with her darker times while continuing to find joy in moments: the joy of working in the gardens and her smile as her plants thrived, listening to the birds and enjoying the dragonflies on the patio, time with friends and family, a good book, research for a trip. Living, for Angela, was not just about her struggles and challenges, but learning to live despite them. She recognized and believed that we all had struggles, and she believed that each person's challenges were equal to hers. Angela did not believe that cancer gave her struggles greater weight than any others.

It is often said that we are born needing care and we die needing care. Angela knew it was how we lived the time we had between that mattered.

As I have learned from Angela, living isn't just about our own challenges, our own struggles. Living is about our resilience, our fortitude; it is about how we persevere despite those obstacles.

It is close to two years since Angela passed away. While I continue to grieve her loss, miss her physical presence in my life, I am aware that I am taking steps to rebuild my life and think about how I want to live. With me in this process is all I learned from Angela. She is always walking alongside me. Despite grief, I seek beauty each day.

Friends, acquaintances, and people who didn't know her but found their way to her blog have shared with me how her life affected them and how they live their lives differently, more fully, with purpose because of what they learned from her. I see that as her legacy. As my grief becomes less brutal, I find Angela's legacy, her voice, becoming a stronger voice for me.

Angela's legacy is about how she chose to live her life. It is about her effect on those in her life, however brief the time. It is how others live their lives differently, more fully, more present in the moment, and the ability to find joy in those moments. When we live our lives differently, that affects those around us, our loved ones. In that way, Angela continues to live on in all of us.

I am sharing the links for the interview and music video, which tell more of Angela's story. It is OK to cry and to smile when watching them!

- INTERVIEW: https://m.youtube.com/
  watch?v=S-jLixeECJ4&feature=youtube
- SONG AND MUSIC VIDEO: *In Lieu Of Flowers* by Charlie
  Chronopoulos
  https://youtube.com/watch?v=JR_eGRZ6mmc

My heartfelt thanks and overwhelming gratitude to the artists Angela was working with—Liesl Clark, Ben Proulx, and Charlie Chronopoulos—who completed this project for her. This would not have been possible without their belief in Angela and her vision.

I wish all of you well. Each step forward can be a challenge, but we always have Angela walking alongside us.

Enjoy moments. Laugh. Celebrate Life. Share your blessings with friends, family, and people you are just meeting.

Posted by Carol Hordis

PART II:

FURTHER REFLECTIONS ON ANGELA'S BLOG

The Haunting of Why and Fair

**"She lives in a world she didn't choose,
and it hurts like brand new shoes."**
—SADE

Why and *fair*: two words that I have developed an intense dislike for.

Fair I developed a dislike for many years prior to Angela's diagnosis, but after her diagnosis, it was a word I grew to despise—a word that I heard so often from people, it made me want to scream. It was not about why or whether it was fair. This was our life, and we had to find a way to live it.

WHY? That little word opens the door to a deep, dark cavern that goes on forever—a space that is easy to get lost in, that can consume me. I feel that if I have an answer, it will ease the grief. I know it won't. I know there is no answer.

I have tried to never go there, although there were times when that effort failed.

The day we sat in the surgeon's office, after the initial call with biopsy results, I said to Angela that the situation should be reversed.

I thought, *It should be her with me, and not me with her.* Why *my daughter? How is this* fair? *She has her whole life ahead of her.*

Was it too many animal products; was it the dairy, nonorganic foods, relenting to her request for packaged mac and cheese in place of the homemade; or was it the hormones in the cheese when it was home-made. Was she exposed to something on a trip, something in our home, something in my breast milk. I even researched the accident at Three Mile Island. We lived 100 miles east of the reactor when the accident occurred, about a month prior to her delivery. I asked the oncologist, who looked at me oddly. I was not able to find any research on individuals and health patterns in those who lived that far from the reactor.

Fair seemed to bubble to the surface of my mind—usually, but not always, after scan results that necessitated a change in treatment. That word would swirl around, taking me into that whirlpool of fear, anger, sadness, and all other negative emotions. Once there, it is a struggle to break free.

Yet getting lost in the whirlpool of negative emotions, I realized, did not allow me to be present with Angela. If I was lost, then I would not have time with her, building memories, being with her. That was what I wanted and needed.

To break free, I started to talk with myself. There is no answer to *why* and what really is *fair*. This was Angela's life and mine. I wanted to live it and enjoy my time with her. Eventually, that worked. Each time those thoughts would creep back into my mind, I would have a talk with them, and they would lose their power over me. I was not going to allow myself to drown in the what-ifs.

Angela had cancer; it was something I needed to learn to live with. It would always be with us; she would always be tethered to an oncologist. Any symptom or illness in the future was a red flag to look for metastasis. Then metastasis occurred.

Angela would often talk about how her friends avoided talking to her about their struggles. She made it clear that although their problems were different from hers, they were equally important. Angela wanted to continue to be a part of their lives and did not want all conversations to be about cancer. She did not want to be the "cancer girl."

As I learned from Angela, we will all have heartaches, struggles, and challenges in our lives. It was not about our struggle, but how we dealt with it and what we learned from it. It was also about what others learned from how we dealt with our struggles. My daughter may no longer be with me physically, but I am trying to take what I learned from her as I build my life.

Initially, in grief, I would still have those *could have, should have, would have* days. I have tried not to look back with regrets, but they have crept in at times. I still struggle with how to put them to rest. There is no answer to any of these questions. I know that we always made the best decision at the time. Was my best always good enough? The only answer is to look at the life that Angela lived, her writing and photos, and recognize that we always made the best decision for her. That is enough.

Breast Cancer Culture

"It's not all pink ribbons and walks for the cure."
—ANGELA AMOROSO

"Hard stuff is hard."
—ANGELA AMOROSO

"Society makes us feel that if you just try hard enough you can beat it, that's the message."
—ANGELA AMOROSO

"...pink is a soft color; breast cancer is not a soft disease."
—ANGELA AMOROSO

"The Culture of Survivorship and the Tyranny of Cheerfulness"
—SAMANTHA KING

I would like to provide definitions of the terminology used when referencing breast cancer for those who may not be familiar with them.

These definitions are from the National Cancer Institute[26]:

Ductal Carcinoma in Situ: (DCIS): Breast cancer that is found in the milk duct of the breast that has not spread to other areas of the breast. DCIS has the potential to become invasive breast cancer.

Invasive Breast Cancer: Cancer that has spread from the original location in the breast to the surrounding breast tissue. Invasive breast cancer has the potential to become metastatic breast cancer. [Angela's cancer was DCIS, invasive ductal adenocarcinoma, and a positive sentinel node: Stage II at the time of diagnosis.]

Metastatic Breast Cancer: Cancer cells have spread from the original site, the breast, to other areas of the body. The cells travel through the blood or the lymph system and form a new tumor in other organs or tissues.

For clarification, Angela has written about breast cancer statistics throughout her blog. I have provided the most recent estimated statistics available in 2024. With that in mind, I originally started writing this section at 3 AM on October 13, 2022, as follows.

It is Metastatic Breast Cancer Awareness Day amidst Pinktober. Angela has written about the breast cancer culture, the idea of survivorship, and the stress it placed on her. This is the public persona of breast cancer, not the lived experience for Angela—and, I believe, for others.

---

26. CAROL'S NOTE: https://www.cancer.gov/publications/dictionaries/cancer-terms.

Every day Angela is with me, and I honor and miss her, but today my thoughts are also about the 117 people that will die, each day, in the US from metastatic breast cancer. This is a day to celebrate their lives and mourn their loss.

Every day of this month is a challenge. The country is awash in pink ribbons, "pink washing," in cheerful stories about finding a cure, happy smiling faces, raising money for research. What is not told, during this month, is the emotional, physical, and financial cost to those living with metastatic breast cancer and their loved ones.

What is shared is an optimistic cheerful attitude. The stories told never include darker days, the struggles, the fear of the individual with breast cancer and their loved ones. There is never talk about the lives that are upended, people struggling just to make it through another day. My experience and Angela's were that days were full of joy, fear, and despair. The list of emotions in living with a terminal illness is unending.

I recognize that the pink ribbon organizations and perhaps the media do not want to instill fear in individuals going through treatment or instill fear that may prevent women from getting mammograms. However, a dose of realism would be helpful, perhaps especially for those newly diagnosed who may have a false impression of what to expect—and for those supporting them. For Angela and me and for her friends and family, it was our first experience "up close and personal" with breast cancer treatment. None of us was prepared for the struggles of that first year of treatment or that when Angela walked out of the cancer center after her last treatment, she was not able to pick up her life where she left off a year previously.

We were educated by surgeons, oncologists, and their staff; obtained a second opinion; reviewed treatment options. No amount of education could have prepared us for the reality of living with breast cancer or metastatic breast cancer. It is my belief that some of this is because of years of exposure to the toxic optimism of the pink ribbons.

While I appreciate all that they are doing to raise awareness and money for research, it is a disservice to those living with breast cancer and/or metastasis who are struggling. It does not validate their lived experience. Angela always felt that there was a lot of pressure on her, and I felt it also. It is hard to keep up the happy face when your heart is breaking.

Fight, fight, fight, as if that is the answer. Positive attitude. Stay positive. Angela said she didn't fight the first year; she showed up. Getting through each day was a challenge with surgery, chemotherapy, and dealing with the side effects, some of which were permanent, and working to keep health insurance, pay her medical copays, and manage the financial implications of living with cancer.

This is the unfortunate part of the culture: the lack of information or talk about the full experience. That lack of information, education, and the acknowledgment of fears is a disservice to everyone with breast cancer and their support systems. Despite the education provided, it cannot fully prepare you for the emotional and spiritual effects of cancer and treatment. I acknowledge that others may have different experiences. However, because most organizations do not present the full picture of cancer and treatment—the physical, psychological, and spiritual toll of those in treatment—for Angela and others like her, their feelings and experiences are not validated. Because of this, Angela felt that her feelings were wrong. Yet the struggles, dark feelings, and fears are as real as the beauty of living.

The lack of experiential information also meant that Angela's support system was unprepared for her lived experience. The glossy public perception of breast cancer leaves those who are living with it unprepared for reality. What is not shared is the lifelong tether to the medical community. Metastasis can occur ten-plus years from the original diagnosis of early stage breast cancer. Every symptom, every illness raises a red flag: Could this be breast cancer?

I have heard from others with breast cancer how angry they are every time an advertisement for breast cancer or a new medication is shown. These advertisements feature only perfectly groomed individuals who are energetic and bouncing through treatment, which was not Angela's experience nor that of others whom I know.

There is a common belief that a person can just fight harder—that they can and should rely on a positive outlook. But staying positive and fighting hard is not going to change the medical outcome. Metastatic breast cancer is a terminal illness with an average life expectancy of three years. I often felt that Angela's voice was drowned out by the "pink" community. There was a constant push, message, that if she just stayed strong, fought harder, then she could overcome metastatic breast cancer. I saw what she struggled with daily—lived with daily—and was in awe of my daughter.

Recently I sat down with the journals I took to Angela's appointments. We recorded questions, symptoms, concerns, and side effects that she was having from treatment. We kept track of the information provided, testing results, new recommendations, and medication changes. I recommend everyone do this. Often you get so much information, it is helpful to have the journal entries to later refresh your memory on changes. Angela's care was quite complex. For Angela, this was her full-time job: managing appointments, treatments, symptoms, and side effects. Managing her care independently was more difficult due to the side effects of chemo ("chemo brain"), in addition to the cognitive effects of brain metastasis, four craniotomies, and radiation. For many years, it took both of us to manage her cancer.

When Angela passed away, she was on sixteen scheduled medications, additional supplements for some of her side effects, scheduled narcotics with additional medications as needed for pain management, and as-needed medications for the side effects of medication, cancer, and treatment.

Over the seven years Angela lived with cancer, this is my count:

Surgery:

- 15 surgical procedures.
- 2 cancelled surgeries.

Radiation:

- 6 weeks (30 treatments) to the chest wall.
- 12 weeks (60 treatments) to the brain over 5 years.

Chemotherapy:

- 20 IV chemotherapy treatments in the first year. A clinical trial given IV every three weeks for at least six months. A medication used to reduce brain swelling for three weeks (unfortunately, it caused a brain bleed and had to be stopped).

Stereotactic Radiation (technically considered a surgical procedure):

- At last count fifteen tumors were treated (eventually I lost count), some requiring multiple treatments due to the size. Eventually, Angela needed sedation for her treatments, which required a few hours of pretreatment and post-procedure recovery. All treatments required pretreatment with Ativan and three days of high-dose Ativan post-treatment to prevent a seizure, which left her sleeping for three days, further affecting her balance and cognitive abilities.

Ongoing Medications:

- At least sixty-two different medications, many with multiple doses daily; multiple dose changes; some were stopped and then restarted. One of her medications was given monthly by injection in the oncology office. One of her chemotherapies was six pills daily. Other chemotherapy was IV as well as multiple pretreatment medications, which are not included in the list.

As-Needed Medications:

- No count of the number of medications she used when needed to treat side effects.

Supplements:

- Multiple taken to help with long-term chemo side effects.

MRI, CT scans, bone scans, lab draws, X rays, cardiac testing:

- uncounted.

This is part of the darker side of metastatic breast cancer that is not spoken of.

The estimated 2024 statistics for breast cancer are overwhelming. These statistics are from the National Cancer Institute[27] and confirmed by other cancer organizations. These statistics are for the U.S. only.

It is estimated that in 2024, 310,720 women and 2800 men will be diagnosed with invasive breast cancer in the US. An additional 56,500 will be diagnosed with ductal carcinoma in situ.

Estimates are that 42,250 women and 530 men in the US will die with breast cancer in 2024. Each day 117 people will die from metastatic breast cancer.

1 in 8 women, 13 percent, will develop invasive breast cancer. It is estimated that 20 to 30 percent of individuals with early stage breast cancer will progress to metastatic breast cancer. This is more common in women diagnosed under 40. Angela was Stage II when she was diagnosed with invasive breast cancer at age 34. There is a higher risk of developing metastasis in women under 35 at the time of initial diagnosis. Metastatic breast cancer is not curable or considered a "chronic" cancer.

---

27. CAROL'S NOTE: https://seer.cancer.gov/statfacts/html/breast.html.

For women and men with metastatic breast cancer, only 31 percent will survive five years.

The goal and hope are that metastatic breast cancer will become a chronic illness, but we are far from there.

There is a lack of knowledge and a misperception about metastatic breast cancer. I believe that this is because the conversations about breast cancer rarely include metastatic disease. Many people whom I spoke with were not aware that it is a terminal illness.

Angela died from metastatic breast cancer not because she didn't want to live, not because she didn't have a positive outlook (she had a realistic outlook), not because she did not fight hard enough. She died because it is a terminal illness; there is no cure.

Each year, October 13, Metastatic Breast Cancer Awareness Day, to honor Angela, all those I have met living with metastatic breast cancer, and all those who have died from this disease, I will gather with other cancer-impacted families at the Memorial Bridge in Portsmouth, NH. I first attended this event with Angela; now I attend with her spirit. Each year on October 13, the bridge and other locations around the world are lit with the colors of metastatic breast cancer: green, teal, and pink. There are no speeches or scheduled activities. It is a time of quiet contemplation and remembrance. I always light a candle for Angela and remember.

Finances

"Financial stressors ... Struggle of saying f*** it,
just travel ..."
—ANGELA AMOROSO

Dealing with the financial aspects of cancer contributed to Angela's physical and emotional challenges.

Angela had her first job when she was sixteen, mucking stalls and caring for horses. She loved going to work, just to be with the horses. Until 2015, the year after she got cancer, she had aways worked, except the three years she lived and went to college in Australia. Her Visa did not allow her to work, which was a challenge for her. Angela did not like the feeling of being financially dependent.

When she lived at home, she always contributed to the household. She helped with groceries, fixed meals, did chores, ran errands, and participated any way she could help.

As I have noted, Angela continued to work full-time during her first year of treatment. She had her home, with Oskar, and she needed to continue her health insurance. She started to acquire medical debt during that first year of treatment, often on her credit cards, which allowed to her collect miles she used for travel, although she also accumulated interest.

It was recommended that Angela reduce her work hours during that first year of treatment. She was physically and emotionally exhausted, was having a difficult time with side effects, and had lost a lot of weight. She had been cautioned about the risk of "burn out" from working full-time during surgery, chemo, and radiation. Twice, for a week each time, they postponed her chemo to allow her to regain strength and try to stabilize her weight loss. I could not convince her to accept help from me with her expenses, which would have allowed her to work less and care for herself more. She was also concerned that if she reduced her hours, she would lose her health insurance. Angela referred to this year as her dark period. It was a dark time for both of us.

Once she completed treatment, she started on a hormone blocker. Initially, she resisted the suggestion of taking more medications and treatments, but then she agreed to try it. Unfortunately, she experienced multiple side effects. After a few weeks, she stopped the medication. Angela was aware that this placed her at risk for recurrence, but she needed to balance quality of life with the medication.

Her decision to stop taking this medication frightened me. I was also frightened to see her going backward, drifting back into that dark place from the year before. We never discussed whether her choice may have contributed to metastasis, nor is it important. Quality of life was important. One of her oncologists told her that the brain tumors, due to their size, may have been present when she was initially diagnosed. For Stage II breast cancer patients, the brain is not scanned unless or until there are symptoms.

A year after her diagnosis, she spent a week ice climbing with First Descents, joining a group of other twenty- and thirty-year-olds with cancer. When I took her to the airport, she was still a shell of her pre-cancer self. To my enormous relief, a week later, the Angela whom I had always known got off the plane.

On her return from ice climbing, she had energy, physical and emotional strength, and a desire to change her life. She made the decision to sell her home, resign her position, and take close to a year off. Angela moved back home with me, using the equity in her home to pay off her accumulated medical debt and pay off her car. The equity also allowed her to support herself for that year, travel, and recover from her year of treatment. During that year off, in addition to the ice-climbing trip, she went to Turks and Caicos with me on her chemo graduation trip, and she went to a yoga retreat in Costa Rica and then on her cross-country trip.

At the end of her year off, when she was ready to return to work and was setting up interviews, she was found to have two brain tumors.

Angela always had a hard time accepting financial help. After the cancer spread to her brain, she needed ten radiation treatments to her surgical site. She was still physically fatigued from the surgery and the emotional challenge of metastasis. We decided that she would spend the two weeks in Boston to limit the often-long journeys to and from Boston. She could not drive, and, I think, she wanted me to return to work and not take another two weeks off. One of the side effects of radiation is also fatigue, compounding the fatigue from surgery.

We decided that she would stay in Boston during the week, friends would visit and stay with her, and I would come down for an overnight each week. A friend set up a Go Fund Me account to raise money for the apartment that she had rented, although, initially, Angela was resistant. At first her name was not used, but then she relented, and it was listed as a collection for her. She was humbled by the support and donations, which were enough to cover the rental.

In her blog posts, Angela sometimes mentions the challenges of insurance coverage and eligibility tied in with Social Security. Fortunately, Angela was able to supplement the money she received from Social Security with the equity from the sale of her home and withdrawals from her 401(k), along with travel miles she had accumulated, miles that were gifted to her, and additional help from me. However, none of this was straightforward or easy. Once she was considered disabled, Angela had a five-month waiting period until she received Social Security. Then, Medicare had a two-year five-month waiting period after her date of disability until coverage could begin. During that time, she needed to maintain her own insurance. Initially she had COBRA, followed by a year under the Affordable Care Program. However, Angela received too much in Social Security to qualify for assistance with premiums. The year after brain cancer was found, the Affordable Care program changed, and she was no longer covered to receive treatment in Boston. Angela had a local oncologist as well as three oncologists, a neurosurgeon, and access to clinical trials in Boston that she would not have been able to participate in if she had received all her care locally. Also, she was unable to access a neurosurgeon locally if she needed additional surgery.

To address these challenges, Angela found an individual program with a premium of $500.00 monthly, which was 30 percent of her Social Security. It had high deductibles and copays, but she could continue her care in Boston. Of course, she knew that she and Oskar would always have a home with me. That is why she considered herself to be lucky. She had to accept that she would never live in her own place again.

Debt started to accumulate. In 2016, her medical expenses were over $11,000, which was $3000.00 more than her income. In 2017, her medical expenses were again over $11,000, which was $8000.00 less than her full year of Social Security. Initially, she was able to use her 401(k) to pay the insurance and medical expenses, but she exhausted those funds before she became eligible for Medicare.

Once she was covered by Medicare, things eased a bit, although medical debt continued to accumulate due to high deductibles and copays. Her copay for an MRI alone was $350.00. As an example, her share of one of her chemo treatments was over $350.00 a month. Later, that seemed like a bargain after she was changed to a different chemo for which her share was over $2700.00 monthly, *$10,000 more than her yearly income.* I did check other Medicare plans, but oral chemo co-pay is always 20 to 30 percent of the cost. Grants are available, but only if the treatment is started in the beginning of the year, and the amounts available are quickly exhausted. Added to the cost of her chemo, she still had her fifteen other medications, copays, and deductibles. It adds up quickly. I now understand how people often file for bankruptcy when they have a serious health problem like cancer.

Carrying the debt was an emotional challenge. I was always available to help with her finances, and I researched different supplement plans, but the premiums were prohibitive. The younger you are when you are on Medicare due to a disability, the higher the premiums are. Angela finally asked me to help with the paperwork when she found she could no longer review the medical bills and negotiate the payment plans. Even I—with my brain not addled with multiple craniotomies, weeks of radiation, and the effects of chemo and medications—felt overwhelmed as I reviewed medical bills, which were often fifteen to twenty pages long. Once we reviewed them, we needed to make certain that everything had been sent to the insurance company. Then the negotiations started with the individual medical centers over the amount they wanted her to pay and what she could afford. Angela was always adamant that I was not to pay her medical expenses. She felt that providing her and Oskar with a home and other assistance was enough.

Another issue Angela wrote about is the cost in time: time spent in appointments, in travel to and from appointments, in tests, and in days in a chemo chair. Additionally, there are the travel costs and parking fees. We had an agreement: I drove, I paid for gas, I covered the parking fees—and she bought lunch!

I understand why hospitals and medical organizations work so hard to receive copays and deductibles. Angela's Medicare plan, with copays included, only reimbursed 20 to 25 percent of the billed cost. The organizations needed to "write off" the 75 to 80 percent remaining of all her visits, procedures, and treatments.

When Angela was initially faced with a life-altering illness that became terminal, she faced the question of how she wanted to live her life. In this situation, the question becomes *What are you willing to give up so that you don't die with medical debt, and how can you balance that with how you want to spend the short period of time that you have to live?* The options are endless, from a meal out with friends, taking care of your dog, maintaining a car, to traveling, all of which bring such joy. Angela lived with the knowledge that even if she gave up everything, she would still die with medical debt.

Living with a terminal illness takes and takes from each person. It is often a struggle to maintain your dignity, and independence, but I don't believe that it should be allowed to take your joys. Angela and I recognized that quality of life was a consideration in all her decisions.

During her illness, Angela was able to continue to travel, and she knew how to do it inexpensively. Travel to her was not about a fancy hotel; it was about the experience, meeting people, immersing herself in the culture of the area. In addition to using travel miles, oftentimes she would stay with friends, share a one-bedroom rental, and eat meals in. Having a small apartment when she traveled allowed her to respect her fatigue and rest comfortably.

I often felt helpless and hopeless as a parent of an independent, adult child with a terminal illness. She did eventually allow me to pay for her "less" expensive chemo. She also allowed me to help with some of her travel expenses, although when we traveled together, that was my treat. She accepted it as her inheritance from me. Similarly, traveling with her dad was his treat. For me, it was a chance to share experiences and build more memories, which are now so treasured. Accepting some help was a gift she gave me, to counter my hopelessness.

In the end, Angela died with medical debt. That was going to be the case regardless of her choice to live a full life during whatever time she had. This was a choice that I fully supported.

PART III:

LIVING WITH DYING

Open Communication

"Struggle - dealing with FEAR
Not fear of dying
Fear of suffering"
—ANGELA AMOROSO

"Talking about death doesn't bring it on any faster."
—KRIS HALLENGA

"Aid in dying is for people who don't have the choice to live. They're choosing the way they will die ... this is not suicide."
—DIANE REHM

"...a positive mental attitude does not cure cancer— any more than a negative mental attitude causes cancer."
—SIDDHARTHA MUKERJEE

I want to start by saying again that both Angela and I were realists. As I've noted, we both heard—frequently—about the importance of being optimistic—of not letting the fears take hold. Unfortunately, in situations with people who felt we must always be optimistic, I was not able to address my fears, and so my feelings were not validated. This placed walls—barriers—in relationships. Being truthful and honest about an experience, whether that involves recent scan results, treatment changes, or another surgery, is being realistic. Being able to talk about our feelings was important for both Angela and me. It is open communication that I believe helped us to maintain our relationship, and perhaps even strengthened our bond. The open conversations allowed me to support Angela and the life she wanted to live, her fears, and what was important to her after her death.

. . .

Angela and I worked to keep communication open. No topic was off limits. That did not make discussions easier, but it did make them helpful for both of us. We frequently talked about our relationship, my perspective on parenting and her perspective of being a child. We talked about both of our challenges. This allowed us to resolve any issues we may have had, to say all that needed to be said, and to apologize when we felt that was due. We had the privilege of resolving any issues that may have been lingering between us. Nothing was left unsaid. For me, it was a blessing, a gift. Grief is hard enough without creating or leaving behind unfinished business.

. . .

As I consider the seven years that Angela had cancer, the early conversations with her oncologists and surgeons felt difficult, often devastating. We had conversations about surgery, pathology, staging, chemotherapy side effects, and the risk of recurrence—the list is long. I came to realize that these discussions were traumatic, although they were not the heavy, onerous conversations that we would have with her oncologists and each other after she developed metastasis.

Angela first talked about medical aid in dying while she was in the hospital after her first craniotomy. Her goal was to avoid suffering. This topic then seemed to drift into the background, popping up occasionally, until a few months prior to her death. We had both kept up with states that had enacted laws approving this—noting the legal issues and the process for approval—but we had not discussed it with each other. We were aware that it is legal in Maine.

During the last year of treatment, we had many conversations with her team and each other about palliative care, hospice, prognosis, and limited treatment options available. On a drive home from Maine in early 2021, we tuned into an NPR program on the radio. It was a conversation with Diane Rehm about her book *When My Time Comes*. I offered to change the station, but Angela wanted to hear the conversation and opinions. This triggered an in-depth conversation between us. Neither of us could escape the discussion; it needed to occur, and being in the car meant our time was undisturbed. We talked about the steps she would need to take to be considered and approved for medical aid in dying. At that point, we knew she was out of treatment options and her prognosis was six months or less. Inside, I was crumbling.

Angela's concern was whether I would support her decision and if I would be with her if she made that decision. I believe that for Angela, it was not just a fear of suffering but also a fear of dying alone—fears that I shared also. I assured her that I would be with her. I never had a doubt that I would support whatever decision that Angela made: hospice at home, Hospice House, medical aid in dying. I would be present when she made that decision, and I would be there to care for her. Now, she needed to hear me say that. I reassured her that I would have plenty of support if she wanted to be at home with hospice.

Although I wondered how I would manage to provide that level of care for my daughter, I knew that I would.

I understood Angela's wish to consider medical aid in dying. Angela did not choose to have cancer; however, she had chosen how she wanted to live with it. Cancer controlled much of her life. While Angela was in control of her choice to accept or decline treatment, those considerations were always due to the effects of cancer. That was her life for seven years.

Medical aid in dying, for Angela and for me, was not a choice of living or dying. We knew she was dying. There were no further surgeries, no additional chemotherapeutics, she was not a candidate for any further radiation. Her only choice was how she would die.

Angela often talked about her fear of suffering at the end of life, her fear of a Grand Mal seizure. Choosing medical aid in dying would have allowed her to have control of when and how she would pass away and the knowledge that she would have a peaceful death surrounded by loved ones.

I assured her that if that was her choice, I would support her. I would help her see whomever she needed, and I would be with her when she made that decision. She wondered about her pillars and if they would be with her. I hoped and believed that they would.

Angela never took the steps she needed to choose medical aid in dying. I didn't ask.

. . .

Angela and I also had many conversations about me. After her initial diagnosis, we were told about my increased risk for breast cancer due to her having cancer. There was a recommendation for me to take medications and reduce that risk. Angela was devastated to hear that my risk had increased. I was aware of it and had already looked at the statistics. I made an appointment to talk with her oncologist and review options. I decided not to take the medication. Angela and I discussed my decision, and, thankfully, she was supportive.

Angela's other concern about me was that she would not be there to take care of me as I had been taking care of her. Despite the consistent reassurance that I could manage, that I could live on the first floor of the house we built in Maine, that I could hire help if needed, and that I had a support system, it was still a constant source of worry. While I focused on her and how she was doing, she worried about me. Angela's worry about me felt—to me—like a burden for her that I was not able to fully relieve.

. . .

Similarly, Angela worried a lot about her pillars, including that something would happen to them or to me before her. She often said she did not know what she would do if something happened to any of us. It was hard to see her worry and talk about those fears. I wanted her to be focused on herself; instead she worried about her support system.

. . .

There were many conversations about prognosis over the years, starting with the initial diagnosis. Initially, discussions on prognosis focused on her risk of recurrence. After the disease spread, it was about longevity.

Those conversations about prognosis and risks were some of the hardest ones we had. In fact, *hard* is too gentle of a word. They were brutal. These are the times that I had to control myself and not collapse into a sobbing mess, although tears and shock were present for both of us. These are the conversations that I always knew would come, but I kept that knowledge packed away, someplace deep within me, so that I did not focus on them until necessary.

Over the years Angela had metastatic disease, she would go through stages of giving away some of her things. This usually occurred after a "bad" scan result. It was hard to come to grips that she was planning for things after her death, although I recognized how important it was for her.

During Angela's first post-craniotomy visit, she asked about prognosis. Her oncologist recommended that we talk about prognosis after a year, and then we could see how she was doing. I was initially upset, because I felt that at that time we could be provided with some information, some type of expectation. I believe that Angela was troubled by this also, since we both apparently did some research on our own after that visit. We were later told that less than 5 percent of individuals with her type of breast cancer have the brain as the first place of metastasis. I realized that the prognosis we wanted and the prognosis that we found online were not accurate to her situation. There were too few people in her situation for the medical professionals to be able to accurately establish a prognosis, but neither of us realized that at the time.

Over the years, I missed one appointment. That was the one when Angela had a serious conversation about prognosis. Unknown to me, she had wanted that time alone with her oncologist to ask the question, without me there. When she picked me up from work and we started talking about her appointment, she revealed that she had asked about prognosis. Then she was silent. Eventually, Angela asked if I wanted to know. I told her I did, although I did not really want that information. The prognosis was that Angela might have one more holiday. I wasn't ready to hear that, but I would never be ready. Instead, different treatment options came along, and that initial prognosis was tossed out. Until her final year, it was not something we discussed again. We recognized that Angela was paving a new path—her own path for metastatic breast cancer to the brain—and there was no prognosis.

At the time, I didn't recognize these conversations and information as grief. I only saw my fear. Now, after Angela's death, I find that, for me, grief and fear are linked. I would not accept or deal with grief, and I put the fear aside. I wanted to deal with and live in the present.

In the first years, Angela was resilient. She always seemed to bounce back, and for a while there was always another clinical trial that would give her stability for months or another surgery or treatment option. Then there were no more trials, and the only treatment option was the one she had declined from the beginning: whole-brain radiation.

As the last option, Angela hesitated and then asked her prognosis. The oncologist said it was harder to say what the prognosis would be with treatment, since Angela had been paving her own path with brain cancer, but without treatment, the prognosis was one or two months. We both sat in stunned silence. After the appointment, Angela said that she was not ready and did not feel bad enough to think that she would have only one to two months.

I was not ready either, but, again, would I ever be ready for my daughter to die. I monitored Angela's symptoms carefully and was aware of the changes she was experiencing—changes I was not certain she saw or remembered. I saw how cancer continued to steal bits of her but at a greater pace than a few years earlier. It was hard to think about her having so little time. I was not prepared to think that the spread would increase that rapidly. But I was wrong.

Twice in the past, I have been present with family members when discussing hospice and/or a lack of treatment options. Those were heartbreaking decisions to make, but they pale when talking about my daughter.

Initially, Angela resisted palliative care. She didn't want another physician or more appointments in Boston. I understood. The days were already long and emotionally exhausting. Her local oncologist was also a palliative care specialist, so Angela was able to incorporate palliative care into her visits.

In that last year, hospice was discussed many times. It was time to think about what she wanted, and Angela wanted to know what I could support.

Those prior experiences did not prepare me for having that conversation with Angela and her providers. There were warnings. Being told that they were running out of treatment options. Being told that they do not have a lot of experience with patients who live this long with metastatic brain cancer. She was receiving palliative care.

I could see the changes in Angela: a progression of the brain cancer symptoms, and an increased difficulty tolerating the higher dose of medication being used to try to reduce the symptoms. Palliative care and hospice discussions had been part of her appointments for many months. Still, each time hospice was mentioned as part of the appointment, I was never prepared for it. Each time I would tear up and feel like I could not take a breath.

At home, we had multiple conversations about hospice: home vs. Hospice House. Angela wavered, but in the end she wanted to be home. Each time we had this conversation, we both became teary. I knew my emotions were making it harder for her; nonetheless, the tears would come. I was supportive of her decision and wanted her to be home. I assured her that I would have help to care for her. As a nurse I had many friends who were nurses and would be able to help with her physical needs, and we both had good support systems to help with our emotional needs.

In the past, I had experienced the opportunity and privilege to help my parents and Grandmom at the end of their lives, and I had seen it as a gift that I was able to give them and myself. Being present with them, helping with tasks, taking care of hygiene, maintaining their dignity, honoring and participating in rituals when asked, holding their hand, and just being present to talk had all been a gift to those I loved. I wondered if I would feel the same when I cared for my daughter.

As a "just in case," Angela wanted to tour the Hospice House to know where she would be if needed. Unfortunately, she was not able to get the tour, and she died before getting to Hospice House. Another unfortunate: despite our best intentions and plans, in the end, her needs were too great for me to have her at home.

I was in the ER after Angela's seizure. I was told that the seizure was caused by cancer and not a brain bleed. There were no options for her. I don't remember how the ER physician asked the question or the words that were said, but I had to say the words aloud: "She is a DNR" (Do Not Resuscitate). It was a struggle to get those words out. I brought her living will with me and shared it with the physician. Angela and I had both hoped that she would drift off to sleep at home in hospice care. She had entrusted me to respect her wishes, although there was no way that I could be prepared for uttering those three letters.

. . .

Over the last few years of Angela's life, we also talked about her wishes for after she died. Angela knew what she wanted, and she needed to make certain I was comfortable with her decisions. These were not *if* something happens, but *when*. Angela knew she wanted to be cremated and what she wanted done with her ashes. We talked about how to handle her blog and a post to notify her readers, her social media accounts, a friend who would be my IT guru, church service (no), and wake (no). Angela had talked about having a Life Celebration and her wish for the day. (She was very specific that it is not referred to as a Celebration of Life.) She had told me she wanted it to be held in Maine, and she was aware that the location might make it hard for people to come, but that was her wish. End-of-life documents were reviewed.

Angela also talked about money and finances, expressing concern that I would be responsible for her debt. I clarified with her attorney that she was an adult, and I would not bear responsibility, which was a relief for her. Angela made me, multiple times, promise that I would not pay her debt. It remained her belief that I had been supporting her emotionally and physically with a home, etc., and that I should not pay her bills.

. . .

During one of our conversations, Angela asked me to make a list of things I wanted her to do. What wasn't said in her request was that she wanted to make certain she took care of my concerns while she was able. It was a challenge to hear her planning for her death and considering ways to make things "easier" for me. It was important to her, and I knew it would help me when I needed to have information about her estate and belongings, but it was not a request I wanted to hear.

I told her the one thing I wanted was her passwords and then, over the next week or so, I thought about it and made a list. After she asked, she never wanted to talk about the list. It was left on the table for weeks, possibly months. I am not certain if she looked at it, but we never discussed it. Eventually, I put it away. I couldn't continue to look at it, and I did not feel that she was ready to discuss it. As I shared earlier, I found Angela's own "to do before" list on her desk after she passed away.

. . .

A few months prior to Angela's death, we talked about her blog and how she had wanted to have it published. That was also when she told me that I should write a book about my experiences, which is how this combined project came about. I did not realize it at the time, but now I believe that she wanted to help me find a sense of purpose after she died. Angela was, in a very subtle way, trying to take care of me. All prior conversations were focused on her wishes; now she wanted to focus on me and my survival.

. . .

There are so many things that Angela and I talked about over the years—all hard but necessary conversations that were helpful to both of us. Angela's desire to have those talks and my willingness to share them with her kept communication open between us and kept us open to sharing and supporting each other. I can look back now and be grateful that we had that open relationship and ability to have those talks. I believe that it allowed Angela to be at peace because I knew what was important to her and would respect her wishes.

In the end, our conversations about her passing did make taking care of the arrangements after her death "easier" for me. Although *easy* is not the right word, because I was numb and nothing was easy, our previous discussions meant that while I was not in a place to make decisions, I did not have to. I did not have to think about what Angela would want, because I already knew. Everything was about honoring her wishes.

. . .

Hard conversations, as I have learned, are about being present, being comfortable with the uncomfortable. They didn't occur at a single setting, but over time. Wishes change. It was clearly important for Angela to be able to freely share her wishes so she could take comfort in the knowledge that I would respect them and that I was comfortable with them. She knew I would speak for her when she was not able to speak for herself.

There is no blessing in Angela having cancer or in her death. Not putting blinders on to those challenging and heartbreaking talks, I believe, improved our relationship and brought us closer. There wasn't any topic, fear, or emotion I would not talk about with her. Keeping communication open is a gift we gave to ourselves and each other. Avoiding or preventing open and honest communication about joy and fears, happiness and darkness would have robbed Angela and me of the loving and supportive relationship that we had. I would have lost the opportunity to add seven years of memories to my treasure chest, which is what sustains me. The ability of both of us to be present throughout the waves of emotions, the bright and dark times, is the beauty I am now blessed with.

Cancer—Blessing and Curse

"Cancer is taking my passions from me slowly."
—ANGELA AMOROSO

"Cancer is my blessing and my curse."
—ANGELA AMOROSO

Angela started to look at cancer as her blessing and her curse. It seemed odd to hear her talk about living with a terminal illness as a blessing. She found that cancer gave her the ability to focus on the activities that she enjoyed, a blessing. It was this attitude that could lift me up when I was struggling with any blessings, seeing only the curse.

Despite her attitude, cancer had a way of taking from Angela, me, and those who loved her.

At the end, it took her life, and we all miss her and mourn her loss. While she lived and thrived, it was all the other things that it took.

As I look back over the seven years, I see all the big and small losses. It is not the finances, her ability to work and to manage her own affairs, her independence, although they are losses.

It is the activities, her creativity, the purpose that she had found in her life and in living and writing about her experiences with cancer and travel. The ability to enjoy the three things she referred to as her gifts from cancer, the blessing of cancer: writing, photography, and travel. It was her dignity. It is all the little pieces that broke away, that were lost. Each time Angela lost a piece of herself, a piece of me broke also.

The losses were slow, at times almost imperceptible. Both of us were aware of the subtle, gradual changes.

Burden of disease was a term we heard during medical visits, more frequently in the last one to two years of Angela's life. When her oncologists spoke of disease burden, they were talking about progression and treatment options. While they always considered quality of life, I watched Angela live with the burden of cancer daily. To both of us, it was more than just disease progression, effects of cancer and treatments. It was the long-term physical, emotional, and spiritual effects.

For me, disease burden is the curse of cancer. Angela developed neuropathy in her first year of treatment. She was unhappy with her breast implants and was never able to have the second revision, or—her preference—to have them removed. This affected her self-image and comfort, another burden. She spent many years bald and once told me how much she missed her hair. People disappeared from her life who later told me it was too hard. This caused Angela to refer to herself as the invisible cancer girl.

After developing brain cancer, we quickly learned how to live life in two-month increments. Making plans for more than two months was a risky venture. They would often need to be cancelled due to scan results, treatment complications, and all the many barriers that were thrown at her. A burden, but both of us figured out a way to live with it.

As cancer progressed, she had more surgeries, more radiation, chemo changes, medication changes, stressors, and grief, and so the burden of disease became heavier. She was aware of memory problems after her first surgery. Angela learned strategies to deal with these. As changes occurred with increased rapidity, that became harder. Those struggles became my burden also.

Independence and dignity. Angela was always an independent person, even as a child. Independence was lost when she needed to call me and ask for help to take a bath and wash her hair. She wrote in her journal about the embarrassment and humiliation of needing help with what would seem, to most of us, a simple task. She lost her financial independence. As the cancer progressed, Angela needed help with some of her daily activities and to manage her complex medication regimen. Angela lost the ability to drive. The list is endless. The burden of disease interfered with her ability to live her life independently. Again, these struggles became mine.

Angela loved writing her blog. She loved doing the research when she was planning a trip. She felt it was important to understand the history of the area prior to traveling. Writing her blog became harder as she struggled more with words and speech. Hence, she stopped writing and was never able to pursue publishing her blog. Writing her blog gave Angela purpose. Losing that ability due to cancer and treatment effects was devastating for both of us.

Photography stopped bringing her the joy she had found with it.

Travel became more difficult. She could not travel alone, treatments were becoming more frequent, and she was having a harder time tolerating her medications. She also had to deal with the challenges caused by the pandemic.

Reading became more of a challenge. For Angela, a literature major, reading was a lifelong joy. After her initial diagnosis and surgery, she was disappointed that she struggled to read. I thought it may have been a side effect of the pain medication, but once she was off those medications, the struggle continued. The struggle to read was from the emotional turmoil, shock. It was cancer. Eventually, she was able to resume reading, which brought her great happiness.

With the progression of memory loss from brain cancer, she struggled to remember characters and events in the beginning of the book by the time she reached the middle and end. To support her, I would read the same book so that we could talk about it, so that I could remind her of parts of the book and characters that she had forgotten. Reading was a source of pleasure for her throughout her life, a place to escape. Reading together became a solution.

Reading and writing were something she enjoyed during those quiet days. It helped fill the void of not being able to work.

Cancer took those things from her, where she found joy, satisfaction, a sense of purpose and pride in her accomplishments. Those things that she enjoyed in her quiet, private times. Those activities that Angela initially considered a blessing, a gift from cancer, were disappearing.

I am not certain I have found a blessing in cancer, as Angela did. I will never say there is a blessing in her death. However, seeing Angela find so much joy in activities she had always loved I would say was a blessing. Inspiring others from her writing and how she viewed life and living with cancer is a blessing. Keeping our relationship open and honest was a blessing. I learned from Angela about living with adversity—finding tidbits of joy and beauty despite the adversity. I hope that I am a better person for all she taught me.

In health care, the burden of disease refers to the amount of cancer, spread, location. To Angela and me, it was more personal. The Burden of Disease and Burden of Treatments led to our Burden of Loss—and they were all accelerated over the years she lived with cancer. Yet despite the curse of cancer, we found a way to keep our relationship open and honest. We sought moments of beauty in our days. We were both shattered by cancer in different ways; however, our relationship was not shattered.

When Is Enough, Enough?

'Somedays - reminders of things "can't do"'
—ANGELA AMOROSO

"Defeat - constant battle of starting over. Exhaustion.
Readjusting to new limitations."
—ANGELA AMOROSO

"Constant struggle good and bad, beauty and gloom,
deep breath vs shallow ones, weak to strong and back
again, heaviness of starting over."
—ANGELA AMOROSO

"…saying you have had enough is not failure.
It is just as brave and OK to say, 'Enough,' and to 'fight'
no more. Death is not a failure. It is not a test:
we don't succeed or fail at it."
—KRIS HALLENGA

As I have noted, during 2019 and 2020, Angela and I were both aware that treatment options were running out. Her oncologists had informed us that most people with brain metastasis don't survive as long as Angela. There was a lack of experience with which to draw recommendations. She was exhausting her treatment options, and there were no new clinical trials available. As Angela had always done, she continued to pave her own path with her disease. We talked about hospice together and, eventually, with her oncologists. The practical side of Angela occasionally took over, and she needed questions answered about options.

She was tired. The physical and emotional fatigue was affecting her. Some of her friends have told me Angela was having those thoughts about having had enough. Angela was weighing continued treatment vs quality of life. When she talked about stopping treatment, she would always come back to saying that she just wasn't ready for her life to end. If this was to be the last year of her life, how did she want to live it?

How do you determine when or if enough is enough? How do you make that decision—and if you do, will the time you have left have quality to do things you still wish, or will the symptoms of cancer interfere with quality of life? These questions cannot be answered.

Her last year, 2020, I believe, was as hard as the first year of treatment. She had two craniotomies two months apart. The first was followed by two weeks of radiation in Boston, the second was amidst COVID, and radiation seeds were used to keep her out of the hospital for ten radiation treatments. A new chemo was started in the summer with life-altering GI effects. Angela became more homebound due to the side effects despite dose reductions. Symptoms persisted despite medications recommended to minimize them. She was so tired of taking pills that she resisted a higher dose of medication to mitigate the symptoms. There was progression of cognitive and physical symptoms. It was often hard to determine if her symptoms were related more to medications or to cancer.

Throughout the seven years that Angela was in treatment, she/we always balanced treatment options with symptoms, level of disability, and quality of life. It is a narrow beam to walk without a right or wrong answer. It is about balance, but this scale has more than two sides.

It may sound like all days were bad. They weren't. We had a lot of good moments and good days mixed with more challenges.

If I want or need to find a blessing in any of her symptoms, it was that she seemed to be aware that she was needing more help. Angela let go of her fight to maintain independence and began accepting my help. I took on more of a caregiver role, while being a mother first.

Our last appointment with her oncologists was in early March 2021. She made her wishes clear—hospice at home—but she wanted to wait for that scan in April to see if the last brain radiation had worked, prior to starting hospice.

Again, this is cancer. I saw my independent, fierce daughter needing help with daily activities, in a wheelchair to get to appointments and so that I could take her for a walk. It robs people of little bits of themselves until it grabs you with both hands and finally forces you to say, "Enough."

PART IV:
LIVING WITH GRIEF

Grief

"I acknowledge that it will be harder for my mother et al.
to mourn/miss me than it is for me to live with
a terminal illness."
— ANGELA AMOROSO

"To love deeply is one of life's most profound gifts,
and the loss of a loved one is one of life's most profound
tragedies."
—JOANNA CACCIATORE, PHD

"The pain of grief is just as much a part of life as the joy
of love: it is, perhaps the price we pay for love, the cost of
commitment. To ignore this fact, or to pretend it is not so,
is to put on emotional blinkers which leave us unprepared
for the losses that will inevitably occur in our lives and
unprepared to help others with the losses in theirs."
—COLIN MURRAY PARKES MD

March 21, 2021, 8:20 pm

I had been sitting at my daughter's bedside for three days, holding her hand, talking to her, reading to her, watching her breathe. While sitting with Angela I sent out silent pleas to all those we loved, who loved us and had passed away before us, asking, begging them to be waiting for Angela. I did not want her to arrive at her next life and be alone and frightened. I gave her permission to let go, telling her I would be fine, not certain if that was true. I knew I had to be. I spent those three days saying goodbye. Angela was finally peaceful, her face relaxed. I knew she was tired. She had talked for a few years about having had enough. I knew when she took her last breath. I sat there holding my breath and watched, hoping she would take another breath, hoping she was not gone.

It had been three days since I had to utter the words in the ER that she was a DNR (Do Not Resuscitate). For three days, I knew she was going to die but could not comprehend it.

A representative from hospice had been in. Her oncologist had been in a few times to see Angela and talk with me. Angela's friends had gone to our home to move furniture and make room for the hospice bed and equipment. Her oncologist then came in and told me she could not go home. She knew that was Angela's wish and mine; however, her needs were too great to be managed at home. Angela would be going to Hospice House. We had talked about taking a tour, because she wanted to see the facility in case she went there, but we had not made it.

Covid was still ongoing, but I had received permission for three of her friends to come and see her and say goodbye. I knew that would be important for them, for Angela, and for me. I had notified my family and a few friends. People called, and I held the phone to Angela's ear so they could say their goodbyes. I had a hard time thinking of friends whom Angela would want to hear from, my mind and body numb.

I sat with two of her friends and we talked about all they had shared together. Fun stories, chuckles, wonderful memories. I do believe Angela was with us, listening, smiling, and basking in the love that surrounded her.

It was Sunday evening when Angela died. She had been admitted after a seizure in the early hours of Friday and never regained consciousness. Those three days, still a blur, still a nightmare. I don't remember thinking that she was going to die, that she would never go home. I did not think that when I left the hospital this time, I would be alone. I would go home to a house that she would never return to. I do not believe that this was denial, but my daughter's death was something I could not comprehend, contemplate, could not think about. All I could concentrate on was each breath she took.

I understand that when in shock, you continue to function, take care of things that need to be managed. But that also leaves that time a bit of a blur, without clear memories. Numbness sets in. Perhaps that is because it is too painful. Perhaps it is self-preservation.

During those three days, I held her hand, slept in the recliner, which I was able to position so I could hold her hand. Touch was so important. It was hard to let go so the nurses could provide her with care. I talked to her, read to her, and just sat with her.

I did get one slight response: the corner of her mouth turned up briefly (I believe that is what I saw) when I told her that I was going to make a cup of tea. Angela always teased me about drinking tea all day. I could hear her voice saying, "More tea Mom!"

I sat with her for a while after her last breath. Time had no meaning. Leaving Angela was painful, impossible to turn my back on her. I then went home to a house with furniture rearranged to make room for hospice, without Angela. It was then that I knew, grasped, that she would never be at home again.

Once home, I went out on the deck, looking up at the stars. I felt a bit of peace when sitting outside, as if Angela would be able to see me unobstructed.

I called her dad while I was outside but decided all other calls would have to wait. That was all that I was capable of.

Eventually I went into her room, wandered around touching her things, items she had touched. I looked at her jewelry and fingered her pieces. Seeing the ring I bought her on our first trip to Hawaii, with her Hawaiian name on it, I put it on. I have taken it off once, briefly. It felt wrong to remove it. I have been wearing Angela's ring consistently since then. I climbed into her bed and fell asleep for at least a bit. There was comfort in being in her bed, with her things, my head on the pillow her head had been on three nights earlier. Fia, one of her cats, joined me in bed.

The next day all the chores, tasks, the business associated with my daughter's death would start, but this night was for me.

March 22, 2021

It is the day after Angela died. The intense grief is deep within the numbness. I know that I have things to do, calls to make, people to notify, but taking those steps feels impossible. I just want to sit in the house, curl up on the couch, and sob, while knowing that I can't.

I wonder how I am going to survive. I make this constant plea to the universe: How will I survive this? It is not that I feel suicidal; it is a shout out to the unknown, despair. Despite losses in the past, this life that I now have is foreign to me. The level of pain and despair I am feeling is foreign.

Arrangements

The list is made, calls started. Family is notified. Angela's pillars and my pillars are notified. Word is spreading, and texts and emails start from Angela's friends and our family. For hours I sit on the porch trying to keep up, then allow myself to stop. I will get back to people when I am able. I put the call list away. It has been a few hours trying to manage all of this, and I cannot continue. Maybe later, maybe tomorrow, maybe never.

I have this sudden realization—panic—when remembering that Angela is still in the hospital. I realize that I must handle the arrangements. The funeral parlor is called, and an appointment is made for that afternoon. A friend fixes lunch for me and goes with me. I am not certain I could have managed alone.

I have asked to see Angela again. I need to see her one last time, but I have not thought about how hard it is going to be to walk away, again. My friend, who has known Angela since she was a toddler, is with me, both of us in tears and both with the same struggle of walking away. We both back up out of the room, unable to turn our backs on her, wanting that last look.

Angela and I had discussed her wishes; she had legal documents drawn up. I did not realize how helpful this would be until I was sitting at the funeral parlor. I did not have to make decisions; they were already made.

Once home, things would suddenly come to me. Angela had told me items she wanted with her when she was cremated. I wanted her in her own clothes and not a hospital gown. Going in her closet and touching her clothes, looking for what I thought she would like, felt like a violation of her space, her belongings. I couldn't find her newest favorite pants and asked Angela for help. The next day, I still could not find them but remembered that I had bought her a new pair for her birthday. It felt good to be able to give her one of her birthday gifts.

A few days later I decided to take a day off from the tasks that needed to be done. I needed a respite from grief, or myself, the phone. I am not certain what I needed, but I hoped that my friends and their glass studio would provide that, and I spent the day with them. I was not certain if I would be able to enjoy this time or if I would collapse in a puddle of tears. I knew that it would not matter. I was safe there however I spent my time.

I left some of the grief at the door with my coat and knew it would be waiting for me when I picked it up in a few hours. It was a wonderful day—a chance to rest my mind from the grief and watch artists at work. In a studio with molten glass, you must be focused. Although I am not a glass blower, I have taken a few classes and am able to lend a hand when an extra one is needed. Grief was still with me, but it was helpful to leave the couch, sobbing, and wandering around the house lost.

The need to write the obituary was on my mind. I wanted it to be personal, about Angela's life, joys, who she was as a person. I wanted it to be more than just the facts of her life. Another challenge. They seem to keep coming. It took at least a week to feel that I was satisfied with the obituary.

Something needed to be posted on her social media page. Her friends and family were already making posts, but I felt I should make a post.

These activities seemed to interfere with grieving, although it felt that they needed to be done.

I found during this time that mornings were spent in tears on the couch. Afternoons I was a bit better and able to complete at least one task or a few phone calls. Nights were, again, a loss.

Tears

Tears, they were constant. From gentle crying to being curled in a fetal position on the couch or in bed sobbing, there was no stopping them. I knew that I had to let them flow. I tried to just be with tears, but there was an internal battle to stop them.

If I can stop crying, will I feel better? I tried, and the answer was no. I felt worse. Intense crying leaves me exhausted, which then allowed me to have an hour of sleep. I learned to accept the tears, the sobbing. They allowed me a brief respite from the grief in sleeping.

In grief, I lost all concept of time. When I think back, I recognize that, after months, tears were becoming less intense at times. I was curled up on the couch sobbing less, but every day there were tears.

I would be doing a task in the house, thinking about what I was doing, and would find myself crying. I spoke to a family member who had also experienced this type of grief many years ago, and he told me that he had the same experience. We can be doing anything and tears just flow. As with everything, more acceptance.

Then something new. At least six months after Angela died, I found myself waking in the early morning, and I was crying. My face would be wet, the pillow damp, and tears flowing. I must have been dreaming, but don't remember a dream. I wonder if it was a good dream, a good memory, reliving something joyful—or some of the trauma. I choose to believe that it was a good memory, a joyful dream, and the tears were a longing for those times.

Now, it is over a year since Angela has died and I still cry, no longer daily.

Sleep

When Angela was first diagnosed, I went weeks with only a few hours of sleep at a time. Then up and wandering about the house. This became a regular pattern. Rarely was I able to get back to sleep later. This pattern waxed and waned over the seven years.

After Angela died, I slept little. A few hours, possibly, were all I could manage. Rather than just lying in bed, I would get up and find something to do or just stare out the windows. If the weather was nice enough, I would sit outside and look at the stars. I have always liked the quiet of nighttime and early mornings. When in Maine, I can watch the sunrise. I am learning to accept that this is grief, accepting that my body is talking to me. I have learned to find peace in these early hours.

I became comfortable with naps when needed, paid attention to my eating habits, made certain to be outside daily and try to take a walk. I have never cared about alcohol but found that it made my sleep worse and was triggering worsening nightmares. After trial and error, my best treatment was a cup of mint tea, sitting on the deck, looking at the stars and moon, talking to Angela prior to bed.

One day, I was sitting in Angela's room and saw a stone that I had given to her that was wrapped with a piece of weaving grass. There was no beginning or end visible to the grass; it was about continuity. I held the stone in my hand, and it felt comfortable, comforting. I took it with me and that night held onto it while falling asleep. I had a tangible item of Angela's with me to fall asleep, and it was helpful. I still sleep with that stone in my hand. I have had nights when I wake after a few hours and my fingers are numb from grasping the stone so tightly. Other nights it is under my pillow or in the bed with me.

Over many months, sleep started to improve. During the first year (plus some months) after Angela died, I would not sleep the week prior to the twenty-first of each month. I would not be thinking of the date, but then I would still find myself up walking around during the night. I realized that there was an internal calendar affecting my sleep. Another aspect of grief that I needed to accept.

Memories

After Angela died, all memories caused tears, occurring simultaneously. It was nine months until those memories were not accompanied with immediate tears. Eventually I found that I had a few moments to embrace the good memory, enjoy the happiness before tears occurred. It was a gift. I was able to start to feel less fearful of my memories. I realized that I was, hopefully, starting to reach a place where good memories brought moments of comfort, although that did not change the longing, missing Angela.

Attempted Respite

About a week after Angela died, I decided to go to Maine for a few days. The beach was calling, salty air, the sound of waves, and the home we built and loved. Angela's presence is everywhere in Maine. I didn't know how long I would stay, but I had decided to turn off all technology. I needed relief from the tasks associated with grieving. I needed to be present with Angela and grief, not distracted from the pressures of calls, texts, and emails.

I pulled my car in the garage, but that felt wrong. Angela used the garage.

I walked in the door, unpacked, opened blinds, looked around the house, and ended up on the couch sobbing. I allowed the tears to flow, and I fell asleep crying. Once awake, I could not get myself under control. Anxiety hit, my mind raced, and I paced, thinking that I needed to go home and put the house up for sale. I thought, *It is not the place of respite, peace, comfort that I was expecting. Why?*

I am suddenly hit with the answer. Usually Angela arrived first, when she was able to drive, and had the house open. She would put away the food that I brought with me while I unloaded anything else. Now, Angela was not there to greet me. Oskar was not there to greet me. I walked into an empty home. Angela would never be there to greet me. Her car would never be in the garage.

Other times, when Angela was well enough and I would come up by myself, I would text her to let her know that I had arrived. Now, I could not text her.

Everything was different. All our routines were gone, both at home and in Maine. I was no longer checking on her, staying nearby when she bathed, worrying about a fall or seizure, helping her with medications, shaving her head, answering questions about dates, schedules, appointments, and all the other things I helped her with daily. Walking into the house in Maine, without her with me or there in advance, hit me differently than the loss of the routines at home.

At a singular level I had known how much help I provided for Angela every day, but I also had not known this on a wider scale. The caregiving role had expanded gradually over years, but walking into Maine, it hit me with full force. There was a physical response to the intensity of grief, the loss.

Yet even while my initial thought was to leave and sell the house, I also knew that doing that would be as heartbreaking as being there. I had to learn how to live without Angela's physical presence.

Grief Brain

I felt lost every day. As I have noted, over the last few years, as Angela developed more cancer-related complications and needs, my caregiver role increased. New tasks and responsibilities were added to my daily routine. Initially, after she developed brain cancer, the changes were gradual, not as significant, and we both had time to adjust. But during the last few years, her care needs progressed quickly. While we had both disliked the constant adjusting to a "new normal" in the earlier years, now there was no time to adjust.

From the moment I got home from the hospital after Angela died, all those routines and responsibilities were gone. I found that all the activities I had done for Angela every day had been blended with those I did for myself. I now had all this extra time that I had previously spent caring for Angela—and she was not there. I had not realized how much time I spent helping her daily.

When I lost all my caregiving for Angela, I found that my own self-care and routines were lost too. For years, I would make a pot of tea each morning. Now I still did that, but often I neglected to put the leaves in the pot. It was only water. I would find my toothbrush by the sink with the toothpaste on it. I had forgotten to finish brushing my teeth. I could not remember if I had changed clothes, my last shower. Simple routines that I have done without thought were lost.

I could not remember if I had fed the cats, and so I believe they often got an extra meal. Of course, they were always looking for food, so they would not tell me!

I have since heard about "grief brain," and I believe that was me. If I was not on the couch crying, I would walk around the house—lost.

Fill My Day

I was overwhelmed with the lack of control I had over any area of my life after Angela died. There was never control over cancer or the direction it was taking. We tried to find control by monitoring and addressing side effects to treatments, keeping a journal of appointments, eating healthy much of the time. Angela continued with yoga whenever she was allowed, and I continued to exercise.

In grief, there is no control. I was drowning. I had no appetite, and the food did not taste good; sleep was poor; I struggled to leave the house to take a walk. All the strategies that I had been using for seven years to help with stress, anxiety, worry, and grief no longer worked. I was living in this swirling storm of grief, and all I could do was sit and stare, wander the house, spend time in Angela's room with her things, and cry and cry and cry.

I had to find something that I could control, since it wasn't emotions.

I started by getting out her hankies. I couldn't continue to go through boxes of tissues. I knew if I ran out, it would mean a trip to the store, being in public to purchase more, which I did not think I could handle. Angela had started using hankies—cloth napkins that were soft from frequent washing and use when she was on chemo. I pulled out her cloth hankies and started using them.

I started cleaning out my closets. I found a box of letters from my grandparents and sat on my bed rereading them. I was reminded of my grandfather's sense of humor and smiled at some of his writing. I was not ready to manage any of Angela's things, but I could manage mine.

Some days I did nothing but sit, stare, and cry, but other days I was able to manage a chore, which I found felt good. It felt that for the hour or two that I would work on something, it was a respite from grief; it was something to occupy my mind, however briefly.

Life felt foreign, unrecognizable. It felt that I did not recognize this home that I had lived in for over twenty years. I turned to books and movies that I had read or seen. There was comfort in the familiar. I also chose some of Angela's favorite books and watched some of her favorite movies. Again, knowing the story was helpful since my concentration was poor. There was also solace, a feeling of being close to her when watching and reading what she enjoyed.

Mingled with reading Angela's books was reading about grief and memoirs people had written about living with cancer or grief. I was able to see myself in those books, which helped me to feel less alone and understand that my experiences were often like others'.

Learning About Grief

Grief and isolation were my constant companions. I felt safe when I was isolated. No need to make small talk. No need to wonder if the person I was talking to was uncomfortable and might not know what to say. No need to worry about the tears that would suddenly flow.

I began to wonder if this was normal. It is what I needed, so I allowed myself to isolate. Still, over a year later, often I found myself still isolating, although less often. I wondered, *Do I need to force myself out? Should I just go out and get the mail and not first check to make certain there are no neighbors outside?* If there were, I would walk away from the window and check again later. I took a different street to the beach, so I wouldn't see any neighbors. It was starting to feel pathological. I talked to my counselor and was reassured that I was not "crazy"—my word, not his. How long will this last and will I just wake up and feel that I want to see someone, or do I need to push myself? Going to the grocery store was a chore, the need to be pleasant and polite to the person at the register or bagging my groceries. I did my best to have dark glasses on when out, so I didn't need to make eye contact. I walked along the beach with a hat pulled down and dark glasses on. I didn't want to be recognized; I didn't want to be seen.

To try to gain a better understanding of grief, I started reading books about grief and loss. This may seem odd when in the deepest, darkest point of grief, that I would reach for books about grief. I found them comforting. It gave me the knowledge that I was looking for.

In health care, there are protocols for everything. I kept looking for protocols for grief. How long would the tears last, the despondency, the isolation? There are no protocols, no timelines. There is no guidance that if I do something, the pain will lessen. This was hard to accept, but I have gradually learned that there is no schedule. I have also learned that when I have an activity on my calendar, I need to allow time for myself in the days following to feel that I am in my pre-event place. There may be days or weeks when I am isolated again. I do recognize that, with time, those periods do not last as long as they did in the months after Angela died, but they are still there. I have learned to respect them. I have learned to respect that grief may be in control and I must be present with it. Reading also reassured me that isolation was normal. If it is what I need, then I allow myself to isolate.

I have found, though, that it doesn't just disappear. I kept waiting, thinking I would wake one day and feel like I was better with that stage, for now. That has never happened. I found that it was gradual, a subtle lessening. I found that I might sit on the deck in Maine and if a neighbor waved, I would acknowledge them but would not get up and initiate conversation. This was a change from sitting in the backyard where I would not be seen. I eventually stopped checking for neighbors outside before getting the mail.

I am learning to accept those small changes and respect my needs. After so many years of placing Angela's needs above mine, first as a parent then with the development of cancer as Angela's caregiver, it is a hard transition to place my needs first. Having worked my professional life as a caregiver, I suspect that has always been my nature. It is a very foreign feeling, considering my needs.

As I am learning, if I don't make self-care a priority, I am not sure I can recover—although I have no idea what "recovery" will look like, or if that can occur or is the correct word. I have learned that grief will always be with me, but it will become less brutal, less intense.

Journaling

I started journaling regularly after Angela died. I wrote about my feelings, fears, good memories, and those that I struggled with. I wrote about grief. Over weeks I started to journal a description of my grief. It was slowly taking shape into a tangible being. It needed to be more than a feeling or an emotion. Giving grief structure and form was important to me. Eventually I realized I was describing an octopus, its tentacles wrapped around me. I could not see, breathe, or scream for help. I could not move, my arms pinned to my sides. The tentacles were wrapped tighter. It was a physical pain as much as an emotional pain. Although I knew I could not fight it, at times I tried—which made everything worse. I learned I needed to let go of my desire to fight; leaning into grief and collapsing in sobs would lessen the pain. I could not run from it or bury it deep inside me. Grief was with me.

I continue to write regularly. I have found it helpful in processing grief. Often, it may be a letter to Angela. I talk to her, although at times, writing a letter helps me to feel closer to her. I hold onto the thought that she is reading over my shoulder.

Counseling: Grief and Trauma

Angela encouraged me to get counseling a few years after her diagnosis with metastasis. I knew I needed a counselor—someone outside my support system to help me with the emotions, fear, anger, and anxiety that I had developed but struggled to admit to myself. I was aware that I needed someone who could bring objectivity and honesty when my fears were spiraling out of control. My counselor talked with me about grief and trauma during those early years. I did not think of it as grief; I saw it as fear and sadness. I fought the word *grief*. I would not accept it. If I was grieving, it was a disservice to Angela. It felt that to acknowledge my grief and trauma minimized Angela's. After all, she was the one with cancer. With each surgery, new treatment, scan result showing disease progression, each conversation about prognosis, each palliative care visit, each discussion of hospice, witnessing disease progression, new symptoms, incorporating each new medication into an already complicated regimen, I was grieving. Even so, none of those seven years of grieving compared or prepared me for the grief of Angela's death.

After Angela's death, I attended a parents' retreat and spoke with a bereavement counselor there. After hearing both Angela's and my stories, along with my symptoms, she talked with me about trauma.

I finally let it sink in: trauma and grief were the cause of the multitude of symptoms I was having, and denial of that would leave me stuck in this cycle. It was not how I wanted to live. It wasn't living, and living was important to Angela and to me. I knew I would need to return to the world, leave the safety of my porch, and—sometime—take a step toward building a life without Angela.

I had the same feeling about the word *trauma*. I fought with my counselor on that word. I was aware of and could remember every traumatic event over the seven years and refused to accept it. It took sessions with my general counselor, a bereavement counselor, nightmares, panic attacks, and flashbacks before I would finally accept that trauma and grief, for me, were traveling together. With help, I accepted that—which was the first step in treatment.

I was grateful that Angela had encouraged me to seek counseling during her illness. It was helpful to be established with a counselor I knew and trusted, who knew my story when Angela died. When I was deep in grief, I would not have been able to seek a counselor.

Panic Attacks

I have always loved sitting on my back porch. It is a place where Angela and I would sit, talking or just enjoying companionable silence. It had been a place of peace and relaxation. After Angela died, that peace was broken. I would go outside to sit and breathe, but each time, as I relaxed, a panic attack would hit me. I had never had panic attacks. Initially I did not recognize it as one. I kept going out to sit, breathe, and relax and it would occur again. I found that all efforts at relaxation would trigger a panic attack. I did not know how I could live this way. I did not want to give up my place of peace. With the help of my counselor, I learned how to manage panic attacks by recognizing when the symptoms were starting and then taking steps to stop them.

Months later, I was able to sit and enjoy the sounds of the birds, the quiet. I was trying to learn to just sit and be present, no phone, no book, no electronics. There was only me, my memories, and my tears.

Nightmares

Nightmares started a few months after Angela's death. I had started getting interrupted sleep. I would wake up in the early morning hours with fear, panic, heart racing. I never remembered Angela in the nightmare. I was unable to calm myself down. Instead, I would get up, check all the doors, make certain blinds were closed, turn on every light in the house, and then pace, telling myself that it was not real. I would take multiple deep breaths to slow down my heart rate, but I was never able to get back to sleep. I didn't even try; the fear had taken over. My counselor told me the nightmares were related to grief and trauma. I could acknowledge the grief and started to acknowledge trauma. With trauma counseling, the nightmares started to occur less often, but for those first few years, they never resolved.

Flashbacks

I have had two flashbacks since Angela died. The first one was of a traumatic event with Angela. It was as real as the first time the event occurred. Unlike a memory, I felt like I was standing in the exact spot as when the incident had first occurred. In the flashback, everyone in the room was clear, faces sharp, in the same places as they were the night it occurred. I was frozen in place. I was left in a panic, thinking that I was developing some form of psychosis. But when I spoke to my counselor the next day, I was told that it was a flashback, which can occur with grief and trauma. This was not psychosis. Since then, I have done the work with counseling and trauma therapy.

There was one further flashback, but it was a wonderful, happy one. In the flashback, I was on the beach with Angela, and she was in the sand looking for sea glass and stones, in her favorite spot. I just held by breath, watched, and did not allow myself to move. I did not want it to end, although she was so close I felt if I reached out, I could touch her and hug her.

Auditory Hallucinations

Auditory hallucinations occurred in the weeks after Angela died. These were not frightening. I found comfort hearing Angela's voice and Oskar's bark. Each time it occurred; I would look for her. Once, I was making calls to let people know she had passed away. There was a name on my list, and I was not certain she would want me to call that person. I sat with my phone trying to decide what to do. I heard Angela in the chair next to me say, "Don't do it mom. Don't call him." I looked at the chair and she was not there. I sat for a while longer and picked up my phone. Again, I heard her tell me not to call him. Eventually, I did call, and Angela was right. He said hurtful things to me, so I said goodbye and blocked his number. After the call, I told Angela that I would listen to her from now on! The auditory hallucinations lasted for a few months. I miss the comfort of hearing her talk to me and Oskar's bark coming from her room.

Dreams

As the days, weeks, and months pass, I find that I am grieving for more than the loss of her physical presence. I grieve for the unfulfilled dreams; I grieve for the things she wanted to do in her life that were not accomplished. I grieve for my dreams for Angela and myself, the future I saw for myself with Angela present, times we would spend together, a call or text, sharing a meal, events, celebrations. We knew Angela had terminal cancer, and we had talked about me outliving her. Despite this knowledge and these conversations, I never thought of what my life would be like without her. It was beyond my comprehension. I don't believe this was denial; it was a desire to enjoy and live in the present.

Gifts For Loved Ones

Angela had told me about items that she wanted gifted to family and friends.

When Angela turned twenty-one, I gave her a charm bracelet for her birthday. It contained charms that I had been collecting from our trips and other charms as a memory of important times in her life. During her illness, we had been talking about her jewelry and what she wanted to do with it. She had decided that she wanted to give the charms to her female cousins on a necklace. A few weeks prior to her death, she was working on this project, trying to decide who would receive each charm. Sitting on the table was the list of charms and who she wanted to have them. There were a few that she was stuck on but had ideas.

I decided to finish this project for her. I couldn't deal with any of her belongings but felt that I could manage this.

I sat with her list of charms and list of cousins, and then I asked Angela for guidance on the few that she was uncertain of. I believe that she guided me in making the choices. Then I took the bracelet to the jewelry store to have the charms removed, and I purchased chains for each one. Each cousin received a note from me about the meaning of the charm bracelet and why Angela had chosen that charm for them. I could only handle writing one or two notes a day, but eventually I finished and mailed them off.

Standing at the postal center while they made the arrangements for shipping felt both heartbreaking and good. I knew how much her cousins would appreciate this gift from Angela, although it was difficult to let them go.

Now, when I see her cousins, they are often wearing the necklace, which makes me smile.

For her male cousins, she had other ideas. One received one of her heart-shaped stones, which is a treasured possession to him. He brought it to Angela's Life Celebration to share and talk about Angela. Our other family of boys received a wooden plane that had been at her grandmother's house. Her intention was always to refinish it. I sent it as it was, showing that it had been a well-loved toy.

Eventually, I will distribute the rest of her jewelry, but I am not ready to do that. Angela had told me who she wanted to have each piece.

Cancer Bed

After Angela completed her first year of treatment, she decided to get a new bed. She referred to her bed as the "cancer bed." For that year she felt that she had lived in her bed and needed to get rid of it—not just the mattress, but the headboard and frame also.

A friend wanted the headboard, but Angela refused to give it to her. She knew the bed did not give her cancer; however, did not want anyone she knew to have it. A junk truck was called, and it was removed. I did let them know that there was nothing wrong with it if they or someone they knew would like it.

The summer after Angela died, I kept looking at my pocketbook. Some of the features were stretched out from carrying things to her appointments. I started to view my pocketbook and the messenger bag I used for Boston trips as "cancer bags." I understood how Angela felt about her bed. It was time to get a new bag and wallet.

As I was taking things out of my bag to put in the new one, I came across items of Angela's. There was the bottle of three days of pills I carried, just in case. One of her lip glosses, Medicare card, extra license, medication list, and other items. Everything I pulled out that was Angela's was like a kick in the gut. I had to struggle to catch my breath. Tears flowed. I would sit and hold the item in my hand and think about it, wondering what I should do with it.

There are items that I have not been able to let go of. The bottle of pills that I carried with me is still sitting on my dresser. The jar containing all the partially used lip gloss that I found on her coffee table is still on my windowsill. Angela's sunglasses are still in the bowl on the credenza, with an extra pair in the car pocket where she kept them. Although her phone is locked, I have not been able to disconnect her number. Her wheelchair sits in the corner of the dining room. Oskar's treat jar is still in her room along with his basket of toys. I found a "barf" bag in the glove box that we had for possible problems on the ride home after a chemo treatment. As with all of these and other items, I sit and look at them and decide if I am ready to let them go. Gradually I am letting them go as they lose their pull, their hold on me. When ready, I have developed a ritual that allows me to peacefully move them to their next life—to dispose of these and other items, a way to say goodbye.

Recurrent Grief

I never realized how many sounds my house made: the refrigerator cycling, a creak or groan, the wind, noises from outside, the cats moving about. After Angela died, each sound made me jump up and start looking for her. Had she fallen, was she struggling, did she need help? There was a delay in my thoughts and then I would remember: Angela had died. Each time it was as if she had just died again. It was many months until I could stay where I was and remind myself that the noises were the house and not Angela. All these benign noises, which my brain had filtered out while she was alive, were now constant reminders of Angela's death. Each sound triggered an initial jolt of fear, then grief. My home had become noisy—making grief more present and robbing me of any moment of peace that I had found. I wanted silence but could not find it.

Angela loved to walk along the beach collecting shells, sea glass, driftwood, and heart-shaped stones. When she was no longer able to walk the beach, I would go out briefly, collecting whatever I could find for her. Angela was always sitting at the table waiting for me when I would return. After her death, I would come home and look to my left, and she was not there. I started reminding myself that she would not be waiting for me at the table when I got home, which did not stop the shock of not seeing her there. Another reminder, another smack of grief. I considered not taking walks, although being on the beach was peaceful. I continued to walk and would come home and put my findings on the table as I did before. Then I would sit down and look at the collection, believing she was looking with me.

Tasks of Death

Financial business. Bills were coming in, and I was not certain how to handle anything. A call to her attorney allowed me to put off the financial piece. It was almost six months until I was ready to start the process with probate. In the interim, there were medical bills, collection agencies, calls, mailings, and insurance issues. Every bill, every call was another shard of glass piercing my heart. Open accounts went to collections. I sent letters to agencies with a copy of her death certificate. This forced me to open the envelope with her death certificate that had been sitting on my desk. I had been unable to open it or look at it. The collection agencies advised that the accounts would stay open until probate was settled. As I have explained, Angela knew that I was willing to pay her medical bills and was adamant that she did not want me to. She felt that I had cared for her and provided her with a home. That was enough. She had elicited a promise from me, which I respected. I quit trying to manage the bills and turned everything over to Angela's attorney.

The attorney recommended that I notify the credit agencies so that her Social Security number would be locked to prevent identity theft. More letters and copies of her death certificate. I also was able to obtain her credit report so that I could verify the list of creditors, make certain it was accurate, and include it as needed with probate.

Initially, I was also overwhelmed by cards, letters, and calls. After a few days, I gave myself permission to open them when I felt able, and if I had read enough, then I stopped. The same with calls and texts. I learned to allow them to go to voice mail. This was a hard lesson for me; it felt that I was being rude, but it was necessary.

So many people wrote letters full of wonderful memories, kindness, and generosity that I would just sit and weep. I understand that this is often referred to as a small act of kindness. There was nothing small to me, the person receiving these notes. This sharing was a source of comfort, sadness, and longing. Every story became a treasured memory.

I eventually was able to respond to each card and letter. It was not an everyday project. When I felt up to it, I would sit at the table and write a few notes in return. Many of those days, cardinals would come and go from the bushes in front of the window and watch, keeping me company. If I was feeling that I could not write another note and the cardinal had left, I took that as a message from Angela that it was time to stop and take care of myself.

Belongings

In the first month after Angela died, I distributed specific items to those whom she had named as receivers. Since then, her belongings have trickled out. I did not feel pressure to clear her room. Since she was living with me, there was no need, no initial pressure to clear things, no home to sell or apartment to empty. Instead, when I see an item she bought when traveling with a friend, or one that someone gave to her, I give it to them. I believe that is what Angela would have wanted. I believe that she is directing me, and I would like items that have shared meaning with someone special in her life to be with them.

As I would find items to give away, I collected them on my dining room table. When I felt ready to let them go, I did. Every time I gave something away, people were very grateful. It reminded me that while I struggle to let go of her things, we are all grieving. To me, these are Angela's belongings. To her friends, these items are tangible reminders of time spent together, places they traveled.

After giving the items away, I found myself rearranging her closet and bookcases. The empty spot was a visual reminder of my loss.

Travel

About six months after Angela died, I decided I was going to take the trip to Acadia that we had planned many times, but cancer had different plans for us. It was a beautiful few days of hiking, watching the sunrises, and sitting on a beach. On September 21, six months after Angela died, the B & B where I was staying had pancakes for breakfast. Angela loved pancakes. I enjoyed them in her honor and for her.

I was up early that morning and headed to the beach. I wanted to watch the sunrise, and it was beautiful. I thought about how much Angela would have loved the hikes that I did. I believe that she would have had her camera. I chose not to take it with me and did not take a single photo. I did not want anything between me and the views. I had to see everything for Angela and for me, although I know she was always with me, the angel on my shoulder.

Pets

Angela's cat Fia became very sick about ten months after Angela died. A vet trip determined that she had renal failure related to both age and her long history of an overactive thyroid. The vet prescribed a medication to see if it would help, but it was not successful. She had to be euthanized in March. It was like watching Angela go downhill again from the year before.

At the vet, the tech came in wearing a scrub top with sloths on it. Angela loved sloths, and I mentioned it to the tech, who said she also loved sloths and had spent time in Costa Rica at a habitat caring for them. Angela loved Costa Rica and had traveled there multiple times. The tech looked at me and said that she believed in messages. I do also. I felt Angela's hand on my shoulder as I stood patting Fia as she died, and I knew she was with me. The vet tech, with her sloth scrubs, confirmed that.

Once home, I sobbed for days. It felt like too much grief. In just over a year, we lost Oskar, then Angela, and now Fia. I had the same feeling again: *How will I survive this?* I was drowning in a pool of grief. Finn, Angela's other cat, and Fia had been together since they were kittens, sixteen years. Finn was grieving also. She would no longer lay on the ottoman where they always snuggled and napped together. She started with this mournful meow and howl. Like me, she would wander the house looking for her sister, as I did when looking for Angela. Like me, nothing comforted her.

Nine months later, Finn, Angela's last cat, passed away from cancer. I was shattered again. Back in that black abyss, black pool drowning in grief. In almost two years my daughter and her three pets that were our family, passed away.

Medium

After Angela died, I developed a fear that she was suffering. I knew that she had been peaceful when she passed away, so this fear seemed irrational, but it consumed me for many months.

On one of my walks, in tears as I found a lot of sea glass, I started thinking of each piece of glass as Angela's tears. This increased the sadness of a once enjoyable activity. This fear that the glass was Angela's tears was part of my motivation to see a medium. It contributed to my fear that she was still suffering.

Fortunately, my visit to the medium provided me with the reassurance I needed. She shared many messages from Angela, although most important was that she was not suffering. She also passed a message from Angela that everyone I had asked to be with her when she arrived was there. She was not alone.

After seeing the medium and knowing that Angela was not suffering, I was able to think of my walks, sea glass, shells, and heart-shaped stones differently. Finding Angela's favorite items on the beach were not her tears; it was Angela sending me love, a hug, a kiss. When I see the sun glint on a piece of glass, I am reminded of the glint—the light—in Angela's eyes when she smiled. It is Angela's light still with me.

With each piece of glass that I find, I imagine that, eventually, the shards of glass that fill my heart will start to lose their sharp edges. I am not certain they will all develop smooth edges, but I accept that.

There are often still tears when walking. I still look to the left when I walk through the door. It was over six months, at least, until the shock that Angela was not sitting, waiting for me, had started to dissipate.

I returned to the medium a few months later. Through the medium, Angela told me where her journals were. I had found them but had not looked at them. I felt that it was a violation of her personal space and private thoughts. I had no intention of ever reading them. However, I was told that she wanted me to read them. Still, it was months before I could open the box they were in, and months to be able to read through them. I have now included many of her thoughts and poems in this book. I am thankful that she gave me permission to read them.

The medium asked me if I was writing a book. I told her that I was trying, and she gave me a message from Angela: she wanted me to know that I was rambling! I agreed that I needed to sharpen my focus, and it was nice to hear that she was reading over my shoulder.

How Are You?

"…words often fail during tragedy…"
—ROB DELANEY

Angela and I both received this question frequently over the years. It has continued since her death.

I found that it always left me questioning how to answer. There were many times when I really was "good" or "fine." Other times not so. I wondered if the person asking really wanted the true answer or was it just that automatic question that was asked when seeing someone. More importantly, did I really want to talk about how I was?

If I was struggling, I had to decide if I wanted to give a true answer or just throw out "fine."

After Angela died, the answer was usually "managing" or "functioning." Occasionally, after asking me, the person would look at me and say, "That was a stupid question." I appreciated that. It took the pressure off me to figure it out and decide how to respond.

Often, even now, I want to respond with a bunch of swear words. Angela always said that I learned to swear when she got cancer.

Truthfully, I always knew how to swear, but in trying to set a good example when she was young, I avoided it. She learned anyway. I never found a strategy that would stop her swearing. Swearing seemed to come in handy after cancer and her death. There were times when no other words were suitable.

Fine is a nebulous word. Since Angela's death, "fine" meant that I may have gotten some sleep, fixed a meal and ate some of it, took a shower, put on clean clothes, remembered to brush my teeth. Those everyday activities that I never thought about became a struggle. Even remembering if I had done them was a struggle. At one point I thought that I should take a picture of myself each day so I could look back and see when the last time was I had put on clean clothes.

It is hard to say how you are. The bigger question for me was *Who am I?* I am aware that I am not the same person I was before Angela got cancer, while she was in treatment, and now since her death. The entire experience has changed me. Figuring out who I am is the task ahead of me.

I will try to remember not to ask "How are you?" in the future when seeing someone with a loss. Instead, I am simply going to say that I have been thinking of them.

Invisible

"To care is to be present."
—DR. RANJANA SRIVASTAVA

Angela learned quicker than I did that not everyone could deal with her illness, could travel with her through the process. It is often referred to as a journey, but I do not like that word. I think of a journey as a joyful time. Although we had joy in our lives, the path was a blend of joy and heartache, happiness and fear. I remembered hearing from others with a serious illness about how people disappeared from their lives. Angela said that when this occurred, it made her feel invisible. She would refer to herself as the "invisible cancer girl." While some people disappeared, others only saw her as someone with cancer. They could not see the whole person, the person she became living with cancer. She learned to accept this disappearance and to let go of the anger and hurt. I continued to carry that anger, but in the months since her death, I have started to let it go.

Someone whom she met after her diagnosis wrote, honestly, about being nervous about meeting Angela—to be so close to someone with a terminal diagnosis. He acknowledged that he thought it was natural to want to distance yourself from death. On meeting Angela, those fears were resolved. He found her happy and brutally honest, making jokes. They remained friends. What he said was very true. I appreciated his honesty and his willingness to share his fears with others. Both of their lives were enriched by their friendship.

I met with a different friend of Angela's for coffee one morning after she passed away. He told me that he often did not know what to say to her when they were together, so he listened. I let him know that he provided Angela with what she needed: someone to be present and listen to her. As Dr. Ranjana Srivastava, an Australian oncologist, has written, "When we stop to listen, people become visible to us in all their complexity" (p. 81). It is easy to forget the power of listening.

I was surprised that people also disappeared from my life. Calls, texts, and emails were not returned. I was not prepared for that loss; I was not the one with cancer. Having a child with cancer is not contagious, which is what I felt. Some people later told me that maintaining our connection was too hard, or it made them too sad. I had expected hard times to be when people would rally around us, not walk away. Unfortunately, those relationships are forever altered or still absent from my life. Again, I feel that I have let go of my anger, accepting what Angela learned: not everyone will be able to walk this path with you.

I am left, for now, with a bit of sadness for those who disappeared. The sadness is knowing all they lost in not being present, in not being a part of her life or in not allowing her to continue to be a part of their lives—in sharing her experiences, in learning her story. They lost her presence and the richness of shared lives.

I am not certain if Angela recognized that she was not invisible. She was very present in the lives of those who were at her side. It was those who disappeared—they were the ones who were invisible.

Advice

**"...it doesn't matter what you say because no words are
going to help. And that's OK."**
—ROB DELANEY

I had originally written this section a few months after Angela died.
It was a long rant full of pain, grief, and anger. It contained what I
needed to say at the time. Since then, I have learned to breathe again.
Time has allowed me to obtain perspective, and I began to soften
my writing. Then I attended a bereavement group, and others who
had lost loved ones shared some of the hurtful things other people—
well-intentioned or not—had said to them. They encouraged me to
revise the piece to include some thoughts and recommendations for
readers who want to reach out to someone who has experienced a
loss. As a result, I am sharing my perspective, and I understand that
others who are grieving may not feel as I do.

I will start by admitting that I now know that I have not always said
the right thing to someone who has lost a loved one. It is not that I am
uncomfortable with grief, but I struggled to say something thoughtful.
Looking back, I am not certain if things were said when my parents
and grandparents died that I also found difficult to hear, or if then I
was in a place to just ignore what I didn't want to hear.

I do understand that it is hard to know what to say to a mother who has had her daughter pass away. Grief is hard for everyone, and the "right" words are often not known. Perhaps there are no "right" words. Here is what I would like to share today.

If I seemed short when you asked what you could do for me, I am sorry. I appreciated the offers of help, but I could not figure out what I needed. A better option for readers may be just to say you are dropping off a meal or a bag of groceries and leaving it at the door. I often did not want visitors.

Be honest! In place of cliches, I would prefer to hear that you don't know what to say and that you are sorry. As the bereaved mom, I am not certain that there was anything that could have been said that would soften my grief.

If I see you and you want to give me a hug, please ask. There were times when I did not want to be touched. It caused a physical response and was painful, both physically and emotionally.

Tell me that you are thinking of me and Angela.

Tell me you loved my daughter.

Tell me a good memory or funny story. I wrote down the ones people shared with me and looked at them on difficult days to remind me of happy times. I bought myself a "happy journal" so that I could keep all the wonderful stories in a single place.

Tell me what you learned from Angela, and how you live your life differently because of what you learned.

Tell me how Angela changed your life for the better. That lets me know that she lives on in the people who were an important part of her life and in those who only knew her from her blog. It is a gift to me knowing that she will not be forgotten.

If you called and I did not get back to you for a few days or a week, it is because I could only handle a few calls a day. About a week or more after Angela died, I thought I should check texts, emails, and messages to make certain I had seen them all and responded. There were a few that I had no memory of seeing, but they showed that I had replied. I know that I was not functioning at even 50 percent during those first few weeks or months. Be patient with the bereaved mother. I was trying to call people, respond to messages, and handle the "business" side of death.

Sending cards is fine. If you don't know what to say, or we don't know each other, a card is better than an awkward phone call or a visit. You can always call a few months later with the hope that I am in a better place to answer your call. I did try to respond to every card and note, although it took a while. A card, a note, sharing a story with me allows me to respond when I am ready, and for those who don't know what to say, with a card you don't have to figure that out. I received so many cards with wonderful memories of Angela, and I treasured them. Often, I would pull out one and reread it. I found them comforting.

Remember, you do not need to say anything profound that will be hung in calligraphy on the wall.

Take time to think before you speak. Just because you are thinking about it, does not mean that you should say it! Example: "I don't know how you recover from this." Neither do I!

Please don't tell me Angela is in a better place. I am not certain what that means. Recently, a grieving mom I was talking with said she had the answer for that statement: "Which of your children would you want to be in that better place?" What place is better than here with people she loved who loved her?

I don't want to hear that it was her time to be with God and he called her home. I have never blamed or been angry at any god for Angela's cancer, and I feel the same about her death.

I don't want to hear her work in this life is done. She was only forty-one!

Please don't tell me that her pain and suffering is over. That reminds me of the hard times, and I am struggling not to be focused on those times.

Do not call three, four, or more times a week to check on me. Nothing has changed, and it places a burden on me to respond. There were many days, initially most, when I spent most of the day curled on the couch crying. A call that I must answer or return later is not helpful. If you need to be in touch almost daily, send a text to let me know that you are thinking of me—a brief message that I do not need to respond to. A text allows me to respond quickly without, at times, long conversations that I am not up for. A friend would often send a heart emoji or a picture from a walk she was taking. It was a way to let me know she was thinking of me; it was not intrusive and did not require a response. She started this when Angela was receiving treatment, and I found it helpful. Those texts would always bring a smile.

However, four to five texts daily is too much. It took me a few weeks to figure out that I did not need to respond to each text, and then I would answer once a day or every few days. It took me awhile to give myself permission not to be 100 percent available. I eventually gave myself permission to turn off my phone for a day or more. I had to remind myself that I needed to take care of myself—and, at times, that meant being alone with grief. I know that people care and that they were also grieving, which is why it was hard for me not to be available, but it was also important for me.

If you are one of the people who disappeared from her life when she got cancer, I don't want to hear about how hard it was for you and how you didn't know what to say, so you said nothing. You are one of the invisible people that made her feel invisible. Your guilt and regret are yours, and I am not able to absolve you from it. Forgiveness must come from within. I accept that Angela's cancer was hard, possibly harder when you are in your thirties and forties, just beginning your life. Angela was just beginning her life also. Just managing each day is difficult enough. To those of you who reached out to Angela, reconnected, and were honest with her, thank you. Angela and I both appreciated and understood how difficult that was for you

Please don't tell me that Angela's scars were gruesome, and you could not handle them. Did you forget who you were talking to? I received a note from someone who read her blog after seeing her obituary. She had never met Angela but told me that she was living her life differently after reading her blog. She told me how beautiful Angela's photos were, even the ones that were hard to look at. She admired her courage in sharing her story. In contrast, I felt angry and sad for those who felt her scars were gruesome. I believe that they never knew Angela, despite knowing her for years. Those who never met her recognized her courage and honesty.

Please don't ask if you can come over and go through her room to look for mementos, and don't tell me what you want of hers. I have not gone through her things, and when I am ready to share them, I will take those steps.

What was most hurtful was the people who said nothing—people who knew Angela had died and did not acknowledge it to me. Again, grief is hard, and I know that you are grieving also. But sharing our grief can be helpful for both of us. I found it helpful to sit and cry with someone who loved Angela, who was an important part of her life and/or mine. When her death is not acknowledged, it feels that you have forgotten her. It was also helpful when a friend of hers came to the house and we were able to sit outside and share good memories.

. . .

Now, over a year later, I have taken many steps toward letting go of the anger and hurt. It interferes with grieving. It requires too much energy. I know and now understand that while I may have found comments hurtful or insensitive, they were not said to me with meanness. We were all grieving, feeling lost.

As there is no word for parents who have lost a child, I am not able to come up with a word for the level of grief, the severity, pain, fear, hopeless and helpless feeling that is grief. Perhaps there is no word to fully express sympathy and condolences.

I remember something Angela wrote, something she had heard, how she came to peace with those who disappeared from her life when she got cancer: *Not all who start this journey with you will be there at the end.* As I have grieved and learned more about grieving, I recognize how that was true for her and for me in grief. When I see those who have not acknowledged Angela's death and who cannot look at me—when I feel their discomfort when seeing me and then they quickly excuse themselves—I realize that this has nothing to do with Angela or me. It is about them, particularly about how they can or cannot grieve. There is no anger for me any longer, no hurt, just acceptance that this is about them and not about Angela or me. Here are a few more suggestions.

Please be comfortable sitting in silence. I may not have always wanted to be alone, but most of the time I did not know what I wanted. I knew I did not want to talk. There is no need to fill a silence with chatter.

There were other times I wanted to tell Angela's story. If you are with me, please listen. I am only able to tell some parts of her story. Do not ask me to elaborate or fill in holes. You may be asking me to go places that I do not want to go to or cannot go to. Often, we are both grieving and each need to share.

Please don't try to fix anything or to fix me. Grief cannot be fixed or cured. If you are uncomfortable with that, please don't visit.

Don't be afraid to use Angela's name. When you won't say her name and don't want to talk about her, it feels that she has been forgotten. If you want to talk about her, but are uncertain if I am receptive, please ask. I am always willing to hear a happy memory or a story.

Accept tears and allow yourself to cry with me. Those tears may be both joyful and sad. Shared grief, while difficult, is helpful to both of us.

With time, I realized the anger was not as much about what was said. I was angry that Angela had died. I was lost and grieving. I am aware that I was very sensitive.

I know that I have been blessed by support from family and friends, both Angela's and mine. Many of us are comfortable sitting and talking, sharing memories, laughing. I find that being with people who loved her is more important than words.

What Do I Say?

Just as Angela wondered what to say to new acquaintances about what she did and why she was traveling, I now have a similar concern about what to say when I meet someone new and they ask if I have children.

I will always be and see myself as a mother. What do I say to someone I am just meeting? It was a concern that I had spoken about with my counselor, and we had come up with a few options, but I kept such a tight lid on my interactions during the first year after Angela died, the situation never arose. Eventually, it occurred as I was taking a walk and found myself unable to avoid encountering some new neighbors.

Initially as we chatted, I hoped that I could just say hello and leave. However, as I was looking for a chance to make my escape, they asked the question: "Do you have children?"

Frozen for a long moment, my mind in freefall, I finally said that I "had a child." They looked almost frightened, said they were sorry, and quickly gazed elsewhere. In the few minutes we stood there, they never made eye contact again. I believe they were looking for an escape, and I was planning mine.

When I got home, I realized that I had made it through that first dreaded question, but my response felt wrong. I felt like I had discounted Angela. I decided that in the future, I would say that I have a daughter who has passed away and is always with me. I have chosen not to use the word *died*, which feels a bit more shocking for many people. Since I have responded in this way, I have had some people tell me they are sorry and then ask about my daughter: what she was like, things she enjoyed; some ask what happened. I enjoy the opportunity to introduce people to Angela and tell a bit of her story. Others have also averted their eyes and ended our meeting. I accept this as who they are. Being honest may not be the easier path, but it is the right one for me.

The second year after Angela died also included some family gatherings. With vaccinations and lower COVID, everyone was catching up on events. When I received the first wedding invitation, I considered not going. I was concerned that my presence—grieving mom—would put a damper on a happy and celebratory event. In the end, I chose to go. I will always be a grieving mom, and if that makes others uncomfortable, then they can choose not to invite me. I find these events are bittersweet. I am surrounded by celebrations, joy, love, and people who have loved and still love Angela, and the awareness that Angela is not physically there is painful.

I remember Angela struggling about going to a friend's wedding during her first year of cancer treatment. Like me, she was afraid her presence would put a damper on the happy event. Her friend emphasized that Angela was an important person in her life, and Angela's presence was requested to celebrate. Neither the friend nor her fiancé was uncomfortable with the situation, and they assured her that their reactions were the only ones that mattered. I remember this now when I attend a celebration, although I do try to place some controls on the situation, such as taking my own car. Then if I feel that I need to leave, I can.

Angela went to her high school reunion after her diagnosis. I found in her journal an entry describing her anxiety about what she would say when faced with that inevitable question, "What have you been doing?"

Angela's response: "Dying, how about you?"

We always found humor helpful, even though it was often dark.

March 21, 2022

"We mustn't hurry our sorrow merely to accommodate a world that's uncomfortable with the idea of mourning."
—DR. RANJANA SRIVASTAVA

"...grief does not have an expiration date."
—DR. RANJANA SRIVASTAVA

One year!

This day had haunted me, challenged me, and consumed me with anxiety for months.

- How will I honor Angela?
- How will I handle it, manage it?
- Where will I be?
- Do I want to be with others or alone?
- Will the panic attacks return?
- Will I have another flashback?

I tortured myself with this anxiety. I felt consumed by grief again. Not just the grief of Angela's death, but grief from recently selling her car, taking steps to resolve her debt, wondering if I am ready to give away more of her belongings, and grief of Fia's death that month.

I decided to pack up Finn and headed to Maine. I needed to be in a place that Angela and I each enjoyed so much both before and after she got cancer. I needed the salt air, sand, beach, sound of the waves. It has always been healing and relaxing for me.

Somehow, I had survived the first year. I had been warned that the second year could be harder—more painful and intense as the numbness wore off—than the first. During the first year after Angela died, I could look back a year and have memories of time with Angela. Many of those memories were challenging, but she was alive and with me. Looking back during the second year, all I would see would be heartbreak, grief, and pain. Even so, I was not certain how anything could be worse than the first year. I was trying to learn and accept that I must live life moment to moment—allow myself to be present with feelings, grief, emotions, memories.

Once I arrived in Maine, I decided it was time to stop worrying about what would happen. I knew I couldn't control how I would feel and that it was not healthy to put up walls and block my emotions. When I did that in the past, I not only had blocked grief but also had felt a barrier that blocked my feeling of Angela being with me. I knew I had to be open to whatever I was going to experience. If I chose to be present with my emotions, I knew I would feel Angela's presence. I made a choice to be present with whatever I was going to feel, allowing my heart to be open to all emotions.

I gave myself permission to have technology off. I knew her loved ones were still grieving, but I needed to be alone. I would check messages if I felt up to it.

I spent the evening of the twentieth curled on the couch sobbing. It reminded me of the first time I came to Maine after Angela died.

Earlier that day I had taken a long beach walk and found a piece of crescent-shaped yellow sea glass. I held it in my hand and could feel Angela walking with me. Yellow is a color that always reminds me of Angela. The crescent shape can also represent feminine energy and empowerment. I needed that.

On the twenty-first, I was walking and sitting for hours on the beach. During my walk, I looked down, and there was a large heart-shaped white stone in front of me. Surprisingly, it didn't immediately bring me to tears, but it brought comfort and joy first, then tears. The stone is now central in my memorial garden.

I sat for a long time in our favorite place to collect sea glass. Then I experienced that second flashback. I could see her sitting in the sand looking for pieces of sea glass. It felt real to me that she was there with me. It was more than a memory. It was as real to me as the first flashback that brought so much pain, but this time, the flashback brought good memories and a smile. I watched Angela, the concentration on her face while looking for glass, and the smile each time she found a piece. Wonderful, happy memories filled me. In the past, these memories would lead to tears. Today I felt only joy.

The blessings of this day, so fraught with anxiety for so many months, were a blend of joy and sadness when I chose to be present and opt out of worry, fear, and anxiety.

There were tears, but with my open heart, Angela was with me, and it was a day of peace and good memories.

I wonder if this is the blessing and the curse of grief: learning to let go of expectations, fears, and anxieties. As I am learning not to fight the pain of grief, I open myself up to being present with grief, joy, love. By doing that I have a greater awareness of Angela's presence and the gifts she left for me—both the tangible gifts on the beach, and the gift of her love, her joy, her presence in my life. I am learning that by letting down the walls, I open myself up to joy mixed with pain. I am learning that I can survive.

PART V:

LIFE CELEBRATION

Miracles

Angela wrote about miracles and talked about miracles. People talked to her about miracles. We both heard frequently about prayers being made on her behalf asking for a miracle. With each new treatment or clinical trial, we heard about wishes and prayers for a miracle—that this would be a cure.

We would occasionally talk with each other about miracles, but not in the context of Angela having a miracle cure. My wish with each new treatment or clinical trial was that it would give her more quality time. I was not able or willing to live my life and spend the time I had with Angela waiting for a miracle. As I learned from Angela, life is about living—something we both did.

I believe that we need to think about miracles differently. I believe that Angela did receive a miracle, just not the one that everyone was praying for. She got the miracle of time.

When Angela was diagnosed with brain metastasis, her life expectancy was twelve to fourteen months. She lived for five more years: four years longer than her life expectancy. That was her miracle. Angela was able to live, enjoy life, and share her message about living with a terminal illness. Those years were time for us to learn from

Angela—if we hadn't already—about living and loving.

This is not to minimize the dark and challenging times during those years. They were there, interspersed and combined with joyful times.

I have learned not to think about metastatic cancer in terms of years. It is about how we choose to live with the time we have. It is about good moments, days, weeks, months, and sometimes years. We will all die, but Angela taught me that it is about how we live that is important.

To all those who prayed for a miracle: Thank You. I believe that your prayers were answered.

Signs from Angela: Happy Stories

Angela and I have always believed in signs sent from those who have passed away. Since her death, I have had many signs from Angela and even from Oskar, who died a few months before she did, and Fia, who died a year after Angela. Many of her friends have told me about the signs they have had from Angela, which I would like to share. In each case, when I heard about the visits from my daughter, I was filled with joy. While I know that she is always with me, the signs feel like a tangible presence.

A friend of Angela's and mine had a dream that she came to the house to check on me. When she was leaving, she turned to look back at the doorway, and there was Angela. She was smiling, healthy, and had long hair again. They ran together and gave each other a big hug. She woke happy.

Angela's friend was with her the week prior to her death. They worked on a butterfly puzzle. After Angela passed away, the friend asked Angela to send her a butterfly. It was March, and there are no butterflies that early in the year in New Hampshire. A few days later, she was in the car with her husband, and the vanity plate on the car in front of her said BTRFLY!

Angela's friend was out for a hike the week Angela died. She felt pulled to a spot to sit. As she looked around, she saw a pinecone chewed into the shape of a pineapple. Angela loved pineapple, but due to an allergy she could eat only a few bites at a time. When the friend picked up the pinecone, a heart-shaped stone was sitting next to it.

Angela's friend was driving and thinking about Angela. Angela's favorite song came on her friend's playlist, a song she was not aware was on her list.

A friend of both of ours was sitting on her porch and was visited by a male and female cardinal frolicking in the yard. She recalled that cardinals are often considered to be a sign from our loved ones.

I was sitting at the table writing a letter to one of Angela's friends. I did not have the friend's phone number, so I had not been able to let her know that Angela had passed away. I was crying; putting it on paper made her death feel more real. I looked up from the table and saw a female cardinal on the bush outside the front window. When I put the note in the envelope, she flew away. I found this happened often, whenever I sat at the table writing a thank-you note.

A friend of Angela's planted a memory garden for her. She was sitting on one of the chairs she placed in the garden, and her fence gate opened. No one came in. She started crying, and the gate slammed shut!

Angela's friend was making the urn for her ashes, and she incorporated carvings from some of Angela's tattoos. She felt Angela was with her all day, sitting in the chair and watching.

One of Angela's friends was taking a bike ride through a nature preserve in Florida on Angela's birthday. This was a ride that Angela and I took every year that we went to Florida. It was a special place and a special day. On the way to the preserve, the friend asked Angela for a big sign that she was with her. When she got there and headed into the preserve, there was an alligator sitting in the road. As she went past, it hissed at her. Angela always did have a sense of humor!

One of Angela's friends will occasionally pick up her phone and find Angela's contact information on the screen.

My niece let me know that she had a dream about Angela. She was smiling, had her long hair, and was able to give her one last hug. My niece woke up happy.

A friend of Angela's had visited when she was first in the hospital and brought her a bag of her favorite books. They were both avid readers. Angela had never had the opportunity to return them once she read them all. The books were kept together in her closet. After Angela died, I had the opportunity to return them. When she went home and unpacked them, there was a book about Ryan Gosling in the bag. We were both laughing at Angela's sense of humor!

I was talking on the phone with a friend of Angela's on a beautiful day. It was stormy where she was, and she was sitting with her daughter watching TV. She commented that this was not one of her better parenting days. I told her that I did not have a problem with spending a nasty day watching a movie together when Angela was small. It also reminded me of when Angela was just a few years old. She was not able to change the channel on the TV, which had a big, stiff knob.

I had never liked cartoons when I was a child, so I did not introduce Angela to them, but one Saturday morning, she enjoyed them at Grandmom's house with her cousins. Later, when Angela requested cartoons at home, I told her that we did not get them on our TV—only on Grandmom's TV. Angela was not happy but accepted my "story." As I shared this with her friend, we both laughed. Then I realized I never told Angela this story or apologized for not being honest about cartoons. I said, "I guess she knows now." When we hung up, I told Angela that I was sorry about it all. About five minutes later, there was a crack of thunder that made me jump. This was followed by a big storm and lots of thunder. I had to smile at Angela's response to my cartoon lie.

I brought Angela's ashes home from the funeral parlor and placed them on the mantel, as she had requested. Fia, one of Angela's cats, had not gone onto the mantel for many years, so I assumed that Angela would be safe. After a few days, I came home to find the shells Angela had placed on the mantel on the floor. This continued to happen. Fia, like me, just wanted to be close to her.

After Angela died, I started taking Finn and Fia to Maine with me. Up to that point, I had been traveling back and forth to care for them. After Fia died, it was just me and Finn. One day, in Maine, I found Finn on the floor staring up at Angela's bed crying—howling. Finn had never been to Maine with Angela. I believe that she sensed that it was Angela's room, and that Angela and Fia were there with her.

In the first few months after Angela died, I would hear her say, "Hi Mom." Each time it was so real that I would stop and look for her. Oskar also visited. Sitting on the deck, I heard his bark. It sounded just like when he would bark when he was in the house—his deep, loud but slightly muffled bark. There are dogs in the neighborhood, but they are all small dogs, so the bark is very different.

At the end of the day that Fia died, as I was just falling asleep, I saw a cat fly across the room over my bed. Immediately I opened my eyes. I felt comforted that Fia was saying goodbye. As I fell asleep, there were a lot of cats playing just above my bed. I believe that they were all of Angela's cats that passed away over the years, playing together, and I am certain Fia was with them.

I am finding that when I try to just be present with my emotions, however painful, and let go of anticipation and worry about how I am going to feel in a situation, I have a stronger awareness of Angela with me. During those times, the signs are there, and they are easier to see.

Blessings, Acts of Kindness

There have been so many acts of kindness and generosity since Angela died. They may seem small to the person offering them, but they are grand to me, the receiver. They have run the range from sending a kind word or note to providing a meal, making a donation in Angela's honor, writing a song, and completing her Photo Essay project. I am humbled by these generous people, and it reminds me of how Angela affected people, how much they believed in her, and how many lives she touched.

During Angela's first year of treatment, she received a gift from an unknown person. She kept the card on a board in her room with other treasured possessions.

At Angela's Life Celebration, a friend of hers shared a memory. The girls were in elementary school. After school one day they were at my home, and they decided to dye their hair with Kool-Aid. I believe they walked to the market and bought Kool-Aid without sugar in a variety of colors. My kitchen was full of large bowls, which they used to dissolve the Kool-Aid and then soak their hair. I do remember the mess. Some of the friends eventually went home with Kool-Aid colored hair. Now it is such a wonderful memory, which I cherish, so I was grateful that Angela's friend reminded me of that time. I only wish I had remembered these hair-coloring adventures during her last year, when she was bald. We could have laughed together. It may have cushioned Angela's sadness at missing her hair and mine at shaving her head.

This story also reminded me of when Angela decided to use a purple Manic Panic dye on her hair. It turned her hair into a purplish gray color. That was her hair color in her first passport picture, which I recently found in one of her memory boxes.

More than fifty people visited with Angela during the weekend of her fortieth birthday party. At my request, my sister-in-law's daughter made a two-layer cake: the bottom was a mandala and the top a brain with a tumor. Angela scooped the tumor out and, later, we went outside, where she fed it to the seagulls with everyone cheering her on.

Angela's cousin had to write an essay about someone she admired.[28] She wrote about Angela and how she was living with cancer. It was moving and very special to both Angela and me.

Angela's birthday was a few weeks after her death. My niece called and asked about setting up a Zoom family gathering to remember Angela and to share happy memories with each other. It was a special time and a thoughtful way to honor her birthday.

During the Zoom gathering, her cousins shared their memory of playing soccer with her many years ago when they were visiting Maine. Angela was wearing a maxi dress, and she was able to trap the ball in her dress and make it across the yard. This brought smiles to everyone.

---

28. CAROL'S NOTE: The essay can be found on page 383.

During that same visit to Maine, her cousins remembered when she sent them to the beach to find heart-shaped stones, with a reward for whoever found the most. They returned with a treasure trove of heart-shaped stones!

The evening of Angela's birthday, her friends took me out for dinner to a favorite restaurant. They had arranged ahead of time to make her favorite drink, which was no longer on the menu: lavender gimlet! I made them blondies, one of Angela's favorites.

Angela's oncologist called me after she passed away to express her condolences. She reminded me that at one of her appointments, Angela had blisters on her feet. We were not certain if they were related to the clinical trial or from hiking a 4000-footer that week! The oncologist shared that she admired how Angela lived her life.

A friend and her husband wanted to do something special for Angela and Oskar. They obtained a police vest for the newest K9 for Nashua. They were making the donation anonymously; they wanted it to be about Angela and Oskar. It was a kind and generous gift in their memory and something that would have made Angela very happy.

The dedication ceremony for the new K9 was special and moving. We saw a demonstration of Yukon and his handler at work. There were pictures of Angela and Oskar in front of the podium. When I saw them, I started crying, and when I looked at a friend standing next to me, she was also crying. The dedication was read, which brought me to tears. I couldn't get through the few minutes of comments that I had prepared to thank our friends without crying and getting off track. Luckily, it was just a small group of people, and I knew everyone. There were tears among the group, so I was not alone.

A friend wrote to me after Angela died and said she hoped that my treasure chest of memories would bring comfort. I love the idea: the visualization of a treasure chest holding those most precious memories. The chest is not locked. It is filled with my memories and the stories Angela's friends shared with me after her death. Their memories have become my treasured memories. It is always open, and when I remember another wonderful moment with Angela, I place it there, to be retrieved when needed or when it wants to visit again.

I had landscapers come to the house to help me with a large project. When I was talking with them, they told me they had met Angela once when they were working at the house. They remembered how she came out to introduce herself and talk with them, and how much they enjoyed meeting her. They expressed their condolences. Again, we were all crying together. People who had met her once were crying with me that she had passed away.

A year later, one of the gentlemen was working next door. He saw me sitting outside and took the time to stop and say hi. He let me know that he was thinking of me and hoped I was well.

The office manager at the funeral home called me and let me know that she knew Angela in high school. She was a few years ahead but knew who Angela was. Every time she saw her in the hallway, Angela had a smile. She was aware that Angela was a force.

Another person from the funeral home contacted me after reading Angela's blog. She admired her zest for life, beautiful writing, and spirit. She told me she was honored to get to know her through her blog.

When I need to go to the hospital for tests or my mammogram, I see receptionists or phlebotomists who remember Angela. They all tell me how much they miss her coming in, always with a smile and a few minutes to talk. They knew her diagnosis and what she was being tested for, but she still was pleasant, chatted with them, and always asked them about their lives. They let me know that they missed seeing her, and we were able to cry together.

Angela had a way of meeting people and letting them know that she saw them, knowing that their presence was important to her. She had a gift of making strangers feel special. I believe this is a gift she gave others, who have returned that gift to me in their kindness and sharing of their memories of Angela.

Life Celebration

**"The imperfectly beautiful life that was once ours
doesn't exist in the same way, and we try to find a steady
ground from which to be reborn."**
—JOANNA CACCIATORE, PHD

June 4, 2022, 1 PM at our home in Maine.

Due to Covid, like so much of this country and the world, Angela's Life Celebration was delayed. Planning it a year after she passed away, I was left wondering if it was better to wait. I wondered if I would be less numb. More importantly, would I be in a better place to plan the Life Celebration that we had talked about, that she had told me she wanted. Talking about her wishes over the years, this was one of those important conversations that I never wanted to have. However, I knew that it was important to her and important for me to know and be able to respect her wishes.

Most of our family came and stayed for the weekend. Friends came from around the country. Angela's spirit was here with me and all those who loved her.

Angela's cousins took over all the food and household issues, which allowed me time to visit with many of Angela's and my friends.

I was blessed that so many of Angela's friends and family came to celebrate, to share their memories, to share the effect she had on their lives, to share all they learned from her, to share how they live life differently because of her.

The day was what Angela and I both wanted: a day to celebrate her life—the life she lived, not the life lost (although that was there also).

It was a day of laughter, joy, sharing, love, caring, and tears.

I had been talking to Angela for weeks prior to her Celebration to emphasize that she had one job: she needed to work with Mother Nature and provide nice weather. As expected, Angela came through, blessing us with a gorgeous spring day on the Maine coast.

After Angela's death, as I was looking for her insurance card, I found a Target gift card. At the time, I left it in her wallet. When I was planning the Celebration, I remembered the gift card, so Angela bought the beverages for her Life Celebration.

Wonderful memories were shared—things that I had forgotten. Her primary care provider came and played "Blackbird" for us.

We set up a journal and chair in the memory garden I planted for Angela so people could share some thoughts and memories—anything that had meaning to them—if they wished. It was months before I could look at what was written. Here are some of the most consistent themes.

- Admiration
- Looked up to
- Always do uniquely you.
- Promise to carry on the strong, independent, life-loving spirit you spread and shared with us all
- Forever inspired by you.
- Awesome soulfulness will be an inspiration forever
- Collecting heart shaped rocks together - now see hearts everywhere and know it is you saying Hi.
- I love you for the role model you have been to me and most especially to my girls.
- Living life unapologetically free
- Don't wait for the right moment, take advantage of the now.
- In awe of your fearlessness.
- Forever inspiration to live my life - ACTUALLY LIVE IT

It has been hard to know when to bring our story to an end for this writing. I have decided that this is the time.

Epilogue

"Today was a good day. That's enough for now."
—ANGELA AMOROSO

"If you are seeking a time when you will be finished,
you will never be done."
—TIBETAN SAYING

"i carry your heart (i carry it in my heart) . . ."
—E. E. CUMMINGS

". . . the acute, raw, all-encompassing grief was too
exhausting to sustain and would eventually dissipate,
leaving in its place a dull ache that would flare without
notice from time to time as a reminder that death never
completely lost hold."
—DR. RANJANA SRIVASTAVA

During the years since Angela's death, I have learned a lot about Angela, myself, grief, and grieving. I have reread Angela's blog many times, and each time I see and learn something new.

There were times when I wasn't certain I would survive Angela's death, emotionally and spiritually. The grief and pain were so intense, they consumed me. It was a cry out, a lament during those long days and nights when I was so lost, so bereft. Yet—although I did not know how to do that initially—I have learned that I can survive Angela's death. When I fall into that black hole of grief, I just sit with it. When I am ready, I find the strength to crawl out of the hole. I accept that it still occurs, but less frequently and for shorter periods of time.

I have twice attended the Selah Carefarm in Arizona for parents and families who have had a child pass away. Each visit has been a truly helpful and life-changing experience for me. I have learned about myself and grief. I am not alone; there are many other parents I have met who share the loss of a child or children. I am blessed to still be in touch with some of these parents.

Before these encounters, in grief I had often felt alone, knowing few people who have lost a child. The Selah Carefarm was safe. We were all searching for help, support, and guidance in a safe place to talk about our fears and to talk openly about grief and our children with others who understood the pain of having a child pass away. The Selah Carefarm is a place of support and knowledge. We all grieve differently, and I learned that what each of us was experiencing was "normal." I felt that I could share fears that I was often afraid to say out loud.

When it was time to leave, I felt anxiety crashing back. The knowledge that I was leaving this safe place to return home was frightening. During my time there, I was fully focused on grief, fears, and all that accompany it—without the distractions of home. Having a professional to support us for hours every day was a gift. Sometimes I worry that the panic attacks and flashbacks will return, but thanks to counseling, I have the tools to deal with them.

For the seven years that Angela lived with cancer, I also lived with her cancer. I did not allow myself to experience the grief that I was living with during that time, or even to acknowledge it. There were also other losses during that time, which I now realize I did not have time to grieve. Both my counselors at home and the counselors at the Selah Carefarm have helped to guide me in accepting my years of grief and trauma. I now accept that there was trauma for both of us. I now recognize that cancer became a family member: our family of two became a family of three. Whether cancer was taking a back seat or hitting us full force, it was always present. I still see myself as a family of three: Angela's spirit, grief, and me.

From all my reading about grief and the time I spent on the Carefarm, I have learned that I cannot bury grief. I am better if I allow myself to be open to it and let it be a part of me. I cannot fight it. I have learned that I do not need to "get over this"; to "move on"; to find "closure." There is no cure for grief. I will never be healed. I am not going to get over grieving Angela. Grief will be, forever, my constant companion, along with Angela. I am slowly coming to a place of peace with this. However, I have also learned that grief does not have to be my *only* constant companion.

When I need to cry or just be alone with those feelings, when I need to retreat to my cocoon, I do that. It is a gift that I give myself. I allow myself that time. I am learning to take care of myself and to respect grief. When I tried to fight it and find a way around it, life was harder. Now, although difficult, I embrace it and allow myself to be present with grief—in the same way I have allowed myself to be present with

Angela and the messages that she sends me. There are no shortcuts, no easy answers, no protocols.

Grief will always be with me, but Angela is also still with me. I still say good morning and good night every day. I still feel her walking alongside me, always on the right, while grief is on my left. I have developed small rituals that help with grief. The days when I need both to hold me up are fewer, but they are still there. Most days, grief is no longer suffocating me. As I have hoped for, the shards of glass that fill my heart have a few edges that have started to wear like the sea glass Angela loved to collect.

I continue to miss Angela every day. I have learned to just be present with those feelings, because then I am open to feeling her with me. I thought that once Angela died, I would not make any new memories. I have. Each time I feel her presence or find an item that I believe is a gift from her, I am making a memory. I am trying to be present and open so that I can hear her.

Alongside my days of tears, there are days when I find happiness in the beauty that surrounds me and my treasured memories of the life we lived. It is nice to feel joy, even for a moment, without the sadness fighting for a presence in that moment.

As grief has become less brutal, I am still working to learn, understand, and figure out who I am in this new life and how I want to live. I know that I am not the same person I was before Angela got cancer. I am not the same person I was when Angela was alive, living with cancer. I am not the same person I have been since Angela died. This experience has changed me as it changed Angela. That is okay.

With each new day, I am still looking for a new foundation, as mine has been shattered, on which to rebuild my life. I am starting to think about what I want to do with my time, trying to find purpose and meaning. I am trying to look at life in more than a two-month window now, but I still find it hard to look too far ahead. I am not setting goals or making a timeline. Things will happen as I am ready to take that step. Regardless of where that step takes me, I do know that Angela will be with me.

I remember that during the year that Angela's cancer metastasized, she told me that she saw herself as "a lucky one." When I asked why, she said that it was because both she and Oskar would always have a home with me. Angela wondered what would have happened to her if I had not been there to provide her with a home. No other option seemed ideal or suitable for the long term. Consequently, she was concerned about those who did not have someone to live with, a support system. That concern has always stayed with me. It is a reminder to me as I look toward my future and how I want to live life. It has guided me as I have supported others who are not as "lucky" as Angela through multiple organizations. I am happy to be able to do so in her memory.

I rarely find myself isolated, although I do enjoy my solitude. I find I need to be alone with my memories. I am not certain that will ever change; that is grief for me. I have always cherished my solitude, long before Angela got cancer, and I still do. Isolation, which I first experienced after her death, always came with a sense of desperation and an anxiety that built up whenever I was forced to leave it. In that way, isolation is different from solitude, which gives me a sense of peace: no anxiety, no fear of going out. I believe that Angela's feelings were similar. We would often sit on the porch or in the living room or take a walk, spending time in companionable silence.

I have realized that since Finn passed away, for the first time in my life, I am truly living alone. Although Angela had moved out multiple times in her adult life, I always had multiple pets with me. I was always responsible for these four-legged family members, so it is strange to realize that I am now only responsible for myself. My daily companions at the present time are my memories, the birds singing, the sun, a breeze, the gardens, friends and family. I am starting to think about bringing another pet into the home, but for now, I enjoy the pets of friends and those I see when walking the beach.

There is life all around me. I look for it, seek it out, and revel in it despite my need to be alone with life.

On March 21, 2023, I was again in Maine. Angela and Mother Nature blessed me with a beautiful sunny day, with temperatures in the fifties. I started my day on the Cliff Walk, heading to a small cove at the end. It was a walk that Angela and I had done in the past. At the cove, I sat on a boulder and enjoyed the quiet and solitude, the sounds of water lapping on the shore and birds overhead. This is a perfect place for meditation. Then I looked down and saw a perfectly shaped heart stone. This was not a stone that required me to use my imagination to see the heart. Despite cracks, missing pieces, and jagged edges, it was still a perfect shape. I sat holding it, still warm from the sun, and realized that it reminded me of my still-fractured heart, fractured self.

Eventually I went to stand at the water's edge, looked down, and spotted another perfect heart-shaped stone. This one had one small chip in it, but the rough edges had been worn smooth. I believe that Angela left those for me to remind me that my heart will not always be completely shattered, although a piece of my heart will always be missing. The time may come when I have moments when I am more whole than broken. Small cracks and sharp edges will always reappear, but I feel that she was letting me know that I will feel nearly whole again, just different. I carry that perfect heart with me as a reminder of her message.

I have also learned that her presence continues in her friends, family, those she never met who learned about her through her blog, her message, the song that was written for her, and her interview. Each person is a life she touched—and through her story, they carry her message.

I have found joy and happiness at times. I no longer approach those moments by adding, "BUT Angela is not here." I have learned that joy is mixed with missing her, with grief. There can be both; they coexist. That was Angela's message in her writing and her photos about cancer. Beauty and darkness coexisted with her when she was living with cancer, and they now coexist with me in grief.

In writing about Angela, myself, and our relationship, I have tried not to idealize either of us. As a child/teen, she challenged me, and I am certain I challenged her as a parent. Somehow, we managed to figure out those conflicts. Those memories of conflict are as precious to me as the good ones.

I will not say that the cost of Angela having cancer and her death was worth all I have learned from her. I can say that I hold dear what she taught me as I use it to build a new life for myself—a life with purpose and meaning, a life that continues to carry her message.

I will forever be a bereaved mom. I know grief will be my constant companion. That does not mean that I will not, do not, find and feel happiness and joy, although it is blended with grief and sadness. Finding and feeling joy does not diminish my loss, my love for my daughter.

My treasure chest of memories is full of dark, challenging, devastating times while also being full of happiness, joy, and loving times. All hold equal space, equal importance. I am learning to embrace whichever memory may choose to visit. They are all reminders of a life fully lived.

Angela learned how to live with cancer. In doing so, she shared all she learned with me. She showed me how to live without her, how to live with grief and joy. Cancer, grief, joy, happiness. A blending: a life full of beauty and darkness. Angela taught me that they travel together. I never hid, averted my eyes, or placed barriers to the challenges that we lived with, however tempting. I am now able to look back and see the beauty that accompanied those times, although it was not apparent initially.

The ability to be present with each other, to share our fears and joys, to share our love.

Embracing both beauty and darkness allowed us to live fully, honestly.

"... Over time, grief can morph from a dreaded, unwanted intruder to something more familiar and less terrifying— a companion, perhaps."

—JOANNE CACCIATORE, PHD

Angela's Poems
and Other Writings

Farewell

Angela included the last stanza of her great grandfather's poem at the beginning of each blog posting. It was also one of her tattoos. I wanted to share the full poem with readers.

(To H. L. S.)

Old friend, I know you will not mind
If this lone toast I quaff:
May you, upon your journey, find
A lot of lads who laugh.

And may you find gay field and wood
Where no one stays to weep.
And may you hunt where hunting's good
And fish where pools are deep.

And may you roam where roads are free
And rest where nights are fair.
Then wait a little while for me
Till I shall join you there.

—JAMES CLIFFORD HEPLER

The Bad / The Dark / The Ugly

Anger
Frustration
Irritability

   at
People Wasting My Time
   at
Dishonorable Motives.

Selfishness
   vs
unconditional real love.

Untitled Poem

There are
Many days
When there
Is very little
I can control.

Today there are tears ...

Untitled Poem

There is no joy in life for me right now.
Lost desire
Lost motivation
Lost inspiration
Lost you
Lost freedom
Lost hope
Lost kindness
Lost patience
Lost money
Lost friends
Lost confidence
Lost self-esteem
Lost.

Lost — somedays I am wordless.

Untitled Poem

When I get to the top
and look down at the reality of how far
I've come on this
mountain or in this
life, I am so grateful
and happy. That's the
feeling yoga gives me
every time I practice —

like I just climbed a
mountain

All by myself.
and I have terminal
cancer.

I am incurable...

A Selection of Angela's Writings

Private moments of the Cancerful in Cancerland. Moments no one will ever see. Pain. Suffering. Sadness.

It spreads. I knew.

...alone on this cancerful adventure
Surrounded by people moving forward...

Irony of fear and limits.
Fear of all or nothing
Fear of wasting time.

I am not at the place where I've had enough. Bring it on.

Cancer makes everything harder.

This space that exists inside my freedom is too much sometimes. Result is planning things like travel, my blog, but there is panic within it. I need to stop. I need a break. Right now, I need to LIVE LIFE.

Just keep my feet on the ground and work on my strength. Cancelling Maldives. Staying closer to family. I don't need Asia or Bora Bora, I need my family, my friends, my pillars.

In other words, I need to get my shit together in the next few months. I need to ground myself again.

Feelings: Need to disconnect for a while.
    Alone
    Defeat — constant battle of starting over
    Exhaustion.

I am starting over again, readjusting to new limitations
Somedays relentless reminders of all the things "I can't do"
Others although very rare recently, are small gifts ... walking down
the beach, actually sleeping well, moments of being "awake or alive."

Constant struggle of good and bad, beauty and gloom, deep breath vs
shallow ones.

Heaviness of day after day of inactivity, of defeat, and pills and pain.
A day is a lot of time to fill when you can't do the things you love.

Weak to strong and back again.

2/24/17. One year anniversary of cancer turning terminal. Weird day.
Lots of anniversaries in Jan/Feb — not exactly the fun kind. I'm not
sure if calling them anniversaries given it's not exactly a celebratory
event is appropriate. It is more a reminder of my life changing in an
instant, a split second.

I have so much and so little.

We are the sum of our experiences?
Are we supposed to be more?

Maine — feel free — I hide here — Happy here — I write here. I like
being alone — No appointments.

Favorite Flowers - peonies, daisies, sunflowers, orchids, ferns, lotus

What matters is how people will remember us, me.
I don't know what I will be remembered for ... or who ...

Somedays — reminders of things can't do.

I CAN'T BE STRONG ALL THE TIME

It's not right. I have a home with my mom and my dog

Here is the essay Angela's cousin wrote about her.

Admiring Angela

November 12, 2015
5th Grade

Imagine being diagnosed with cancer at the age of 34. This is what my cousin Angela went through. It's been almost 2 years since this happened to her. She was working in a medical facility as a manager and enjoying hobbies such as reading, writing, photographing, and being outdoors. All of the sudden, her life changed. She needed treatment for breast cancer. She had to have a double mastectomy, reconstructive surgery, 20 weeks of chemotherapy, and 6 weeks of radiation. Now, after almost 2 years, Angela is trying to rebuild her strength and live a simpler life.

I picked my cousin Angela because she went through a very harsh experience. Her treatment for cancer made her incredibly sick. She lost all her hair, including her eyebrows and eyelashes. She had trouble eating because she was nauseous. She lost weight and was very weak. During treatment, Angela learned that it is okay to ask for help and accept help from others. I admire Angela because she had the courage to go through this tough experience. She showed bravery when dealing with the treatment that she knew would make her sick. She has continued to show courage by significantly changing her life, looking at it from a different point of view, and trying to find a different lifestyle. This is why I admire my cousin, Angela.

Angela's Bibliography

Addario, Lynsey. *It's What I Do: A Photographer's Life of Love and War*. New York: Penguin Books, 2015.

Aebi, Tania, with Bernadette Brennan. *Maiden Voyage*. New York: Simon and Shuster, 1989.

Alexander, Eben, M.D. *Proof Of Heaven: A Neurosurgeon's Journey into the Afterlife*. New York, Simon & Schuster Paperbacks, 2012.

Alexander, Eben, M.D., and Ptolemy Tompkins. *The Map of Heaven: How Science, Religion and Ordinary People Are Proving the Afterlife*. New York: Simon & Schuster Paperbacks, 2014.

Alexander, Jessica. *Chasing Chaos: My Decade In and Out of Humanitarian Aid*. New York: Broadway Books, 2013.

Aston, Felicity. *Alone in Antarctica*. UK: Summersdale Publishers Ltd, 2014.

Auden, W. H. *Selected Poems*. New York: Vintage International, 2007.

Beale, Michelle M. B., and Edward Beale. *West By Sea, My Brain Cancer Marathon.* Mystic, CT: Expeditionaire, 2016.

Boucher, Phil. "British Girl Who Died of Cancer Leaves Secret Note Behind Mirror for Grieving Family." People, June 5, 2014. https://people.com/celebrity/athena-orchard-who-died-of-cancerleaves-se-cret-note-behind-mirror-for-family/

Butcher, Holly Ann. "Note Before I Die." www.facebook.com/hollybutcher90/posts/10213711745460694

Callirgos, Jude. *Breast Left Unsaid: A True and Uncensored Story of Survival.* Redding: Green Acres Press, 2012.

Cardall, Paul. *Saving tiny Hearts/Life and Death.* https://www.pandora.com/artist/paul-cardall/saving-tiny-hearts/life-and-death/TRqcp6647PKPX14

Delinsky, Barbara. *Uplift.* New York: Atria Paperback, 2011.

Din, Ravida (Producer), and Lea Pool (Director). *Pink Ribbons, Inc.* (Motion Picture). Canada: First Run Features, 2011.

Dominus, Susan. "Love Lost: When Grief Becomes a Muscle Memory." *New York Times,* October 17, 2018. https://www.nytimes.com/inter-active/2018/06/07/magazine/new-york-love-lost-husband-grief.html

Ensler, Eve. *In the Body of the World.* New York: Picador, 2013.

Fiske-Harrison, Alexander. *Into the Arena: The World of the Spanish Bullfight.* London: Profile Books, 2011.

Franklin, DeVon, T. D. Jakes, Joe Roth (Producers), & Patricia Riggin (Director). *Miracles from Heaven* (Motion Picture). United States: Columbia Pictures.

Frost, Robert. *Robert Frost's Poems*. New York: Washington Square Press, 1916.

Gibran, Kahlil. *The Prophet*. New York: Alfred A. Knopf, 1923.

Goldwyn Jr., Samuel, John Goldwyn, Stuart Cornfeld, Ben Stiller (Producers) and Ben Stiller (Director). 2013. *The Secret Life of Walter Mitty* (Motion Picture). United States: 20th Century Fox.

Greenlaw, Linda. *The Hungry Ocean*. New York: Hyperion, 1999.

Hayward, Susan. *A Guide for the Advanced Soul*. Boston: Little, Brown and Company, 1984.

Hepler, James Clifford. *Simple Things*. New York: Vantage Press, 1965.

Hill, Lynn, and Greg Child. *Climbing Free*. New York: W. W. Norton & Company, 2002.

Jay, David. *The SCAR Project: Breast Cancer Is Not A Pink Ribbon*. The Scar Project, 2011.

Jayatilaka, Hasni. "How Cancer Cells Communicate—and How We Slow Them Down." TED Talk, Mid Atlantic, October 2017, 10.09, https://go.ted.com/6smv

Kalanithi, Lucy. "What Makes Life Worth Living in the Face of Death." TED Talk, November 2016, 16:00, https://www.ted.com/talks/lucy_kalanithi_what_makes_life_worth_living_in_the_face_of_death?utm_source=tedcomshare&utm_medium=email&utm_campaign=tedspread

Lee, Mrs. John Clarence. *Across Siberia Alone.* New York: John Lane Company, 1913.

Markham, Beryl. *West with the Night.* New York: North Point Press, 1942

Miller, B.J. "What Really Matters at the End of Life." TED Talk, March 2015, 22:03, https://www.ted.com/talks/bj_miller_what_really_matters_at_the_end_of_life?utm_source=tedcomshare&utm_medium=email&utm_campaign=tedspread

The Muse. "A Glimpse of Reality: David Jay's SCAR Project." *Forbes,* Oct 31, 2011. https://www.forbes.com/sites/dailymuse/2011/10/31/a-glimpse-of-reality-david-jays-scar-project/?sh=25061444752d

Notaro, Tig. *Happy to Be Here.* TV Special, 2018. https://www.netflix.com/title/80151384

Oliver, Mary. *Wild Geese: Selected Poems.* Northumberland, UK: Bloodaxe Books, 2004.

Rand, Ayn. *Atlas Shrugged.* New York: Penguin Group, 1957.

Service, Robert Willian. "Spell of the Yukon and other verses / Robert William Service [electronic text]." In the digital collection *American*

Verse Project. https://name.umdl.umich.edu/BAD8607.0001.001. University of Michigan Library Digital Collections. Accessed April 23, 2025.

Shepherd, Janine. "A Broken Body Isn't a Broken Person." TEDxKC, October 2012, 18.40, https://www.ted.com/talks/janine_shepherd_ a_broken_body_isn_t_a_broken_person?utm_source=tedcomshare& utm_medium=email&utm_campaign=tedspread

Steinbeck, John. *East of Eden.* New York: Penguin Books, 1952.

Tutu, Desmond. *No Future Without Forgiveness.* New York, Doubleday, 1999.

Van Allsburg, Chris. *The Polar Express.* Boston: Houghton Mifflin Company, 1985.

Carol's Bibliography

Grief

Cacciatore, Joanne, Ph.D. *Bearing the Unbearable.* Somerville, MA: Wisdom Publications, 2017.

Cacciatore, Joanne, Ph.D. *Grieving Is Loving.* Somerville, MA: Wisdom Publications, 2020.

Hickman, Martha W. *Healing After Loss.* New York: HarperCollins Publishers, Inc, 1994.

Kessler, David. *Finding Meaning: The Sixth Stage of Grief.* New York: Scribner, 2019.

Kubler-Ross, Elisabeth, M.D. and David Kessler. *On Grief And Grieving.* New York: Scribner, 2005.

Kubler-Ross, Elisabeth, M.D. *On Life After Death.* Berkeley, CA: Celestial Arts, 1991.

Parkes, Colin Murray. *The Price of Love.* London: Routledge, 2015.

Rehm, Diane. *When My Time Comes*. New York: Vintage Books, 2020.

Sitter, Gerald L. *A Grace Disguised*. Grand Rapids, MI: Zondervan Publishing House, 1995.

Srivastava, M.D., Ranjana. *A Better Death*. Cammeray, NSW Australia: Simon & Schuster, 2019.

Memoirs

Boyer, Anne. *The Undying: Pain, Vulnerability, Mortality, Art, Time, Dreams, Data, Exhaustion, Cancer, Care*. New York: Picador, 2019.

Cruz, Dolores. *Look Around: A Mother's Journey from Grief and Despair to Healing and Hope*. Independently published, 2020.

Delaney, Rob. *A Heart That Works*. New York: Spiegel & Grau, 2022.

Didion, Joan. *The Year of Magical Thinking*. New York: Vintage Books, 2005.

Ehrenreich, Barbara. "Welcome to Cancerland." *Harper's Magazine*, November, 2001.

Fuller, Alexandra. *Fi*. New York: Grove Press, 2024.

Hallenga, Kris. *Glittering a Turd*. London: Unbound, 2021.

Jaouad, Suleika. *Between Two Kingdoms*. New York: Random House, 2021.

Jaouad, Suleika. "Recovering from Cancer Has Showed Me the Difficulty of 'Returning to Normal.' " *The Guardian,* March 8, 2021.

Jenson, Liz. *Your Wild and Precious Life: On Grief, Home and Rebellion.* Edinburgh: Cannongate Books, Ltd., 2024.

Kalanithi, Paul. *When Breath Becomes Air.* New York: Random House, 2016.

Lewis, C. S. *A Grief Observed.* New York: HarperCollins Publishers, 1994.

Lorde, Audre. *The Cancer Journals.* New York City: Penguin Books, 2020.

McInerney, Nora. *It's Okay to Laugh.* New York: Dey Street, 2016.

McInerney, Nora. *No Happy Endings.* New York: Dey Street, 2020.

Nordland, Rod. *Waiting for the Monsoon.* New York: Mariner Books, 2024.

O'Hara, Maryanne. *Little Matches.* New York: Harper Collins, 2021.

Riggs, Nina. *The Bright Hour: A Memoir of Living and Dying.* New York: Simon & Schuster Paperbacks, 2017.

Stordahl, Nancy. *Cancer Was Not a Gift & It Didn't Make Me a Better Person: A Memoir About Cancer as I Know It.* Scotts Valley, CA: Create Space Independent Publishing Platform, 2015.

Stordahl, Nancy. *Emerging: Stories from the Other Side of a Cancer Diagnosis. Loss, and a Pandemic.* Independently Published, 2023.

Additional Material

Aitkenhead, Dekka. "Mukherjee Siddhartha Mukherjee: 'A positive attitude does not cure cancer, any more than a negative one causes it.'" *The Guardian*, December 4, 2011. https://www.theguardian.com/books/2011/dec/04/siddhartha-mukherjee-talk-about-cancer?CMP=Share_iOSApp_Other

Delaney, Rob, and Rachel Martin. "This Comedian Says Words Often Fail During Tragedy. And That's OK." *NPR: All Things Considered*, October 1, 2023. https://www.npr.org/2023/10/01/1202724817/family-cancer-death-religion-spirituality-rob-delaney

Gawande, Atul. *Being Mortal.* New York: Picador, 2014.

Jaouad, Suleika: "What Almost Dying Taught Me About Living" TED, July 2019, 17:29, https://www.ted.com/talks/suleika_jaouad_what_almost_dying_taught_me_about_living?utm_source=tedcom-share&utm_medium=email&utm_campaign=tedspread

King, Samantha. *Pink Ribbons, Inc.* Minneapolis: University of Minnesota Press, 2006.

Mukherjee, Siddhartha. *The Emperor of All Maladies.* New York: Scribner, 2010.

Nhat Hanh, Thich. *Living Buddha, Living Christ*. New York: Riverhead Books, 2007.

Sontag, Susan. *Illness as Metaphor and AIDS and Its Metaphors*. New York: Picador, 1977.

Article Written About Angela Amoroso

Morabito, Jen. "Joy Is The Goal of One's Existence." *Yoga Today*, Volume 25, 49–52, available online at https://theselfstories.word-press.com/publications/

Websites

- American Cancer Society:
  https://www.cancer.org

- Chad Peacock Blog:
  https://thebrainchancery.wordpress.com

- First Descents:
  https://firstdescents.org

- Global Cures:
  https://www.global-cures.org

- Liesl Clark Photography:
  https://www.lieslclarkphotography.com

- Charlie Chronpoulos:
  www.charliechronopoulos.com

- Metavivor:
  https://metavivor.org

- MISS Foundation:
  https://www.missfoundation.org

- National Breast Cancer Coalition:
  https://www.stopbreastcancer.org

- National Breast Cancer Foundation:
  https://www.national breastcancer.org

- National Institute of Health:
  https://www.nih.gov

- National Institute of Health:
  https://www.cancer.gov/publications/dictionaries/cancer-terms/

- Selah Carefarm:
  https://www.missfoundation.org/selah-carefarm/

- World Health Organization:
  https.//www.who.int

About the Authors

After growing up in New England, **Angela Amoroso** studied literature and journalism with a minor in history at the University of Southern Queensland, Australia. Embracing her love of travel, she kept a journal on and off throughout her life, eventually creating a blog called "Beauty and The Dark" after her diagnosis with breast cancer at age 34. Angela wrote honestly about her experience, sharing the joys, the struggles, the dark times, and how she found a way to live life to the fullest—highlighting the difference between just being alive and truly living. Angela continued to write until cancer interfered with her ability to do so, and her message still resonates with a wide audience today.

Carol Hordis, a retired nurse practitioner, is Angela's mother. Viewing her daughter's journey through this personal lens, she completes Angela's story and shares her own experiences of first being the mother of an adult child with metastatic breast cancer and then continuing on after Angela's death, grieving. Angela specifically requested that Carol create and publish this book, which has helped her move toward peace and healing.

www.ingramcontent.com/pod-product-compliance
Lightning Source LLC
Chambersburg PA
CBHW020429130626
46549CB00001B/51